The
Amorous
Imagination

The
Amorous Imagination
Individuating the Other-as-Beloved

D. ANDREW YOST

Cover image: Giuseppe Maria Crespi, *Amore e Psiche*. Wikimedia Commons.

Published by State University of New York Press, Albany

© 2021 State University of New York

All rights reserved

Printed in the United States of America

No part of this book may be used or reproduced in any manner whatsoever without written permission. No part of this book may be stored in a retrieval system or transmitted in any form or by any means including electronic, electrostatic, magnetic tape, mechanical, photocopying, recording, or otherwise without the prior permission in writing of the publisher.

For information, contact State University of New York Press, Albany, NY
www.sunypress.edu

Library of Congress Cataloging-in-Publication Data

Name: Yost, Andrew D., author.
Title: The amorous imagination : individuating the other-as-beloved / Andrew D. Yost, author.
Description: Albany : State University of New York Press, [2021] | Series: SUNY series, Intersections: Philosophy and Critical Theory | Includes bibliographical references and index.
Identifiers: ISBN 9781438484730 (hardcover : alk. paper) | ISBN 9781438484747 (pbk. : alk. paper) | ISBN 9781438484754 (ebook)
Further information is available at the Library of Congress.

10 9 8 7 6 5 4 3 2 1

To Laura

One had a lovely face,
And two or three had charm,
But charm and face were in vain
Because the mountain grass
Cannot but keep the form
Where the mountain hare has lain.

—W. B. Yeats

Contents

Acknowledgments		ix
Introduction: Love, the Imagination, and the Other		1
Chapter 1	The Philosophy of Love: A New Opening	9
Chapter 2	The Lovers Emerge: Marion, Saturation, and Individuation	33
Chapter 3	From *The* Other to *This* Other: Individuation and Imagination	71
Chapter 4	The Amorous Event and the Endless Hermeneutic	85
Chapter 5	Toward a Phenomenology of the Amorous Imagination	115
Chapter 6	The Dark Side of Love	141
Conclusion: Love's Univocity and What's Left Unsaid		155
Notes		165
Bibliography		183
Index		191

Acknowledgments

The ideas expressed in this book could only have emerged as a result of a lifetime of being loved. It was love that set them free. I thank first and foremost those who have tended to me, cared for me, and cultivated me, especially Ann Yost. I am also grateful for the tutelage and wisdom of Dr. Sarah Pessin at the University of Denver, whose oversight and conversations with me transformed this work from one of hunches and intuitions into scholarly reflection and articulation. Thanks also to Dr. Gregory Robbins, Dr. Theodore Vial, and Dr. Adam Graves for your comments and thoughtful feedback. I thank the staff members at SUNY Press, and especially my editor Michael Rinella, who stuck with me despite the chaos of a pandemic. The reviews of two anonymous readers were invaluable, and I am humbled by the thoughtful critiques and careful consideration they gave the manuscript. I am particularly grateful for the charity and commitment of Dr. Benjamin Peters and Jeff Appel, both of whom played an instrumental role in helping me think through my ideas about love and the imagination, and continue to give me the gift of friendship and the joy of philosophical conversation.

Introduction

Love, the Imagination, and the Other

Love and philosophy go hand-in-hand. To philosophize is to love, and to love is to philosophize. But according to French philosopher Jean-Luc Marion, love needs rethinking. "Philosophy today no longer has anything to say about love, or at best very little. And this silence is for the better, because when philosophy does venture to speak of love it mistreats it or betrays it."[1] How can this be? How is it that philosophy—the love of wisdom—has betrayed love itself?

The answer is complex, of course, but part of the answer lies in methodology. Love's enigmatic nature makes choosing a proper method of study difficult. Moreover, all methods run the risk of putting the answer before the question. *What* one studies is always in some way shaped by *how* one studies it. Theories of love can "betray" love by reducing it to something other than itself. These theories adopt a hermeneutic of suspicion, explaining love in terms of a "deeper," more "fundamental" process: love is just a complex chemical reaction (biology), a symptom of our subconscious desire to bond (psychology), or a culturally codified type of relationship (sociology). Love is never what it seems. Others "mistreat" love by pulling it apart, by dissecting its univocity and drawing distinctions along analytical lines such as *eros*, *philia*, and *agape*. While such distinctions may help us highlight the different ways in which we love, they fail to account for what these loves have in common. There are ties that bind, some shared qualities between the different ways we love. But what are they? A strictly analytical approach makes this a challenging question to answer. Some philosophers are suspicious of love in principle. They claim that love is essentially an ideology, arising for example out of an underlying set of material conditions. Wary of oppressive, culturally constructed norms, they claim love does more to reinforce bourgeois power and capitalist values than to tell us something important about what it means to be human.

I don't mean to be crass. Each of these approaches makes a valuable contribution to our understanding of love. But Marion is right to suggest that empirical and analytical inquiries tend to restrict love to the parameters set down by the method, rather than allowing love to show itself on its own terms. We cannot avoid method, but we can acknowledge it, along with its limitations and concealments. Empiricism runs the risk of bowdlerizing love, stripping away parts of it as a truly *lived* experience in favor of a reductive explanation of its so-called underlying causes. Traditional philosophical analysis risks disassembling love in a way that hides its common structures. But love always seems to exceed these modes of inquiry. As Pascal says, it has a logic of its own. Part of what makes love so enigmatic is the *surplus* of experience and meaning it generates. Love resists totalization. As a result, there is always a tension between love and method because there is no one, correct way to explain it. Love is irreducible and, therefore, in a sense, unknowable.

And yet, Marion invites us to rethink love, to try and philosophize about it without mistreating it or betraying it. His is a welcome invitation. But to properly philosophize about love we must be sensitive to the implications of method and cautious when relying on accounts of love that explain it in terms of something other than itself. While there is indeed no one, perfect, way to approach the study of love, the philosophy of love must take seriously love *as it appears,* on its own terms, without explaining it away as a manifestation of some more basic condition. For these reasons, phenomenology is a preferred method because it begins and ends with things as they appear. It starts with life itself, and ends there too. It does not search for a source, but rather, examines what gives itself in experience. It asks, "How does love appear?" In this book I employ a phenomenological method to examine one, even more pointed, question: "How does the Other become the Beloved?" What interests me is the way in which love is marked by a radical particularity; that is, the way in which we encounter an Other and how the Other is "transformed" into someone unsubstitutable, someone whose presence seems to reorder the very way in which we experience life. How does *the* Other becomes *this* Other?[2] That is what I want to explore.

My hunch is that the imagination plays a large part in the answer to this question. The imagination is a powerful faculty and has received a lot of attention in the history of Western philosophy. Thinkers as ancient as Plato and as recent as Richard Kearney have analyzed the imagination's creative-responsive capacity and its ability to engage in the hermeneutic activity of understanding, interpretation, and invention.[3] In this book, I want to build on the work other thinkers have done and develop what I call "the amorous imagination" as part of a hermeneutical phenomenology of love in order to show how love appears as an experience of radical particularity. Jean-Luc Marion's phenomenology is inspiring to me because of its careful attention to the way love appears, as a phenomenon in its own right. And his philosophical concepts are useful in developing a theory of the amorous imagination because of their sensitivity to experiences that exceed our cognitive intentionality. His accounts of givenness, the gifted (*l'adonné*), and the saturated phenomenon are especially useful in this regard. However, in Marion's description of love in *The Erotic Phenomenon* and, oddly, in spite of his own phenomenological concepts, he focuses too much on the lover's advance and does not fully explain the eventual nature of the Beloved's givenness. Marion also mentions the need for an "endless hermeneutic" to respond to saturated phenomena but leaves the idea underdeveloped. Nevertheless, Marion's ideas, especially saturation and the endless hermeneutic, provide a generative opening for a fuller account of the amorous imagination.

Despite its strengths, Marion's phenomenology alone is insufficient to explain in detail the relationship between love and the imagination. For that, we need something more. We need to explore theories of the imagination that do not dismiss it as fancy but take seriously its role in constructing a world and imbuing it with meaning. We need thinkers like Stendhal, Novalis, William Wordsworth, and Percy Bysshe Shelley. We need the Romantics. Building on Kant's account of the productive imagination, the Romantics viewed the imagination as a powerful source of hermeneutical and creative activity. From the nexus of Marion's phenomenology and the Romantic imagination the central argument of this book emerges: *through the amorous imagination, the self-as-lover creatively responds to the saturating givenness of the Other-as-Beloved, individuating her through an endless hermeneutic.*

Now is good time for a comment on my use of pronouns, and my positionality. All thinking happens from a specific location, and that location influences the way one writes, analyzes, considers, and prioritizes issues. Like any thinker, my position carries with it certain inescapable inflections, locutions, and assumptions. In the spirit of authentic engagement, I adopt an "ethics of vulnerability" in assessing my methodological decisions; that is, I acknowledge not only that I am writing from a gendered, racial, and economic position, but that this might well influence my phenomenological sense of structure and may even influence my sense that phenomenology takes precedence over hermeneutics. But as it stands (and given my positionality) it seems to me that there is indeed a phenomenological structure at play in the way in which the Other becomes the Beloved. I will at times use pronouns in describing that structure. Sometimes I will use "he" to refer to the self-as-lover and "she" to refer to the Other-as-Beloved. Sometimes I will reverse the pronouns. Sometimes I will use the same gendered pronouns to describe both the lover and Beloved. Whatever the combination, I do not mean to imply any priority, legitimacy, or value to specific gender combinations. Love is not a heteronormative phenomenon. In places where my use of pronouns seems problematic, I hope that for the reader my word choice does not detract from my overall argument. The best each of us can do is acknowledge our own positionality, its implications and its limits, and then launch into our exploration.

Let us return then to the idea of "individuation" and clarify its meaning. By "individuation" I mean the process by which an Other comes to appear with such radical particularity that she is rendered unsubstitutable for the self who receives her, as a phenomenon. The individuated Other stands out from the milieu of all Others. She appears distinct, arriving with all her "thisness," all her *haccaeitas,* such that no Other could be this Other, no Other could be confused with or replace her. Her specificity denies anonymity. The individuated Other does not appear as an abstract, universal, or unnamed call. The term *individuation* means to capture the phenomenological fact that the Beloved appears differently to me than the stranger. She appears as radically unsubstitutable.

It may be helpful to distinguish between other uses of the term "individuation" to fully explain my use of the term. Some thinkers

(Emmanuel Levinas, for example) use the word individuation to describe the way in which the self comes to stand out from or apart from all that is; that is, from the "world," the *il y a,* being itself, etc. For these thinkers, the self is individuated when she becomes a separate subject. I am not using the term "individuation" in this sense. Other thinkers use the term "individuation" to describe a kind of human flourishing. For example, many Romantics argued that to be "fully human" was to be "fully individuated" in the sense that one was free to express oneself in a genuine, authentic manner. This is not the sense in which I use the term, either. I use "individuation" according to a phenomenological register in order to describe the way in which an Other appears with such a radical particularity that she cannot be substituted for any Other; that she is unique, irreplaceable, specific, and distinct from all Others. In love, this sense of individuation plays out in at least two ways. First, the Other-as-Beloved is individuated through the amorous event and the hermeneutic engagement of the amorous imagination. Second, the lover is individuated as lover insofar as he encounters the amorous event and participates in the endless hermeneutic. In these two phenomenological senses the Other and the self appear to one another as a radical particularity. My goal in this book is to describe how all of that happens.

My account of the amorous imagination relies on three central claims. First, the amorous imagination answers the question of how the Other becomes the Beloved. Second, the amorous imagination highlights something that is missing in Marion's account of the erotic phenomenon; namely, that love emerges not only because of the lover's advance but also because of the eventual nature of the Beloved's givenness, which calls for an imaginative response. Third, a phenomenology of the amorous imagination constitutes a substantive unpacking of the endless hermeneutic Marion signals toward in his work on saturated phenomena. In support of my thesis and these three assertions, this book takes the following structure.

Chapter 1, "The Philosophy of Love: A New Opening," provides a roadmap of the overall argument, explaining in detail why phenomenology is a more appropriate method for the task at hand than other methods (such as empiricism), and provides some important context for understanding how philosophy has traditionally approached the topic of love. I briefly discuss the history of the philosophy of love and explain why the typology of *eros, philia,* and *agape* is an inadequate framework for an analysis of love, and why a hermeneutical phenomenology is better equipped to examine love "as it appears." I then go on to explain the role Romanticism plays in an account of love; namely, that it introduces the imagination into the conversation and opens a line of inquiry inviting an analysis of the role the imagination plays in individuation. After a few examples of "early versions" of the amorous imagination in Romantic thought, the chapter provides a survey of phenomenology to demonstrate the different ways philosophers have used the method to illuminate aspects of lived, human experience.

Chapter 2, "The Lovers Emerge: Marion, Saturation, and Individuation," outlines Jean-Luc Marion's phenomenology, noting its limitations but focusing on its generative openings, in order to lay the groundwork for a phenomenological account of how the Other is individuated through the amorous imagination. I explain Marion's phenomenological concepts of givenness, the gifted (*l'adonné*), and the saturated phenomenon and explore their usefulness in analyzing love and the imagination. The chapter also provides a detailed analysis of Marion's account of individuation in *The Erotic Phenomenon*, highlighting parts of his description that are most compelling and identifying less-convincing descriptions that seem either to leave something important out of the picture (i.e., the imagination) or call for further development (i.e., the endless hermeneutic). The chapter ends by accepting Marion's invitation to explore the process of individuation and claiming that a phenomenology of love should include a fuller account of the endless hermeneutic and the role the imagination plays in transforming the Other into the Beloved.

Chapter 3, "From *The* Other to *This* Other," conducts a focused study of the imagination in order to examine the central role it plays in individuating the Other. It explores five key features of the imagination—its productive and reproductive capacities, its creative-responsive activity, its hermeneutical structure, its embodiment, and its unique mode of consciousness—and describes how they work in tandem to individuate. Anticipating objections that such an account focuses too heavily on the imagination as a purely mental activity, I provide a brief phenomenological description of the enfleshed imagination and argue that the fact of the imagination's embodiment supports the thesis that the amorous imagination is a hermeneutical, individuating faculty.

While the imagination may individuate other Others (friends, family, etc.) the focus of this study is on the Beloved.

Chapter 4, "The Amorous Event and the Endless Hermeneutic," brings together the discussions of Marion and the imagination and returns to the thesis that the amorous imagination is the site of the endless hermeneutic, a hermeneutic that serves to individuate the Other-as-Beloved. Marion's account of the erotic phenomenon overemphasizes the lover's advance and underemphasizes the Beloved's saturation. Drawing upon the previous discussion of the imagination's power to individuate, I argue that a phenomenology of love should describe the saturated phenomenon of "the amorous event" as well as the endless hermeneutic, both of which implicate the amorous imagination. The chapter details the structure of the amorous event, which is given as a call, response, and distance and separation and then examines what an endless hermeneutic might look like, concluding that the amorous event invokes the amorous imagination.

Chapter 5, "Toward a Phenomenology of the Amorous Imagination," provides a phenomenological sketch of the amorous imagination as the individuating site of the endless hermeneutic. Where the preceding discussion identified *the fact that* the amorous imagination is at play with and responds to the amorous event, my phenomenological sketch provides a descriptive account of *how* the amorous imagination individuates. Chapter 5 provides a catalogue of features of the amorous imagination, such as its productive capacity, its narrative function, its impressional affectivity, and the structure of amorous imaginings themselves, in order to show how, through the amorous imagination, the lovers participate in an individuating, endless hermeneutic.

Chapter 6, "The Dark Side of Love," explores the ways in which love can be distorted, suppressed, negated, or misapprehended when the imagination goes too far. It looks closely at the problems of solipsism, narcissism, idolatry, violence, and death as dramatized in medieval and Greek mythology and Romantic literature, as well as some ideas on how love can avoid these dangers.

By the end of the book I hope to have shown something of the relationship between love and the imagination. The degree to which I am "right" about that relationship will turn more on whether my descriptions resonate with the reader than whether my arguments are cogent or convincing. As a phenomenologist, my intention is not so much to put forth "an argument" or "to make a case" as it is to "point out" what's there, to "look at and see" what has always been there but may have been covered over by other methods or modes of analysis. Along the way I will cite literature and poetry as well as lived experience in order to invoke their affective resonances. I call upon the depth of meaning latent in symbol and art in order to direct the reader toward their own experiences of love, not to instruct the reader on proper ways of loving. But I must admit: I think love is important, important enough to consider critically, philosophically. It is not to be dismissed, even in an age of cynicism where there is a strong antiromantic bent. There are few experiences that imbue life with as much meaning as love and for that reason alone it seems to me worth reflecting upon. But I might go a bit farther and say that for many, including myself, life seems flat without love, there is a dullness and an ache that accompanies its absence. And in its presence, life can take on new meaning, depth, and texture. In love, life can become enchanting.

1

The Philosophy of Love

A New Opening

The Traditional Typology and the Romantic Turn

Where to begin with love? Just mention the word and you are sure to get a reaction. Some people worship it, others resent it, and some just roll their eyes at it. "Ah, you're such a romantic," they say, dismissively. But no one is indifferent to it. So how does one start to think about love? And to think philosophically, no less. The question of beginnings is difficult to answer but the answer makes all the difference. I want to begin with a question: *How does the Other become the Beloved?* How is it that someone comes to experience certain Others as radically particular, unsubstitutable, irreplaceable? Philosophy usually begins with divisions. According to the traditional typology, there are different kinds of love: *eros* (love as inquiry, desire, or passion), *agape* (love that does not seek its own), *philia* (love as joyful friendship), *storge* (love as natural empathy), etc. Philosophy has developed a rich history of thinking about love in these terms, but a number of problems arise from the typology too. Once the different kinds of love are pulled apart it is hard to bring them back together again. Perhaps impossible. How if at all do the types of love relate? Beginnings makes all the difference.

On the traditional model, love is multivocal. There are different kinds of love. Each speaks with its own voice. And yet, almost intuitively we know that love seems to be *both* multivocal and univocal;

that is, while love does indeed manifest in different forms, each form seems to share something in common with the others, some *je ne sais quoi* that unites love's various manifestations. I know that I love my wife, and I love my son. Those loves are very different, but I also sense that they "come from the same place," that they are rooted in a certain kind of encounter with another person who holds a unique position in my life, someone who is radically particular, who has a certain "thisness," a *haecceitas,* as Duns Scotus put it. My point here is not so much to establish a logical premise as to signal toward what some might call an "intuition" (in the colloquial, not phenomenological sense), or a lived experience to which most of us can relate. There is something "there," so to speak. While the intuition is elusive from an analytical point of view, it is at the heart of the problem of the traditional typology: love seems to exceed the boundaries set by *eros, philia,* and *agape,* suggesting both a unity and a plurality. An account of love according to the typical categories leaves something important unsaid, unaddressed, or unexplained. This paradox has haunted the philosophy of love for millennia.

The traditional typology is problematic for other reasons too. It carries theological baggage that can divert attention away from the phenomenon of love itself, replacing the rich, lived experience of *amour* with unresolvable, metaphysical problems. Can divine *agape* and carnal *eros* be reconciled? Anders Nygren and Martin Luther say no. Thomas Aquinas and Augustine say yes.[1] The ontology of love implicit in the traditional typology produces intractable logical problems, recasting love as a riddle to be "solved" rather than a phenomenon to be described: Do I really love *you,* or just your qualities? Is love subjective? Are there objective qualities in the Beloved that are universally adored? Are there good reasons to love him? Is love freedom or bondage? Conundrums abound.[2] Some philosophers attempt to think love qua love but end up reducing it to desire, passion, or disposition.[3] Philosophy treats love as derivative, secondary to some other line of inquiry, rendering it the handmaid of epistemology, metaphysics, or ethics. In Plato's *Symposium,* Diotima declares that love (*eros*) is the desire for the perpetual possession of the Good.[4] But love is more than desire, more than an idea. The philosophy of love should not be limited to analytical categories. I agree with Jean-Luc Marion: the whole enterprise could benefit from rethinking.

To do so requires that we breathe new life into old ideas. Romanticism, for example, represents a watershed moment in the history of the idea of love because it introduces the novelty of the imagination as a means by which lovers engage one another and harmonize or even merge their beings with Nature.[5] Thinkers and poets such as Johann Wolfgang von Goethe, John Keats, Percy Bysshe Shelley, and Friedrich Schlegel saw that the creative imagination was the key to sympathy. By imaginatively "reaching out," the protean lovers could experience each other as part of themselves. They could bond with one another, transforming their world and propelling the lovers into a state of ecstatic rapture. At its idealized height, the imagination was even a way to transcend death. Sitting next to his lover's tombstone, imagining her pulling him into the next world, Novalis contemplated the Night's ability to dissolve boundaries and return the lover to his origin. Like the Night, Novalis believed the imaginative faculty was the amorphous site of transcendence that allowed for fusion with the Beloved, even beyond the grave. The Romantics ushered in a new way of thinking about love that up to that point had been weighted down by the theological moorings of *eros, agape,* and *philia.* Thanks to the Romantics' attention to the power of the imagination we can now think about love in a way that was not accessible to us prior to their insights; namely, that love fundamentally involves *the creative engagement of the imagination.* But the Romantics might have gone too far. While they celebrated sympathy as a way to dissolve the self and merge with the Beloved, they failed to see the potential violence inherent in the desire for oneness. They reinforced rather than overcame a metaphysics of the Absolute, which animated the lovers' desire for union. Despite their attention to the experiences love can bring, the Romantics rarely if ever examined love on its own terms. Instead, love became a vehicle, a way to access the Absolute.

These critiques notwithstanding, the Romantics were onto something about the relationship between love and the imagination. They were not beholden to the traditional typology. Many of them saw the imagination's creative-responsive activity as the thing that unifies love's various manifestations. They did not begin by dividing love into categories, and so they were able to avoid many of the problems that come with the traditional typology. Romantic accounts of the imagination opened a new way of thinking about the role love plays in individuating the Other as the Beloved, one that can easily be overlooked in light of our contemporary aversion to Romantic metaphysics and our watered-down use of the term *romantic love*. Three brief examples illustrate the point: Novalis's idea of sympathy, Stendhal's theory of "crystallization," and Percy Bysshe Shelley's concept of merging. Each offers a different Romantic insight into the relationship between love and the imagination, and each depicts what one might call "early versions" of the amorous imagination at play within the broader Romantic movement. These Romantics were the first to articulate a vision of the imagination as a transcendental faculty with the power to "remake" the Other into the Beloved; that is, with the power to individuate him. Understanding their accounts will lay the foundation for an understanding of what I mean by "amorous imagination" as the book develops. We turn to these Romantics now to get a sense of what it means to say the imagination plays a central role in love.

Sympathy, Will, and Imagination in Novalis's *Hymns to the Night*

In *Theory of Moral Sentiments*, Adam Smith describes what he calls "imaginative sympathy," or the human person's ability to become another person and "enter into his body" through an act of imaginative contemplation.[6] Through sympathy we can represent to ourselves what another is feeling, experiencing, or sensing. On Smith's account, "[t]he imagination heightens and vivifies our awareness of another's feelings, until those feelings dawn into reality for us and we feel them just as intensely as he does—perhaps more so."[7] And when the object of our sympathy reciprocates, or when we discover that another has sympathized with us, we experience a kind of binding pleasure. Smith's idea of reciprocal sympathy bears within it the seeds of imaginative projection and ontological merging emphasized by later Romantics such as Novalis and Shelley. Sympathy for the Romantics became one of, if not *the* premiere experience afforded by the imagination.

According to the eighteenth-century Romantic poet Novalis, the imagination held not only the key to sympathy, but was the "one *power*, or way of effecting change and movement."[8] Through it the poet could fuse together art, philosophy, and religion. He could lead humanity into a new world by developing a symbolic language, birthing a new story, or transforming mundane folk life into a "higher and happier transcendentalized existence."[9] The sympathetic imagination provided the poet access to the Other and the ability to poeticize the Other by imbuing her with meaning and significance. And when the Other was gone, when she died, the sympathetic imagination became a vehicle to transcend death and maintain access to the Beloved.

In 1794, Novalis fell in love with Sophie von Kühn. Young Sophie was the "great love of his life."[10] Novalis brought his transcendental understanding of the imagination to bear on his experience of Sophie. The result was the imaginative generation of a new reality, given in a double sense:

> In the first place, imagination lifts and enhances [Novalis's] sense of life, and with this a new, though *entirely subjective reality* is created. But in the second place, imagination works on the *outside world* like a magnet. It draws something out of the other person that is really in her. By the power of the imagination a person *transforms himself and the other.*[11]

Novalis calls this process of transformation "Romanticization," which is "nothing but a qualitative exponentiation" of *both* the lover and the Beloved.[12] Take note: for Novalis, imaginative sympathy does not result in delusion. It is a new way of seeing the Beloved. The old distinctions of "real" versus "illusion" no longer obtain in the new world created by the sympathetic imagination. That is the point of Novalis's project: to collapse the distinction, or to imbue earthly life with beauty and a "higher and happier transcendentalized existence." Sadly, on March 19, 1797, Sophie died. Ever reflective, Novalis seized her death as an opportunity to explore the horizons of imagination by turning inward toward the creative power of Nature expressing itself within him. This strange, unknown power he called "will." "At bottom, each of us lives in his will."[13] The will is the active, "magical" power that animates us, gives us movement, thought, and bodily function. Novalis thought that if we can marshal the will and direct it we can become our "own physician" and even follow the Beloved in death by "crossing over from one form of life to another by the exercise of will alone."[14] For a year, Novalis visited Sophie's grave almost daily, slept in her bed, and imaginatively willed himself into death with her. But he was not looking for an end. He sought a transformation. "The longing for death is in truth the desire for enhanced life, which he will attain by the power of his will and the magical attraction of *the transfigured image of the beloved*."[15] He experienced "lightening-like moments of enthusiasm" sitting next to Sophie's grave.[16] He felt her pulling him toward her. Through the power of the imagination he envisioned himself reunited with Sophie in an imaginary afterlife.[17] A year after her death and his engagement with magical idealism Novalis penned *Hymns to the Night*. In the third hymn he poetically recounts his experience at Sophie's tomb. There, he refashions the image and the reality of the Night (for they are one), reconstituting the Night as an amorphous site of union and fullness rather than an abyss of annihilation. It is his love for Sophie that has allowed him to overcome the night of old and enter into the new Night of origin. "More heavenly," he writes, "than these flashing stars seem to us the infinite eyes which the Night has opened within us."[18] To enter into the Night is to reenter the beloved and the earth: "Just a short time / And I shall be free / And lie in love's womb / Drunkenly."[19] Imagining the world of Night, rendering it real through the act of imagination, Novalis experiences love as an enthusiasm for death; that is, for Night itself, for union with all that is or can be.

We may draw several insights from Novalis's theory of the imagination and its role in love. First, sympathy for Novalis is about imbuing things with meaning, be it other objects, mankind, or the Other. Imagination enriches experience. Through the imagination we can "romanticize" the Other, drawing out her qualities and enhancing what was already there. Second, the imagination is a creative-responsive faculty. It responds to the world that it encounters and it creates anew from that world. This activity does not result in a subjective delusion; rather, it collapses the distinction between "reality" and "illusion," opening up a space to experience the world as a "magical," enchanted, and meaningful place. We come to see the Other as the Beloved not through something as trivial as self-delusion, fancy, or sexual desire but through an imaginative act of "qualitative exponentiation." Finally, the imagination allows the lover to confront, address, and in some poetic sense even overcome death by sympathetically merging with the deceased Beloved. This amorphous experience staves off the finality of death while at the same time embracing it. Taken together, these qualities constitute an early version of the amorous imagination as a creative-responsive faculty with the power to render the Other a Beloved and creatively interact with her, even after her death.

"Crystallization" as Amorous Imagination in Stendhal's *Love*

In his 1822 work *Love*, Stendhal describes how the Other becomes the Beloved through the idealizing activity of the lover's imagination. Through the imagination, he claims, the lover imbues the Beloved with certain qualities that may or may not "really" be there but that the lover sees in the Beloved due to his imaginative engagement with her. He employs a pseudo-scientific method to provide his account and at times implicitly suggests that romantic imaginings are more akin to an aesthetic delusion rather than an ontological transformation, as we saw in Novalis. But nevertheless, like Novalis, Stendhal is keen to the fact that through the imagination the Beloved is transformed in the way the lover "sees" her.

According the Stendhal, love emerges through stages. The lover moves from admiration to delight, to hope, to enjoyment, and so on, deploying a process of what he calls "crystallization" along the way.

> The first crystallization begins. If you are sure that a woman loves you, it is a pleasure to endow her with a thousand perfections and to count your blessings with infinite satisfaction. In the end you overrate wildly, and regard her as something fallen from Heaven, unknown as yet, but certain to be yours.
>
> Leave a lover alone with his thoughts for twenty-four hours, and this is what will happen:
>
> At the salt mines of Salzburg, they throw a leafless wintry bough into one of the abandoned workings. Two or three months later they haul it out covered with a shining deposit of crystals. The smallest twig, no bigger than a tomtit's claw, is studded with a galaxy of scintillating diamonds. The original branch is no longer recognizable.
>
> What I call crystallization is a mental process which draws from everything new proofs of the perfection of the loved one.[20]

Crystallization is a "mental process," an imaginative process. It renders the Beloved beautiful, special, individuated as against all other Others through the creative "visioning" of the imagination and its ability to "see" an object in the *as if*. Like salt deposits clinging to a wintry bough, according to Stendhal the imagination enshrines the Beloved with "a thousand perfections," endowing her with a radiant sheen and idealized appearance.[21] But what is it, exactly, that radiates? The Beloved herself? Or the lover's perceptions of her? Unlike Novalis's creative imagination, the "crystallizing" imagination in Stendhal suggests that the lover imbues the Beloved with qualities that only he can "see" and "realities obligingly rearrange themselves to conform with desire."[22] So while it may be that for Novalis imaginative transformation results in an ontological overcoming of the "real" versus "delusion" distinction, for Stendhal the question remains open: the lover may indeed create only subjective inventions. In either case, the important point is that both thinkers acknowledge the fundamental role the imagination plays in bringing love about. Both Novalis and Stendhal describe the imagination as a faculty with the capacity to envision the Beloved as such; that is, as something or someone *radically unique,* as embodying a kind of "thisness." And this radicality has existential implications for the lover's experience of time, death, value, meaning, and his sense of self. Stendhal playfully describes this phenomenon: "You hear a traveler speaking of the cool orange groves beside the sea at Genoa in the summer heat: Oh, if you could only share that coolness with *her*!"[23] Now the pleasures of the world are incomplete unless they reference the Beloved. If she is not present the lover calls her to mind. Like John Donne's compass in "A Valediction: Forbidding Mourning," whose "firmness makes my circle just, / And makes me end where I begun," the Beloved anchors the lover's existence and grounds what it means to be. The lover's engagement with the world involves an *imagined presence* of the Beloved, heightening and bringing pleasure to life in a way that was not accessible before the Beloved appeared.

Romantic Merging in Shelley's "On Love"

In "Love's Philosophy," Percy Bysshe Shelley expresses Romantic idealism at its height:

> The fountains mingle with the river
> And the rivers with the ocean,
> The winds of heaven mix for ever

> With a sweet emotion;
> Nothing in the world is single;
> All things by a law divine
> In one spirit meet and mingle.
> Why not I with thine?
>
> See the mountains kiss high heaven
> And the waves clasp one another;
> No sister-flower would be forgiven
> If it disdained its brother;
> And the sunlight clasps the earth
> And the moonbeams kiss the sea:
> What is all this sweet work worth
> If thou kiss not me?

The message is clear: love is metaphysical merging. The speaker urges the lovers to "mingle," "mix," and "meet" as one, as all things in Nature do. The poem is an erotic and spiritual pleading, both of which constitute a union.[24] For Shelley, ideal love is heterosexual fusion. It is the event of oneness experienced between two lovers who give themselves to the desire to bind their flesh together. There is in Shelley a strong but not straightforward Platonism that reveals a unique version of the Romantic imagination operating in love.

In his brief essay "On Love," Shelley expounds the themes he developed in "Love's Philosophy." Like Plato and Stendhal, Shelley equates love with a search for perfection.[25] But unlike Plato, Shelley "seeks a oneness that will be embodied in concrete experience of spiritual development that need not have any being elsewhere."[26] And unlike Stendhal, Shelley suggests that the Beloved activates the imagination in a way that subsumes the lovers under an innate, "ideal prototype" of perfection. Shelley begins with otherness:

> I know not the internal constitution of other men, nor even of thine whom I now address. I see that in some external attributes they resemble me, but when, misled by appearance, I have thought to appeal to something in common and unburthen my inmost soul to them, I have found my language misunderstood, like one in a distant and savage land. The more opportunities they have afforded me for

experience, the wider has appeared the interval between us, and to a greater distance have the points of sympathy been withdrawn.[27]

Like Novalis, Shelley recognizes the distance that separates one person from the other, a distance marked by tragedy and alienation. Attempts to know another's "internal constitution" result in misunderstanding. Indeed, the more one tries to know another person, the greater the distance between them. For Shelley there are real and lamentable limits to the sympathetic imagination.

But there is also hope that comes in the form of an innate knowledge of beauty, an "ideal prototype" that resides within all of us, drawing us toward union with the Other. "We dimly see within our intellectual nature a miniature as it were of our entire self, yet deprived of all that we condemn or despise, the ideal prototype of everything excellent or lovely that we are capable of conceiving as belonging to the nature of man."[28] It is unclear whether Shelley is describing a Platonic form or has some other metaphysic in mind. Regardless, the Platonic parallels begin to dissolve when Shelley describes the imagination's interplay with the prototype. "To this [ideal prototype] we eagerly refer all sensations, thirsting that they should resemble or correspond to it."[29] There is an erotic and *imaginative* aspect to this "referral." For Shelley, the Beloved "elicits the imaginative reconstruction of the ideal by approximating perfections that the lover knows to be nonexistent in the world," or at least knows only to exist innately, as a prototype.[30] This "antitype," though, is not a sad insufficiency. It is a happy invitation for the lover to produce an imaginative creation that "moulds and completes the shapes."[31] Love tends toward an "invisible and unattainable point" through "an imagination that would seize upon the subtle and delicate peculiarities which we have delighted to cherish and unfold in secret" and that "vibrate with the vibrations of our own."[32] Here is Shelley's idea of imaginative merging: the ideal prototype is the perfect image of both the lover and the Beloved, indeed, of all that is beautiful, and through the imagination we are able to complete the picture, so to speak, or envision what it is to be one with the Beloved by subsuming *both* the lover and the Beloved under the inborn sense of perfection. The amorous imagination facilitates union. As in Novalis, this new way of "seeing" (or being) is not a delusion. The imagination refers, subsumes, and transforms the "real" into the Real. Through it the lovers can merge with all things. "In the motion of the very leaves of spring, in the blue air, there is then found a secret correspondence with our heart."[33]

Love and the Romantic Imagination: Some Preliminary Observations

We began this discussion of the Romantics in order to get a sense of how they viewed the imagination and its relationship to love. As we can now see, the two are deeply intertwined. That is why Romanticism is a watershed moment in the history of the idea of love. Mimetic theories of the imagination dominated the history of philosophy prior to the Romantic movement. These theories focused on the imagination's capacity to conjure images, images that appear as pale reflections, mirages, or duller versions of more vivid and "real" sensations (Plato, Hume et al.). But on the Romantic view, the imagination gives a poetic charge to perception. It imbues it with vivacity, it synthesizes and enchants the world of experience. Through it we can project ourselves into death and change the way the world presents itself to us in life. As Stendhal describes, the imaginative process of crystallization allows the lover to transform the Other into *this* Other; that is, the Beloved. Although the "objective" world may not witness the diamonds encrusting the Beloved, it is the lover's imaginative perception and responsive play that crystallizes him, rendering the Beloved the source of all joy and happiness. Some go even farther. According to Novalis, the imagination is a means for salvation and transcendence. Like Shelley, he sees the imagination as a conduit or power to bind lovers together. The imagination is the Night, a space of blurred and dissolving boundaries. Stendhal, Novalis, and Shelley valorize the imagination's unique power, insisting that it alone can give birth to enduring love. And for Novalis and Shelley it promises more. It promises transcendence and fusion with the One. Romantic sympathy becomes Romantic union. But we need not go as far as Novalis or Shelley nor be as "scientific" as Stendhal in order to appreciate the insight they've uncovered: love and the imagination go hand in hand. What is key to our study is the observation that the imagination is not merely mimetic. It has a creative-responsive capacity that can transform and enrich phenomena. Through it the lover can come to experience the world in a way that mere perception does not allow. The takeaway is that the imagination plays an important role in how the lover comes to experience the Other as the Beloved. Any account of love must account for imagination too.

Interestingly, none of the Romantic thinkers we've discussed caution *against* the power of the imagination. This is a point not lost on contemporary philosophers sensitive to the dangers of denying difference or viewing it as something to overcome. Postmodern philosophy in particular points out how the desire for union can manifest as ontological violence or mask an underlying desire for violence. If the lovers want to dissolve into each other, is that not a kind of death? And if love is unrequited, isn't the Other's alterity violated by the desire to merge? Although Shelley and Novalis might embrace the idea of love-death, they would almost certainly reject the language of violence. Indeed, Shelley's opening remarks in "On Love" place the very notion of ontological difference between subject and object at issue. It is a thing to overcome, but not through violent means. Love saves us from the "distant and savage land" of alienated being through the sympathetic fusion of imaginative oneness that, like the "winds of heaven mix[ing] forever," promises airy and elevated transcendence rather than grounded solitude. And Stendhal does not seem concerned about the dangers of imaginative delusion, or if he does it is only to admit that the horizons set by the world no longer limit the lover's vision. He admits that crystallization can breed passion but he does not go so far as to suggest it is a sort of violent or narcissistic aesthetic that denies the Beloved her being in favor of the lover's desires. For him, the imagination transports the lover and calls the Beloved forth even in her presence, and enriches life in almost every facet. There is little trace of danger in any of these thinkers, and that is a fair point of criticism. As we will see, the imagination *can* become narcissistic when the lover fails to engage the Other-as-Beloved and simply recasts the Beloved as a *more desirable* object. Moreover, Romantic sympathy can lead to mere duplication of one's own experiences rather than the full "fellow-feeling" described by Smith, Hume, and others. Finally, the Romantic imagination requires a certain level of vulnerability: the lover must be open to the idea of becoming one with the Other and losing the self. The lover can both consume and be consumed by the

Other, or by the lover's own passions. The Romantic imagination is both a creation and an opening. It allows for an outward projection and an inward penetration. Both can be dangerous. In the end, the Romantic imagination remains full of promise but must account for its darker potentialities. Delusion, dissolution, and narcissism are real threats, and it is unclear whether the imagination alone can moor love to itself or if it strains love to the point of becoming something else, something darker and more violent.

Phenomenology and Empiricism

Because today we tend to think of love empirically, according to a scientific worldview, many people consider love as essentially an emotion, albeit an important one. The popular view sees love as something you "feel" for another person. Psychology complicates or problematizes the emotion, suggesting that love is a human disposition rooted in lack; that is, love is the psychological expression of a desire or an impulse to fill the sense of existential "emptiness" we all carry within us. While according to psychology there may or may not be an antidote for our experience of lack, love is ultimately not a "thing" of its own but an expression of a psychological need to fill the void. Biology claims that love is an evolutionary drive masquerading as a transcendent ideal. To put it somewhat crassly: animals need to reproduce to survive, and to do that, they need to mate. Love is essentially the idealized, human term for our more basic sexual drive to procreate and preserve the species. Sociology, cultural theory, and anthropology adopt hermeneutics of suspicion by explaining love in terms of an underlying substructure. Sociologists claim that love is the communal manifestation of our need as people to form groups, a culturally codified kind of relationship. Anthropologists argue humans are better equipped to thrive in family organizations rather than in isolation. Love is a cultural institution arising out of a fundamental survival mechanism. And cultural theorists claim love is essentially a political or economic ideology that reinforces the material conditions of a society and obfuscates the power structures that hold them in place. In each case, empirical methods consider love as symptomatic of an underlying cause that can be explained through scientific or pseudo-scientific observation and analysis.

Despite its limitations, empiricism has its place in a study of love. Its explanatory force and demand for evidence provide a helpful check against our common, less reflective assumptions about love. Empiricism forces us to really ask what love is, why we care so much about it, and what other motivations might play into our idealization of it. Empiricism reminds us that love is not simply some universal concept or Platonic Form "out there," calling us like a siren's song. Love has roots in the basic structures of our human behavior. But empiricism cannot provide a complete picture of love either. Two schools of philosophical thought—phenomenology and hermeneutics—offer strong critiques of empiricism and suggest that there are aspects of love that call for a very different mode of inquiry.

In *Truth and Method*, Hans-Georg Gadamer provides a warning against the dangers accompanying any method, including empiricism. For Gadamer, truth and method are antithetical. Method conceals as much as it reveals. Because method sets out the parameters of what can be known even before engaging in the inquiry, one must at all times be conscious of the assumptions latent in method and be aware of what it may exclude from view. Heidegger reminds us that in order for a method to formulate a question—including empirical methods—we must have some preunderstanding of what it is we are asking about as well as what might count as a viable answer.[34] There is no such thing as a purely objective method that provides access to a purely objective truth. Psychology, biology, anthropology, etc. are all human projects. They tell us as much about human concerns and orientations as they do about the subject matters they endeavor to study. Moreover, Heidegger points out that any act of understanding is also an act of interpretation which carries certain "decisions" about the way the world is or is not. Faith in empiricism's explanatory power should be tempered by philosophical reflection on empiricism's values, biases, and prejudices. Science has its own hermeneutic.

Phenomenologists provide related critiques of empiricism. For example, Edmund Husserl argues that empiricism must be grounded in some sort of transcendental philosophy in order to justify its claims about the world. For Husserl, phenomenology is more fundamental than empiricism because it accounts for the very conditions for the possibility of experience, what some phenomenologists call the structures of consciousness. Without an account of the structures required to observe the world it is hard to imagine how empiricism can provide an account of it. And for Heidegger, phenomenology provides access to aspects of our experiences that empiricism conceals because it focuses on not only what is given in experience but how we make meaning of that experience. For Heidegger, meaning is built into the very structure of the way we encounter the world. Meaning is the milieu or web of preexisting interpretations we find ourselves thrown into and upon which we rely to make sense of things. Empiricism is a human activity aimed at generating meaning, not some abstract activity that gives access to universal truths, explanatory power notwithstanding.

Hermeneutical phenomenology has several advantages over empiricism when it comes to philosophizing about love. First, phenomenology allows one to bracket the metaphysical questions that underlie empiricism and to focus solely on the way in which love gives itself as a phenomenon. Phenomenology's concern is with love's appearance, not its causes. Second, phenomenology allows space for a rigorous investigation into the way in which what appears does so within a context of meanings. The interplay between (1) what appears and (2) how appearance "happens" within a context of meaning calls for a hermeneutical method, one that takes seriously the way in which interpretation accompanies appearance. Notably, while this study focuses on a hermeneutical supplement (to Marion), it is ultimately informed by phenomenology (over hermeneutics) in the sense that it lays out what it takes to be a universal structure. It is important to keep in mind, however, that there is an inherent tension between phenomenology and hermeneutics. Phenomenology purports to describe phenomena as they appear; that is, to use Marion's term, in their "pure givenness." But hermeneutics suggests that meaning goes "all the way down" and that phenomena always appear within a context of meaning such that interpretation is at the very heart of what it means for phenomena to give themselves in the first place. The tension may be irresolvable. In any event, the fact that love is both a phenomenon that emerges within a context of meaning and itself generates meaning suggests that a proper study of love should include *both* phenomenological and hermeneutical modes of inquiry. Hermeneutically speaking, I consider variations in the cultural expression of love but the phenomenological core of my method recommends that the underlying, "thin" structure of love is the same across time. Finally, as we will see, my analysis of individuation vis-à-vis love is not a search for grounds; rather, it is an examination of contours. It does not attempt an account of the fundamental structures of consciousness, the grounds of being, or a final phenomenological reduction. Rather, this is a study of how one phenomenon becomes another. Metaphorically speaking, a phenomenology of the amorous imagination is a "horizontal" analysis of the conversion of phenomena, not a "vertical" analysis of the grounds of phenomena. A *hermeneutical* phenomenology is best suited for this sort of analysis because it provides the analytical tools needed to examine the way in which love appears as a phenomenon and the processes at play that convert one phenomenon (the Other) into another phenomenon (the Beloved). In other words, it attends to meaning as much as appearance; or better, the meaning *of* appearance. Despite its many strengths, empiricism does not have the conceptual equipment necessary for such a study.

Varieties of Phenomenology

Where Romanticism provides a new conceptual opening to the study of love, phenomenology provides it a method. As we have seen, phenomenology avoids the pitfalls of the traditional typology and the empirical tendency toward reduction. By bracketing metaphysics and looking only at phenomena as they appear, phenomenology focuses our attention at the way things show themselves rather than what's "underneath" them. It takes seriously the appearance of things. But not all phenomenologies are the same. The method evolved over time and a brief survey of its various permutations will provide a sense of how philosophers use phenomenology to investigate different philosophical questions.

Edmund Husserl's Eidetic Phenomenology

Edmund Husserl set out to ground science in transcendental philosophy. He developed phenomenology as a method to describe the structures of consciousness that allow for the possibility of scientific or "naturalist" knowledge in the first place. Husserl argued that so-called objective science fails to account for the role subjectivity plays in constituting the very world it purports to study. Scientific knowledge presupposes a subject/object dualism without investigating its ground.

> Only a radical inquiry back into subjectivity—and specifically the subjectivity which *ultimately* brings about all world-validity, with its content and in all its prescientific and scientific modes, and into the 'what' and the 'how' of the rational accomplishments—can make objective truth comprehensible and arrive at the ultimate ontic meaning of the world.[35]

In order to get to "the things themselves"—their essences—we must first provide a detailed description of consciousness. Only after grounding the naturalistic world in an accurate account of consciousness can we then claim to know what a thing truly *is*. For Husserl, a thing's essence is that which endures after it is examined according to the phenomenological reduction. By stripping away its parts, we can come to know a thing's essence when we have discovered what it cannot be without.

Husserl's method is primarily *eidetic* phenomenology. His is a search for essences. Many scholars read Husserl as concluding that at the ground of experience lies the transcendental ego, which through the process of intending objects constitutes both them and itself. Regardless of whether the transcendental ego is a thing or a posit, Husserl's phenomenological method proved useful in uncovering other central features of consciousness. For example, Husserl discovered that consciousness is always *conscious of something*. He calls this phenomenon *intentionality*. But conscious of what? Husserl's observations revealed another aspect of consciousness: the lived experience of "the world" involves an *intuition* of a phenomenon; that is, phenomena appear to the consciousness that intends them. These two structures of consciousness—intention and intuition—make up the central features of subjectivity and allow for the possibility of knowledge. Husserl noticed something else too: there are a *variety of modes of consciousness*. Perception is one among many. Consciousness also intends in the manner of imagination, judgment, representation, and feeling. Although all modes of consciousness adhere to the intentionality/intuition structure, they intend "things" in different ways. Phenomenology's task is to examine and account for both the *noesis,* or the acts of consciousness, and the *noema,* the entities constituted by them.

Martin Heidegger's Hermeneutical Phenomenology

Husserl's student Martin Heidegger used phenomenology for different ends. Heidegger employed what we might call *hermeneutical* phenomenology. By "hermeneutical" Heidegger means that the task of phenomenology is not to access essences but to uncover the preunderstandings and preexisting meaning-structures that are built into our experiences of the world and allow for our experience of "a world" in the first place. Heidegger's central question was deceptively straightforward: "What does it mean *to be*?" According to Heidegger, Western philosophy has concealed the question of Being and preoccupied itself with the question of beings. Failing to think this ontological difference precluded philosophy from taking up the question of the meaning of Being. Metaphysics, which for Heidegger is the study of beings (what they are, what types they can be, what laws or rules govern them, etc.), does not account for Being itself, which is something like the sheer phenomenality of beings, or their mode of appearing, or how they "presence" or come out into the open in the world.[36] Heidegger distinguishes between the study of ontology (Being qua Being) and metaphysics (the study of beings), privileging the former as the more fundamental philosophical question. Metaphysics not only covers over the question of Being *as such,* when it does address Being it renders it *a being, the supreme Being.* Heidegger critiques this sort of onto-theo-logy (a search for the highest, most general grounds) as mischaracterizing Being as yet another being, albeit a being that is the foundation of all other beings. In any event, that is not the question of Being. The question of Being requires a radical reorientation, a new method for doing philosophy that avoids the ontic pitfalls of metaphysics and examines Being on its own terms. And for that, Heidegger turns to phenomenology.

Drawing from but critiquing Husserl's eidetic phenomenology, Heidegger's method does not abstract out the lived experiences of *Dasein* but starts *from* them and focuses *on* them. For Heidegger, lived experience holds the key to Being. In other words, Heidegger saw the question of human meaning as prior to the question of science and so used phenomenology to uncover how it is that our lived experiences are given as meaningful. For Heidegger, science is a human activity of meaning-making and occurs only because of and within a context of preexisting meanings. He is not concerned with revealing the fundamental structures of consciousness but rather in uncovering the interpretive structure of lived meanings that constitute our human experience. Doing so, Heidegger claimed, gives us access to the question of Being in a way the more abstracted eidetic method cannot. While both Husserl and Heidegger saw phenomenological description as the key to philosophy, they differed in where they directed its gaze.

Emmanuel Levinas and the Limits of Phenomenology

The question of whether Emmanuel Levinas is a phenomenologist helps us think with care about what we mean by phenomenology and whether as a method it refers only to phenomena or whether it can indeed refer to that which exceeds phenomenality. On the one hand, Levinas's close attention to moods and concrete, lived experiences in works such as *Existence and Existents* demonstrate his phenomenological tendencies. But on the other hand, in works like *Totality and Infinity*, Levinas seems to go beyond phenomenology by appealing to an infinite Other that never actually appears, but is given only in its traces. In either case, Levinas is deeply influenced by phenomenology, especially Heidegger's question of Being. Like Heidegger, Levinas moved beyond Husserl's concern with the structures of consciousness. But where Heidegger was concerned with Being, Levinas was concerned with the Other.

Levinas used phenomenology to describe how the Other is given in experience and the implications of our encounter with the Other for subjectivity, time, and ethics. His insights developed over the course of his career, but he began with a close analysis of the way in which the self separates from the *il y a* (literally, "there is," a phrase Levinas uses to express the impersonal and anonymous existence prior to the subject's constitution) and emerges as a being. In subsequent works he explores the self's encounter with radical alterity—the Other—who calls the self's being into question. According to Levinas, "prior" to the encounter with the Other the self experiences the world as a kind of coiling tension between an egoism (marked by enjoyment, in-dwelling, and at-home-ness) and oppression (marked by the experience of an overwhelming plenitude of Being). No effort on the part of the self allows it to escape its ontological suffocation or the sameness of its Being, both of which are two sides of the same ontological coin. Only when the self encounters the Other is it liberated from Being and isolation. But the Other appears as a radical alterity. The face of the other commands the self, placing it in a space of "difficult freedom" in its responsibility to the Other. Levinas's phenomenology of the Other pushes phenomenology to its limits as a method because he characterizes the Other as a phenomenon that does *not* fully appear. The Other is an excess, transcendence, or infinity that resists any attempt to render it an object. Despite his insights (and mindful that the question of individuation is not central to Levinas's project), one finds that his description of our encounter with the Other as an ethical injunction does not help describe the process of individuation that occurs in love. In other words, he does not (claim to) explain how the lover comes to love *this* Other.[37]

Paul Ricoeur's Linguistic Phenomenology

Ricoeur's phenomenology was, like Heidegger's, hermeneutical. "Meaning" for Ricoeur refers to the role of language in the activity of human understanding. While Heidegger did not ignore language, it was not his primary focus, at least not in *Being and Time*. Ricoeur's phenomenology was a linguistic phenomenology. For him, phenomenology must give account of the fact that whatever we experience, whatever appears in the form of intuition, does so through the prism of language. In his hermeneutic phenomenology "experience is to be read *through* expression."[38] For Ricoeur, Being is hermeneutical "all the way down," and so he emphasizes the interpretive and linguistic aspects of lived experience.

Central to Ricoeur's work is the question of selfhood. Who am I? How should I live? According to Ricoeur, philosophy has failed to provide adequate answers to these fundamental questions. Where Heidegger took the "direct route" to Being through *Dasein,* Ricoeur takes "detours" through various modes of inquiry in an attempt to understand how the human person understands itself. Ricoeur determines through a detailed study of the process of understanding and language that the self is no "thing" at all but rather a capacity for agency and ascription. The self "comes to itself" over and over again by attesting to itself and graphing a "who" onto its concrete and abstract experiences, experiences that are fundamentally embedded and intertwined. The self has a "double nature" and exists at one and the same time in a material and a phenomenological world. Ricoeur argues that the self is constructed through narrative and according to time. Our actions only become meaningful and constitutive of our selfhood when they are understood through *emplotment*; that is, a movement becomes an action when it is located within a meaningful narrative. Ricoeur describes narrativization according to three types of activities or structures. First, the human field of action is always prefigured insofar as there are conditions set down for us (e.g., our ability to use symbols, follow a story, etc.). But that prefiguration is also configured according to narrative. We are free to bring together cosmological and phenomenological time by using narrative strategies (pace, order, etc.) so that experiences do not happen one *after* the other but *because* of the other.[39] And finally, the field of action is refigured in terms of possibility. Through narrative, we project and envision the type of world we want to inhabit, and can act toward it in the here and now, constantly re-narrativizing our past in light of the present and future.[40] Ricoeur's linguistic emphasis in his hermeneutical phenomenology highlights the important role that narrative plays in our attempts to respond to events in our lives. As we will see, the creative meaning making that allows for and responds to disruptive events calls for a hermeneutical phenomenology that attends to both Heideggerian and Ricoeurian senses of meaning. That is, it must attend to both (1) the way in which we experience the world as always already full of meaning (Heidegger) and (2) the way in which we use language and symbols to create meaning as we move across the landscape of our existence (Ricoeur). Both are relevant because love "happens" within a preexisting nest of meaning and "calls for" a reconfiguration of meaning in light of its arrival.

Jean-Luc Marion's Reduction to Givenness

Jean-Luc Marion's writings cover a wide range of topics within philosophy and theology, including love itself. Building on Levinas's account of the Other, in his 2003 work *The Erotic Phenomenon*, Marion provides a detailed phenomenology of love and the Other's individuation. But prior to his studies on love, Marion used phenomenology as a method to reveal what he argues is the "final reduction," the reduction to givenness.

According to Marion, Husserl and Heidegger limit the appearance of phenomena to objects and Being, respectively. The task of phenomenology is to liberate phenomena from the confines of intention and reduce them to pure givenness, to examine them on their own terms. Marion attempts such a reduction in *Being Given*. He argues that, properly applied, phenomenology reveals the anonymous and self-giving nature of all phenomena. Liberated from the constraints of the constituting ego, phenomena are shown to give themselves freely—as a gift—and of their own accord. Marion's reduction to givenness exposes the unconditioned nature of all phenomena as well as the self's role in phenomenalizing the given by receiving it. The given is that to which all phenomena can be reduced and the limits of any reduction. As Marion claims: "so much reduction, so much givenness." But Marion's reduction to givenness leads to another, perhaps even more important observation regarding the nature of phenomena. Phenomena give themselves in different degrees. Some phenomena are "poor," providing little or no intuition. Some phenomena are "common," giving intuition adequate to the intention. And some phenomena saturate all intentionality, leaving it puzzled, blinded, or overwhelmed. Like Levinas's face of the Other, these "saturated phenomena" reveal the nature of phenomena as unconstrained by the transcendental ego. Phenomenology exposes the fundamental quality of all phenomena; that is, their givenness. In *The Erotic Phenomenon*, Marion extends his insights regarding the gift, the given, the saturated phenomenon, and individuation and applies them to love. He argues that through love the Other is individuated in a way that ethics cannot accomplish. But as we will see, he does not fully account for the role hermeneutics plays in love, and he fails to adequately describe the evental nature of the Beloved, the one who upends and overturns the lover's preexisting horizon of meaning.

A Romantic Phenomenology?

What do phenomenology and Romanticism have to say to one another? They seem odd bedfellows. Phenomenology, sharp-eyed and reflective, focuses its gaze only on phenomena as they are given in experience, providing rigorous descriptions of their appearances. Romanticism seeks out new territories and landscapes of expression in order to imbue the world with poetic meaning. Where do their paths cross? They cross in pursuit of that elusive mode of consciousness called *the imagination*. Like a leviathan, the imagination is always "out there" (or "in there," if you like) lurking in the background, making sense of the world of sense, breaching the surface of perception and transforming it into something new, only to descend again into the unplumbed depths of the mind. Both phenomenology and Romanticism are keen to the powers of the imagination, recognizing its productive capacity and its ability to shape the world anew. Through the imagination we are able to live in the *as if*—in the world of possibility—engaging in the free play of ideas, images, and concepts. But there's more. The imagination is not just an image-making faculty. As we will see, Husserl's phenomenology reveals that the imagination constitutes its own mode of consciousness, warranting a close examination of its activity and transcendental features. A phenomenological description of the imagination shows that, unlike other modes of consciousness (perception, judgment, memory, etc.), the imagination is not tethered to the *as is*. It intends things differently, according to its own rules. And this raises an additional question, one that echoes Levinas's and Marion's concern with the Other: What role does the imagination play in individuating the Other-as-Beloved? For Romanticism, the imagination is the source of creativity. It produces and projects a world of meaning. Through it, the self becomes a lover, crystallizing the Beloved in amorous imaginings and re-temporalizing the lovers' experiences. More questions come into view: What is the relationship between love, hermeneutics, and the imagination? How does the imagination as a site of meaning making contribute to the Beloved's individuation?

I take these questions head-on. I grant Levinas's and Marion's phenomenological accounts of the Other as a saturated phenomenon, a phenomenon that gives itself with so much excessive intuition that intentionality cannot reduce it to an object. But the Other is not the only saturated phenomenon to appear in love. There is also the amorous encounter, which in its eventful structure, saturates according to quantity. It gives too much information, too many data, too much sensation so that it cannot be explained in terms of cause and effect, linear time, or within our preconstructed "nest" of meanings. The amorous event upends our preexisting world and demands its reconfiguration, a reconfiguration that can only occur in and through the imagination's capacity as a hermeneutic faculty. Because the face and the event saturate, they call for an endless hermeneutic, as Marion points out. We can never exhaust their meanings. Building on Marion's ideas of givenness and the endless hermeneutic, I argue that not only does the saturated phenomenon call for an endless interpretation, it is precisely *in the imaginative engagement of an endless hermeneutic* that the Other is individuated, that the Other becomes the Beloved.

2

The Lovers Emerge

Marion, Saturation, and Individuation

From the Other to the Beloved

Jean-Luc Marion acknowledges a great debt to Emmanuel Levinas for his phenomenological account of the Other.[1] According to Levinas, the Other appears primordially, as an ethical injunction. When we encounter the Other we encounter a demand, a command, "Thou shalt not kill." This command calls us out of the undifferentiated milieu of existence, the *il y a*, and places us in a position of what Levinas calls "difficult freedom," a freedom bound by an asymmetrical responsibility to the Other. But for Marion, Levinas's description of the Other leaves the question of individuation unresolved.[2] It is not clear how for Levinas *the* Other becomes *this* Other. We know from experience that not all Others appear in the same manner. Some Others appear as "other than" or perhaps even "more than" *an* Other. We encounter the Other in different modes or according to different hermeneutical frameworks. Some Others are our friends. Some are our children, co-workers, priests, neighbors, or enemies. Some are our lovers. There is a profound difference for Marion between the Other-as-Stranger and the Other-as-Beloved. How are we to make sense of this difference? If the inquiry shifts from a Levinasian concern with grounds to a Marionian concern with contours then another set of questions emerges, questions that are not concerned with "firsts" or the originary but with "seconds" and the conversion of one phenomenon into another.

Marion's inquiry into the question of individuation turns our focus toward a process or transformation of one phenomenon into another, not a search for foundations. The questions that come into view are subtle but no less profound: How does the Other become *this particular* Other? How is the Other individuated in the face of alterity? How does the Other become the Beloved? In short: How does love emerge?

Levinas and Marion: Ethics, Eros, and the Question of Individuation

Let us take a closer look at Marion's critique of Levinas. His intuition that Levinas's ethical injunction does not adequately explain how we experience the Other as a unique Other points toward a deeper problem rooted in the distinction between *eros* and ethics. As I will argue later, any attempt to describe the phenomenon of individuation that transforms the Other into the Beloved must take into account the productive and creative role of the imagination. In other words, it must describe *the amorous imagination*. While there are a number of ways to approach the question of love, I will use Marion's critique of Levinas's "substitutable Other" as an entry point into a more comprehensive account of the phenomenon of love. As we will see, Marion's critique of Levinas operates in the background of his larger project on love, especially in *The Erotic Phenomenon*, and calls toward a fuller account of the role of the imagination as a hermeneutic faculty. Although some scholars argue that Marion's critique of Levinas ultimately fails, Marion's critique is nonetheless instructive, and it raises the important question of erotic individuation; that is, how we come to experience the Other as the Beloved.[3] We thus begin with a consideration of Marion's analysis.

In "The Intentionality of Love," Marion begins by identifying the "infernal paradox" of the experience of love: "I love only through the lived experiences of my consciousness," and so "[l]ove appears as an optical illusion of my consciousness, which experiences only itself alone."[4] Reduced to my own experiences of my own consciousness, love in this manner becomes self-idolatry.[5] But Marion is not satisfied with this deduction. "Love should," he argues, "by hypothesis, make me transcend my lived experiences and my consciousness in order to reach pure alterity."[6] Marion argues that Levinas's ethics provides an initial way out of the aporia by opening onto alterity. Insofar as the Other exceeds my ability to "capture" him with an adequate concept the Other remains "invisible" to my consciousness, he in some profound way "evades" me, exceeding the limits of my consciousness. "The alterity of the other transgresses, even and especially, the intentionality of *my* consciousness from the moment that consciousness reverts all the more to me as mine in its spreading out ever more intentionally from me."[7] The Other comes from *without,* always appearing as a *surplus.* He "forces himself upon me" by reducing my consciousness to a kind of "unconsciousness" which cannot envision him, cannot "see" him, and cannot render him an object.[8] Strictly speaking, I am not conscious of the Other. Therefore, any love of the Other that emerges cannot be reduced to my own experiences of my own consciousness. But Levinas's insistence that the Other always arrives as an *ethical* injunction does not make space for love, Marion argues, because the injunction issues as a universal command and love appears as a radically particular call.[9] Although the injunction is the first step on the way toward love, it cannot be the last.[10]

In both "The Intentionality of Love" and "From the Other to the Individual," Marion expands his critique of Levinas, arguing that Levinas's account of the Other relies too heavily on Kantian assumptions of ethics as universal and anonymous, qualities that preclude the possibility of love as an experience of radical particularity. For example, according to Marion, Levinas's ethical injunction issues as a duty: it demands that I treat the Other as an end in himself and not an object of utility. It is universal: it enjoins "to every possible other" and "does not in any way depend on the particular identity of this or that other."[11] It universalizes: the injunction renders the Other substitutable with any other Other.[12] And it is anonymizes: the demand for respect issues in the form of a law, "I do not feel for *this* other, *this* face, *this* individual."[13] For Marion, the fact that we experience the injunction in a particular face does not provide a sufficiently individuated account with regard to the radical uniqueness of the Other. Moving from the particular Other to the injunction is a move toward abstract universality: "[T]he moral law—which states that the other man must always count as end and not as means—never uses the face of an individualized other except as a means for accomplishing the universal."[14] The injunction signals to an ethical abstraction that neutralizes the Other as such and cannot lead to love.

The trouble does not end there. In "From the Other to the Individual," Marion goes on to argue that Levinas's account of the Other produces a dangerous solipsism. The face of the Other always carries with it an anonymity because it calls me into existence but it never fully appears itself.[15] "[I]f an individuation occurs, it appears to be not that of *this* other, but my own."[16] The Other only individuates *me*. The Other calls me into being but through the Other I return to myself, to my own experiences of myself. The Other appeals to and enjoins me, calling me into the hypostatic moment. But the Other remains an infinity, a transcendence, the unnamed. "The face stifles and masks individuality, even if, or even *because* it reveals the infinity of its anonymous transcendence."[17]

In both of these essays, Marion argues that what Levinas is missing is a proper account of love.[18] Love individuates by achieving an "atomic particularity"[19] with regard to myself and the Other. It requires "nothing less than *haecceitas*" which "passes beyond beingness in general, but also beyond that which, in the injunction and responsibility, falls under the universal, and thus the Neuter."[20] Marion's critique of Levinas is illuminating for several reasons, not the least of which is that it raises the questions of how and when the Other appears in some cases as not wholly other; that is, how and when the Other appears in relation to myself, as someone to whom I can relate because the Other is in some important ways similar to me. Marion's analysis challenges the Levinasian description of the Other as a radial alterity in favor of a more nuanced account akin to what Brian Treanor calls "relative otherness."[21] It is important to note that Marion's analysis is taking place within a broader conversation between phenomenology and deconstruction, one that seeks to explain what it is we love, when we love. This context is important for understanding the role the amorous imagination plays in navigating the otherness of the Other because it informs a decision to highlight the hermeneutical side of love's appearance.

According to thinkers such as John Caputo and Jacques Derrida, philosophers deeply committed to the program of deconstruction, the Other is wholly other: *tout autre est tout autre* ("every other is wholly other"). Otherness is absolute. Any attempt to reduce the alterity of the Other to the Same constitutes an act of violence and an injustice. For deconstruction, love is not fundamentally about intimacy, union, or similarity, which constitute degradations of the Other insofar as they bring the otherness of the Other under the purview of the Self. Rather, love is about difference, distance, and respect.[22] Deconstruction prefers words more akin to ethics than eros in order to describe the nature of love. Levinas (who blurs the line between deconstruction and phenomenology) appeals to responsibility; Derrida, to justice. Even in a more explicitly Christian form of deconstruction, love takes as its object anonymity rather than particularity.[23] Religious thinkers such as John Caputo advocate for a love of "the impossible," an abiding concern for the "unknown guest whose arrival is *infinitely* deferred."[24] Rather than speaking of love as love of the particular, deconstruction prefers to discuss love toward the universal, or the anonymous, or as the yet-to-come. Deconstruction requires that love maintain distance in order to avoid the supposedly debased forms of love that manifest as a desire for intimacy, merging, or oneness with the Other.

For more phenomenologically inclined thinkers such as Marion and Treanor, this account of love fails to explain the nature of relationship between the Other and the Beloved, relationship that can in some way traverse alterity without collapsing it. According to them, deconstruction cannot account for the experience of radical particularity that characterizes love because its insistence on radical alterity views any reduction of difference as domination. In preserving alterity at all costs, deconstruction does not leave room for the way in which we experience the Other as an individual, as Marion points out. Deconstruction privileges alterity over *haecceitas*. But as Treanor argues, "Absolute otherness cannot surprise us, or jolt us out of economic existence, or call us into question, or question the naive spontaneity of freedom, or found discourse, or any other such thing because otherness qua otherness cannot be encountered, experienced, or revealed." We must therefore find another way to explain the experience we have of the Other as alterity while at the same time accounting for "aspects of alterity imbedded in, or interwoven with, aspects of similitude."[25] I join thinkers like Marion and Treanor in calling for an account of love that rehabilitates a notion of "relative otherness" while still attending to the profundity of the Other's alterity.[26] Such an account must be construed in what Treanor calls "hermeneutic-chiastic" terms; that is, in terms that reject an all-or-nothing account of otherness but that take seriously alterity alongside experiences of similitude.[27] "While there may be some aspects of the other that are foreign and even absolutely obscure to the self, these aspects exist alongside others that are in some measure familiar."[28] In order to analyze the structure of love we must examine the way in which both alterity and similitude appear; that is, the way in which the Other arrives in the form of both distance and intimacy. A phenomenology of the amorous imagination attempts to do just that by invoking the role of hermeneutics and describing the way the lovers engage in a diacritical reading across distance.

So how, according to Marion, does the Beloved emerge? How does she become individuated? Marion's first pass at the answer comes in the form of what he calls the phenomenon of "the crossing of gazes":

> Whence comes what we will from now on consider the phenomenological determination of love: two definitively invisible gazes (intentionality and the injunction) cross one another, and thus together trace a cross that is invisible to every gaze *other than theirs alone*. . . . To love would thus be defined as seeing the definitively invisible aim of my gaze nonetheless exposed by the aim of another invisible gaze; the two gazes, invisible forever, expose themselves to each other in the crossing of their reciprocal aims.[29]

In his earliest writings on love, Marion suggests that the phenomenon of "the crossing of gazes" provides an opening onto individuation, but it is not until *The Erotic Phenomenon* that he fully develops the idea and its implications. There, he builds upon his previous phenomenological studies on givenness, saturation, the self, and the endless hermeneutic to explain how it is he thinks phenomena such as the crossing of gazes create a space for love that is otherwise unattainable in a Levinasian framework. We turn to an analysis of these ideas before returning to the question of individuation and a full account of Marion's erotic phenomenology. As we will see, his account is compelling, but it relies too heavily on the lover's advance and does not explain the hermeneutic structure of love and the role the imagination plays in the Other's individuation.

Givenness

In *Being Given*, Marion sets out his phenomenology of givenness. Positioning himself as third in line following Husserl and Heidegger, Marion performs a "final" phenomenological reduction. Marion argues that "what *shows itself* first *gives itself*."[30] Givenness is the sole horizon of all phenomenality. Husserl claims to get to "the things themselves" but limits phenomena to the confines of objectness. Heidegger claims to reveal the givenness of phenomena but limits their appearing to the horizon of Being (Being as the "ultimate" phenomenon). In *Being Given*, Marion credits Husserl and Heidegger with glimpsing the given in certain ways but argues that neither truly broke free from metaphysics. For Marion, the given is that which is required before any phenomenon can appear. It is the unconditioned call of phenomena.

The central argument in *Being Given* is that givenness is that to which all phenomena may be reduced: "[E]very phenomenon falls within the given, to the point that the terms could trade places."[31] Givenness represents the liberation of phenomena from the limits of the ego. In describing the call of the phenomenon as *se donner*, Marion highlights the double nature of givenness. Phenomena "are given" and "give themselves," according to and on their own terms (*se donner* is a reflexive French verb). It is important not to overstate Marion's critique of Husserl and Heidegger. He does not claim these two philosophers utterly failed to glimpse the given. Rather, he argues that their reductions do not allow phenomena to give themselves according to their own terms. Put another way, objectness and Being do not provide a full or accurate account of phenomenality. Marion argues that phenomena give themselves in degrees and that the reduction to givenness reveals as much. For example, some "poor" phenomena such as mathematical objects provide only a concept-as-intention, which is sufficient to constitute the object. We never have an actual intuition of a circle, only of objects that approximate circularity.[32] And yet these phenomena are fully knowable because we supply most of the content via intention. "Common" or technical objects give (slightly?) more intuition and are constituted via adequation between intuition and intention. Because intention matches intuition we are able to exercise control, mastery, or dispassionate observation over technical objects.[33]

But some phenomena exceed our intentions with the intuition they provide.[34] These phenomena saturate our intentionality, leaving us rubbing our eyes and asking, "What just happened?" The degrees of givenness illustrate the nature of phenomena as having the capacity to give themselves from themselves without the limits set upon them by transcendental or even phenomenological investigation. I will have much more to say about saturated phenomena below.

L'adonné

How is the given received? How does it show itself? We find the answers in Marion's theory of the self. The self for Marion is both receptive and active, the site upon which pure phenomena land and the interpretive movement that shows them in "resisting" or "receiving" them. Marion uses a number of terms to describe that which receives the given. Early in his works he refers to the self as *interloqué,* the interlocuted one who is "taken by surprise" and must give account. He also uses the term *witness* to describe the one to whom an event "happens" and who attests to its occurrence. Later, he refers to the self as *l'attributaire,* the one to whom something is attributed. He finally settles on *l'adonné,* or the gifted, the one who receives the gift, is given over to, devoted to, or even addicted to the phenomenon.[35] Notably, *l'adonné* is not passive, but rather, *receptive.* Receptivity has for Marion a passive dimension insofar as the phenomenon is given over to the self, but it also has an active capacity that may "increase the measure of the given and make sure it happens. . . . [*L'adonné* must] work on itself in order to receive."[36]

Initiative plays an important role in understanding *l'adonné*'s receptivity. Marion leaves nothing to question: the phenomenon gives itself first. It takes initiative. Givenness is fundamental and that to which all phenomena may be reduced. It is only in this primary initiative that saturated phenomena can even "happen" because they are by definition unrestrained by the self's intention. Unlike Husserl and Heidegger, Marion claims to not limit phenomena to any conceptual schema brought to bear upon them. Givenness issues to *l'adonné* as a *call* (not an injunction) that is an "inconceivable, unnameable, and unforeseeable instance which is comprehended less than it surprises and which initially remains anonymous."[37] Marion is not simply reversing intention and intuition, metaphorically characterizing the given as a kind of "subject" while preserving the transcendental "I" that receives it. He is challenging the very question of a transcendental I which precedes any phenomenon. For Marion, the given gives me to myself. It is in receiving the given that I receive myself as a self. The phenomenon "arrives" to and for me but it must be phenomenalized. In receiving a phenomenon, I receive myself and am gifted to myself by the given. But the given is not God. The saturated phenomenon always remains anonymous. As Gschwandtner points out, "It is only in the reception of the phenomenon that we can identify whether the phenomenon comes from God, from Being (cf. Heidegger), from the Other (cf. Levinas), or from the flesh (cf. Henry)."[38] Here we see the important role the self plays in identifying the given: in receiving the given the phenomenon appears, it is phenomenalized. A phenomenon must happen *to* someone. "Beyond activity and passivity, reception gives form to what gives itself without yet showing itself."[39] Marion often describes the *l'adonné* as a screen upon which the light of the given splashes, or a control panel that lights up "at the very instant when and each time the information he should render phenomenal . . . arrives to him from a transistor by electric impulse without initiative or delay."[40] The given calls and *l'adonné* responds. Indeed, *the call itself is shown in the response.*

At times, Marion characterizes the response required to show the given as a kind of resistance to it. *L'adonné* "bears up" against the given, or "holds up" under the pressure of its givenness. Resistance is not a phenomenological act of defiance but a way of describing how the given shows itself in landing upon the receptive self. The self fixes the given by phenomenalizing it, and in doing so shows it.[41] But *l'adonné* can fail to receive a phenomenon appropriately. As we have seen, some phenomena give too much. In Marion's terms, they "saturate" intentionality. *L'adonné* may "misidentify [a saturated phenomenon] or fail to hear it at all, I can be blinded by its excess or experience its fullness as an absence. Instead of giving a 'sensible' account, I may be reduced to fainting, babbling, an inability to speak or even contempt."[42] Receiving the saturated given calls for a proper response, one that does not manifest merely as control, dominance, or manipulation but that includes careful description, attention, and interpretation. Here, Marion introduces his idea of hermeneutics. The given first gives itself, anonymously and of its own initiative, but the given—particularly the saturated phenomenon—calls for an "infinite" or "endless" hermeneutic.[43] The endless hermeneutic is the response to the saturated phenomenon that does not reduce it to objectness, the Other, Being, or any single identity. It is the proper, interpretive response to the saturated phenomenon.[44] The saturated phenomenon gives itself in so much excess that no single interpretation will ever suffice. Instead of *knowing* the phenomenon, *l'adonné* must *understand* it through an ongoing, hermeneutical enterprise. The endless hermeneutic is full of possibility.

Marion's descriptions of *l'adonné* make up the basic contours of his account of the role hermeneutics play in "showing what gives itself." Marion is a phenomenologist, and throughout his work he privileges phenomenological description over hermeneutical explanation. But he does not wholly neglect the latter. As we have seen, he explains the way in which *l'adonné* in receiving phenomena "shows them," and how in being resisted phenomena appear. This is fundamentally hermeneutical activity. In *Negative Certainties*, Marion provides the helpful example of one's birth to illustrate how a phenomenon can remain invisible but manifest through hermeneutical mediation. My birth is a phenomenon that "remains and will remain invisible" to me but that nonetheless happened; that is, was given. Because my birth will forever remain invisible, "complex mediations of speech, language, kinestheses, and intersubjective plots will be necessary in order that it may be *mediately* recognized—moreover, only to certain people, and not to others, for a certain period of time each time, provisionally and unequally."[45] These mediations are always "lagging behind" the event of birth—or any event, for that matter—because "the recipient or givee, initially unconscious of the event when it passes (of) *itself* in the moment, afterward remains . . . in a *différance* crossed by the call and response."[46] This gap between what gives itself and what appears is the space of interpretation, the space from which what gives itself shows itself.[47] Marion's hermeneutics are not without controversy. Some scholars argue that his description of *l'adonné*'s role in "showing" phenomena problematizes or perhaps even contradicts his other accounts of the given, which as we have seen he describes as imposing itself on the self, rather than relying upon the self to play a constitutive role in what is given.[48] This critique has some merit, but because our current concern is with a "horizontal" analysis of how one phenomenon (the

Other) is transformed into another (the Beloved) and not a "vertical" analysis in search of the grounds of phenomenality, the problems that arise as a result of Marion's underdeveloped hermeneutics do not have much to bear upon a phenomenology of the amorous imagination. But Marion's observation that there is a "gap" between what is given and what appears will have important consequences, and we will return to this idea later as we tease out the way in which hermeneutical reception operates as a condition for the possibility of love.

We can begin to see the implications of *l'adonné*'s hermeneutical engagement with the given and its importance in manifesting love in Marion's descriptions in *Negative Certainties* (and in other works such as *In Excess* and "The Banality of Saturation"). Marion explains how variations of phenomenality appear according to the self's hermeneutical interaction with the given. Much of the way in which a phenomenon appears is contingent upon *l'adonné*'s gaze, although—and this is crucial for Marion's project—the reduction to givenness reveals that a phenomenon's "pure givenness" always remains independent of a constituting subject. Nevertheless, according to Marion, a phenomenon appears as an object when intention imposes a "phenomenal restriction" upon the intuition, such that it 'suffer[s] from a shortage of happening." Marion cites the example of a hammer, which "can vary from the status of a subsistent object to that of a piece of equipment according to the variation in my phenomenological gaze." The "viewpoint" of the gaze can "transfigure" what appears from object to equipment, or vice versa.[49] But of course, not all phenomena appear as objects or equipment. As we will see, in the case of the event, which exceeds all intentionality, another horizon of phenomenality emerges: the saturated phenomenon. In *Negative Certainties* Marion goes so far as to suggest that all phenomena give themselves with an eventual character but that *l'adonné*'s gaze determines the way in which a phenomenon appears along a continuum between object and event. He writes, "That even a stone could sometimes appear as an event depends only upon my gaze."[50] Regardless of the consistency of this phenomenological description with the rest of Marion's work, what is important for our purposes is to notice how "hermeneutic variations" are at play in what appears, and the phenomenological observation that *l'adonné*'s mode of reception or restriction of the given has an impact on what shows itself. This idea is important because it opens a space to examine the amorous imagination's creative-responsive capacity and the lover's ability to "see" the Beloved as radically particular, as other than any Other.

The Saturated Phenomenon

The saturated phenomenon is perhaps Marion's most well-known philosophical idea. Although he is not the first philosopher to articulate an experience of excess (see, e.g., Kant's sublime and Levinas's "the face") he is the first to provide a systematic account of the degrees of givenness and the implications of saturation on selfhood, the structures of consciousness, and phenomenality in general. Marion's thinking about the saturated phenomenon shifts throughout his work. He first proposed his theory in an essay entitled, "The Saturated Phenomenon" (1992).[51] In *Being Given* (1997), Marion gives saturation a complete philosophical treatment. And in *In Excess* (2001), Marion delves even deeper into saturation, conducting five case studies of the saturated phenomenon.

In his early texts the saturated phenomenon seems to be an exceptional phenomenon, one that only gives itself at the margins of phenomenality.[52] But in *Being Given*, *In Excess*, and in a later essay, "The Banality of Saturation," Marion explains that the saturated phenomenon is not a special case of phenomenality but rather an everyday phenomenon that most anyone can experience. Saturated phenomena are not strictly religious or mystical phenomena. Marion provides five sense-related examples in "The Banality of Saturation."[53] Regarding vision, Marion notes that one usually experiences the colors on a country's flag as a common-law phenomenon. The colors are given in intuition but disappear into the intention or concept of the country that consciousness brings to them. The phenomenon conveys information and is rendered an object. On the other hand, when one encounters Rothko's canvas *Number 212*, the intuition of the painting's colors exceeds any intentionality consciousness can bring to it. The painting is, phenomenologically speaking, *invisible*. It cannot be intended. Regarding sound, Marion distinguishes between an announcement over an airport speaker, which again conveys information and is a common-law phenomenon, and an opera diva whose voice provides a surplus of intuition that can never be fully heard. An aria sings in the language of saturation. Regarding smell, Marion describes the difference between the smell of gas, which conveys information and warns me of danger, and the smell of perfume, which gives itself as a rich and full abundance. Regarding touch, Marion contrasts the experience of stumbling through a dark room groping for items one can identify as objects, with the caress which provides the fullness of flesh that never gives itself as an object. "I caress in order to love, therefore in silence, in order to console and soothe, to excite and enjoy, therefore without objective signification, indeed, without identifiable or sayable signification."[54]

Recall Marion's critique of Husserl and Heidegger. Their failure was to limit the givenness of phenomena to objects and Being. These sense-based examples illustrate the way in which the transcendental ego hides the givenness of the phenomenon and instead plots it on a predetermined horizon. The horizon masks or obscures the movement of givenness itself as self-giving. Marion's entire project in *Being Given* is to allow phenomena to show themselves on their own terms. To that extent, the saturated phenomenon is the phenomenon par excellence because it cannot be reduced to a predetermined horizon. It exceeds the limits of intentionality, objectness, or Being.[55] "The saturated phenomenon in the end establishes the truth of all phenomenality because it marks, more than any other phenomenon, the givenness from which it comes."[56]

Four Categories of Saturated Phenomenon

In *Being Given* and *In Excess*, Marion develops his idea of the saturated phenomenon against the backdrop of Kant's categories of understanding: quantity, quality, relation, and modality.[57] The categories provide a useful framework for exploring the various ways in which phenomena saturate the horizons of experience. Marion uses them to demonstrate how the given exceeds or overflows what the conscious ego brings to it. While all saturated phenomena are marked by an inability to be grasped, a certain unforseeability, and a kind of "control" or reorienting effect on the self, they do not all saturate in the same manner. Kant's categories are a horizon; or perhaps more precisely, conditions for the possibility of experience. But it is precisely the question of possibility that the saturated phenomenon problematizes. Through his account of the saturated phenomenon, Marion points us toward the impossible.[58] He argues that there are phenomena that give themselves in excess of the categories, phenomena we cannot comprehend. The "possibility of the impossible" has radical implications for the self, the Other, and for love. And yet, Marion's theory of the saturated phenomenon fails to explain the hermeneutic dimension of experience, without which no account of love can be complete. Before we turn to its limitations, however, we must first understand Marion's idea. After explaining each type of saturated phenomenon, I will offer some commentary regarding how (if at all) that type of saturated phenomenon connects to my central argument regarding the amorous imagination. In particular, I will discuss how the saturated phenomenon might manifest in the way the Beloved is given, as well as the hermeneutical dimensions of the saturated phenomenon.

The Event and Friendship: Saturation According to Quantity

Marion first examines saturation according to quantity.[59] In Kant's schematic, quantity is the transcendental category that gives form to an intuition's extensive magnitude by "successive synthesis" of the whole in terms of its parts. "The magnitude of a *quantum* implies nothing more than the summation of the *quanta* that make it up."[60] Marion argues that quantity as an axiom of intuition renders a phenomenon foreseeable "on the basis of another besides itself—more precisely, on the basis of the supposedly finite number of its parts and the supposedly finite magnitude of each among them."[61] But there are some phenomena that give themselves with so much quantity that the phenomenon is "not limited by its possible concept, its excess can neither be divided nor adequately put together again by virtue of a finite magnitude homogeneous with finite parts."[62] Such a phenomenon "could not be measured in terms of its parts, since the saturating intuition surpasses limitlessly the sum of the parts by continually adding to them."[63] Phenomena that saturate according to quantity give too much information, are so rich and complex that they cannot be contained by a concept or successive synthesis.[64] They are "incommensurable, not measurable (immense), unmeasured."[65] Indeed, they are "invisible" insofar they cannot be aimed at (*visé*) by an intending consciousness and therefore cannot synthesize the manifold into a foreseeable totality of which the phenomenon is a part.[66]

Historical events provide a clear example.[67] Marion states:

> When the arising event is not limited to an instant a place, or an empirical individual, but overflows these singularities and become epoch-making in time . . . covers a physical space such that no gaze encompasses it with one sweep . . . and encompasses a population such that none of those who belong to it can take upon themselves an absolute or even privileged point of view, then it becomes an historical event.[68]

A historical event is *evental* insofar as it has the following features. First, it is inexhaustible. It cannot be fully explained or interpreted. It resists any single story. It cannot be seen in its totality due to its vastness, excess, and "amount of happening." The event gives too much information and therefore calls for an endless interpretation. Second, the event's effects precede its causes. The event happens, it wells up according to its own givenness and cannot be contained. It is only after the event occurs that we look back at its happening and give causal accounts as to why it happened. Because the event is unforeseeable, it cannot be predicted. The evental effect takes phenomenological priority over its metaphysical causes.[69]

As we will see, Marion's sense of the inverted experience of cause and effect is relevant to an analysis of the love because love shares a similar structure. The lover's encounter with the Beloved is experienced as an event. Phenomenologically speaking, the Other-as-Beloved is given to the lover as an unforeseeable event that is understood only after the effect has occurred. The Beloved's striking givenness is not merely a romantic experience of "love-at-first-sight" (although not excluding that either) but a phenomenological experience that overwhelms any successive synthesis and calls for endless interpretation. I discuss the importance of this "endless hermeneutic" in later chapters, but suffice it to say for now that Marion's analysis of the saturated event yields the paradoxical result that our very experiences of cause and effect may be overturned or called into question as a condition for the possibility of saturating experience, and that description applies to the event of love.[70]

Marion also cites friendship as an example of saturation according to quantity. In chapter 2 of *In Excess*, Marion describes the evental nature of the friendship between Montaigne and La Boétie. He begins his description by invoking a phenomenon he thinks is unique to our experience of certain others: the phenomenon of the crossing of gazes [*la croisée des regards*]. The crossing of gazes inaugurates the first moment of individuation, catalyzing the conversion of *the* Other into *this* Other through my submission to his radically particular gaze. Marion writes,

> Friendship with the other person first makes it my duty to cast a gaze on him, which does not follow my intentionality toward him but submits me to the point of view that he takes of me, therefore places me at the exact point where his own line of sight waits for me to expose myself.[71]

In his own reflections Montaigne acknowledges the evental and erotic nature of his first meeting with Boétie, as when he writes, "[I]t is I do not know which quintessence of all this mix that, having seized my will, brought it to plunge itself and lost itself in his.[72]" The iconic gaze of the Other calls me forward, but it is in the sudden arrival of the friendship that emerges and is accomplished all at once and as a *fait accompli* that we see friendship's evental character. The friendship cannot be explained. Montaigne recounts that "at our first meeting . . . we found ourselves so taken, so known, so obliged between ourselves, that nothing from then on was as close as we were for one another."[73] The ultimate meaning of the friendship is never disclosed to Montaigne and Boétie. Indeed, it remains inaccessible, hidden, unsayable. Friendship has no cause. It has no reason.[74] And yet for Montaigne and Boétie it happened, it was experienced, it was given. When asked why he loved Boétie, Montaigne could only reply, "because it was him, because it was me."[75]

One is struck not only by the evental but also the amorous tone of Montaigne and Boétie's friendship. There is clearly a radical individuation at play. As I will argue later, love carries a structural similarity to friendship in its evental nature, but love saturates according to other categories as well and implicates the imagination in ways that may or may not be required for friendship. In any event, the key points to note for now are the features of phenomena that saturate according to quantity: (1) they cannot be repeated and are irreversible; (2) they cannot be explained, especially in terms of causality, and therefore call for an endless hermeneutic; (3) they cannot be foreseen or predicted as their (partial) causes are only revealed after the effect and always remain insufficient.[76] Additionally, with regard to the event of friendship the phenomenon of the crossing of gazes inaugurates the first moment of individuation of the Other. The phenomenon of the crossing of gazes plays an important part in Marion's account of individuation between lovers too.[77]

The Idol: Saturation According to Quality

Marion examines saturation according to quality through a detailed analysis of paintings, which can function as what he calls "idols."[78] In *Being Given*, Marion distinguishes between the phenomenon of the idol and the phenomenon of the icon as two "ways of seeing." Idols lure the gaze, which surveys the idol until it is absorbed and filled by it. Icons allow the gaze to travel through and beyond it while at the same time directing a gaze back toward the viewer, envisaging her rather than being envisaged by her.[79] (I provide a detailed account of icons in section D, "The Face: Saturation According to Modality." We focus now on idols because they saturate according to quality.) Marion begins his account of idols by describing the phenomenon of the gaze that turns toward an image and aims at it. When viewing a painting, for example, the viewer becomes "bedazzled" by what she sees. Her gaze is lured to the image. It searches for something that can fill it. It roves around, "looking beyond what it sees," until it finds the phenomenon that fills it, and there it lands, captivated and fascinated by the visible that captures it. Here, the viewer encounters the "first visible."[80] However, because the "first visible" is determined by the intention that searches it out it is actually a reflection of the intention itself. The gaze is "absorbed and filled" by the phenomenon, but the gaze returns back to itself. The painting is a mirror, "an idol—dazzling to the site but made in our own image."[81]

Despite its idolatrous nature (or really, because of it), Marion claims that this experience constitutes a saturated phenomenon in terms of quality. Kant's category of quality refers to an appearance's "*intensive magnitude*; i.e., a degree of influence on sense."[82] Every sensation has a magnitude, a level of intensity that effects our sensation.[83] A sensation's intensity is experienced according to the continuum of possible degrees afforded to the sensation. For example, a shade of red has a particular intensity experienced in terms of the other possible shades of red that may be lighter or darker, or between no sensation of red and a sensation of the most intense degree.[84] Paintings-as-idols saturate in terms of quality because they give themselves in such a way that the gaze can no longer bear the intensity of the sensation it receives.[85] The idol draws our gaze and then "blinds us" with its intensity (although strictly speaking we still "see" it as a perception, the "seeing" is not of an object but of a saturating excess). It is an invisible visible, which "invades all [the look's] angles; it accomplishes *adaequatio*—it fills. But the filling goes by itself beyond itself; it goes to the brink, too far."[86]

Marion's analysis of the idol reminds us of his initial diagnosis of love as an "infernal paradox": that love should by hypothesis transcend my own experience but it seems always to arise from and reflect my consciousness. In other words, love never seems to reach alterity. Love appears idolatrous, an expression of my own desires and experiences. But Marion's analysis of the idol as saturated phenomenon points to a way out of this paradox. Building on Levinas's account of the Other as an excess that comes from without (i.e., as a saturated phenomenon) the Beloved takes my consciousness to the brink and I discover that my intentionality cannot limit the Other's givenness. Moreover, Marion's account of the idol highlights the darker side of love and, as we will see, the dangers of the amorous imagination. In chapter 6 I use the term *idol* to refer to the risks of imaginative individuation; that is, the danger that the lover might fall in love with his own imaginings rather than the Beloved. My analysis borrows from Marion's concept of the idol insofar as I use his idea that the lover's imaginative "gaze" can and often does seek that which captivates it and in doing so reflects his own desires back at him, at which point the lover no longer loves the Other but only himself. The language of love highlights this temptation: we say that a lover is "blinded" by love or that the Beloved has "captured" his imagination. Both terms may betray an underlying idolatry akin to what Marion describes in his work.

The Flesh: Saturation According to Relation

Phenomena that saturate according to relation appear so immediate that they render any relation impossible. In Kant's schema, relation is a condition for the possibility of experience. The transcendental subject synthesizes the manifold of appearances "into a unity in terms of their relations to one another in time."[87] The three a priori synthetic principles of substance, causality, and community regulate the way in which we perceive appearances and allow for their perception to be experienced as a unity. The understanding imposes the principles onto perceptions, laying down the horizons of experience.

Marion argues in *Being Given* that some phenomena give themselves with an immediacy and a "mineness" that is without relation, that is absolute.[88] Take the flesh, for example. I never experience my flesh as distinct from me, nor as related to me.[89] I always experience myself *as* flesh. Indeed, I am my flesh. The phenomenon of my flesh "evades any analogy of experience."[90] It is given as an *auto-affection* that

> refers to no object, according to no ecstasy, but only to itself; for it itself is sufficient to accomplish itself as affected. . . . The flesh auto-affects itself in agony, suffering, and grief, as well as in desire, feeling, or orgasm.[91]

This auto-affection saturates the horizon of relation because it does not appear in relation to any other phenomenon. It always appears on its own and as its own. The flesh's mode of appearing is therefore nonrelational. It overflows or exceeds Kant's regulative idea of relation because the flesh is experienced precisely as outside of or other than relation. It is its *own* experience.

Marion develops his description of the flesh further in *In Excess* and *The Erotic Phenomenon*. In *In Excess*, Marion emphasizes the priority or fundamental experience of my flesh; that is, it is always as flesh that I experience myself. Descartes relies on the *cogitatio* as indubitable evidence of an ego, but Marion argues that it is our sentience that is fundamentally indubitable. The ego's existence as sentient precedes its existence as thinking.[92] "The *ego* gives itself [*se donner*] as flesh, even if one wants to hide it."[93] And through my flesh I am individuated.[94] I am fundamentally connected to my flesh and my flesh is strictly my own (no one else can experience my flesh). My experience of my flesh as "mine" is therefore given to me, it is not something that I constitute or assert. "I do not give myself my flesh, it is it that gives me to myself. In receiving my flesh, I receive myself—I am in this way gifted [*adonné,* given over] to it."[95] Flesh denies the standard phenomenological distinction between *noesis* and *noema* because the perceived is no longer clearly distinguishable from the perceiver. The intentional aim directed toward the flesh is accomplished as an essential immanence where "what I intend is blended with the possible fulfillment."[96] Relation is saturated by and in the flesh insofar as flesh collapses the very relations consciousness uses to constitute the world: intention and intuition.

In the fourth meditation in *The Erotic Phenomenon,* Marion again takes up the phenomenon of flesh but this time within the context of love. Here, he emphasizes less the flesh's auto-affectivity and instead speaks of the way in which another gives me my flesh through touch and *eros.*[97] Marion first argues that worldly bodies affect me only because of the flesh's passivity. In taking flesh I open myself up to worldly bodies, allowing "the things of the world the right to affect me and to reduce me to my passivity."[98] But this apparent hetero-affection of the flesh disguises a more primordial and active auto-affection moving beneath the surface of passivity. Marion states,

> I would feel nothing other (than myself) if I could not first feel myself, with an undertow more original than the wave that seems to result, but which, in fact, announces the undertow and, at once, allows itself to be caught up into it: auto-affection alone makes possible hetero-affection.[99]

Marion then turns to the difference between my experience of worldly bodies and the flesh of another. The fundamental difference is that worldly bodies are given in their resistance to my touch whereas another's flesh affects me by opening itself up to me and for me.[100] Unlike worldly bodies, the flesh of another "withdraws, effaces itself and makes room for me."[101] Then Marion seems to turn back to hetero-affectivity:

> I can only free myself and become myself *by touching another flesh,* as one touches land at a port, because only another flesh can make room for me, welcome me, and not turn me away or resist me—that is, comply with my flesh and reveal it to me by providing it a place.[102] (Emphasis added)

And later:

> *The other gives me to myself for the first time,* because she takes the initiative to give me my own flesh for the first time. She awakens me, because she eroticizes me.[103] (Emphasis added)[104]

Here, we see an unresolved tension in Marion's work between the flesh's auto-affectivity and hetero-affectivity. On the one hand, Marion describes the flesh as radically auto-affective, "it is it that gives me to myself." The flesh saturates relation. But on the other hand, he describes the phenomenon of the flesh of the *other* as that which "gives me to myself for the first time." Which is it? Do I receive myself from my flesh or the flesh of another? Does my flesh give itself as an absolute phenomenon *without* relation to anything else? Or does it give itself *through* relation; that is, relation with another's flesh?[105] Mackinlay makes the astute observation that for Marion it seems as though "I become fully flesh, not by sensing *myself,* but by sensing that I am sensed in the flesh of another."[106] Marion's description of the erotic phenomenon emphasizes both hetero-affection and auto-affection. But his description of the flesh as saturated phenomenon requires strict auto-affection. One way to resolve this dilemma may be to read Marion's account of the erotic phenomenon as beginning and ending with auto-affection but recognizing the unique way in which the other's flesh is given in order to induce my experience of the saturated phenomenon of my own flesh. In other words, I always experience my flesh as strict auto-affection (immediate and mine) but the fullness of that experience is only revealed to me through contact with another's flesh which exposes me to myself in a way that no worldly object can. Marion says as much when he writes,

> And yet the other's flesh is truly phenomenalized, but under a unique mode that must be admitted: it is phenomenalized without, however, making itself seen, by allowing itself simply and radically to be felt. By allowing itself to be felt in such a way of course, that I feel that I am feeling it (by definition of my flesh), but also that I feel that it feels me (by the definition of the other) and what then does this flesh of the other feel, if not that I feel it and even that I

feel it feel me? And, at the end of this interlacing, what do our two fleshes feel, if not each the feeling of the feeling of the other?[107]

But even this charitable reading fails to demonstrate the strict auto-affection Marion requires to show that flesh saturates all relation. Even if it is the case that the flesh is given uniquely as immediate and mine, that immediacy and mineness appears only through the flesh's contact with a world, and especially through its contact with another's flesh. As we will see, my flesh's encounter with the flesh of another constitutes a radical moment of individuation. Marion's strongest argument for auto-affection still reveals a hetero-affection at play. My flesh appears only to me (auto-affection) but its appearance is induced by its contact with another's flesh (hetero-affection). The other's flesh is phenomenalized for me when it allows me to feel it, which actually reveals to *me* that I am feeling it and that it is being felt *by me*. Although I do not experience the flesh of another, the flesh of another reveals me to myself. My flesh is not therefore strictly absolute insofar as it is given to me through a relation with the flesh of another.

Whether Marion is simply inconsistent in his description of the flesh or is instead trying to signal toward a subtler relationship between auto-affectivity and hetero-affectivity remains unclear. For our purposes, however, it is crucial to note that if I am given to myself through the flesh of another then I am given to myself hermeneutically. The flesh mediates. It is a "film," a medium, or a vehicle through which both my self and the Other are phenomenalized. Indeed, on Marion's account, there is a kind of double interpretation that occurs: in the erotic moment it is through the appearance of *another's* flesh that *my* flesh and *my* self appear. The flesh opens onto the space of interpretation. In Richard Kearney's terms, a "carnal hermeneutics" is at play. The phenomenon of the flesh is given not as an absolute phenomenon but in and through a relationship with other things, and in a unique way through a relationship with an Other (which is profoundly *not* "a thing"). The Other plays a special role in individuating me and individuation occurs within both a phenomenological and hermeneutical register. Marion does not speak of the structural role of hermeneutics in the givenness of the flesh. His emphasis on auto-affection conceals the mediating role the flesh plays in understanding and responding to the Beloved. But as we will see in chapter 4, the hermeneutical structure of the flesh is central to the process of individuation. Through the relationship between my flesh and the world and my flesh and another I come to experience an Other as the Beloved. And through the amorous imagination I engage in an endless hermeneutic in which I continuously interpret the Beloved without ever "knowing" her (as an object). Individuation occurs in and is expressed through the flesh. Indeed, the amorous imagination is an embodied imagination and is therefore hermeneutical "all the way down." Any account of the phenomenology of love should include a description of the amorous imagination precisely because of the role it plays in individuating the Beloved, a role that is always already enfleshed. But we get ahead of ourselves. Before unpacking the implications of Marion's ideas for a phenomenology of the amorous imagination we must conclude our discussion of saturation by looking at the final category: saturation according to modality.[108]

The Face: Saturation According to Modality

The fourth type of saturated phenomenon saturates according to modality. These phenomena are "irregardable" because they cannot be reduced to an object and so remain invisible to object-constituting intentionality. In Marion's parlance we can only "see" (*voir*) these phenomena, but we cannot "look at" (*regarder*) them because they cannot be kept "under the control of the seer": the one who in looking at them "guards the visible in visibility" and thus restricts their saturating excess.[109] Marion provides several examples of these phenomena, most importantly the icon and the face of the Other. Each inflects modal saturation differently but for our purposes the face suffices as both a case study of saturation and, more importantly, an opening onto love and the amorous imagination.

Marion relies heavily on Levinas's account of the unseeable face of the Other. According to Levinas, the face of the Other is unlike any other phenomenon. It is experienced as an infinite excess and transcendence. It withdraws. A chasm exists between the subject and the Other that cannot be traversed. The Other is totally other. The Other remains at a distance and yet enjoins us to responsibility through our encounter with it. The face demands, "Thou shalt not kill!" The look of the Other converts the self into a *me* that is seen rather than an *I* that sees. Here we have the first individuation: the Other weighs upon me as a responsibility for *this* Other who stands before me in her concreteness. Marion questions the apparent individuation of the ethical injunction on the grounds that it ultimately renders the Other substitutable.[110] In *Prolegomena to Charity*, *In Excess*, and *The Erotic Phenomenon*, Marion attempts to go beyond Levinas by describing a second, more radical individuation which occurs through love. Rather than insisting upon an asymmetry in the encounter with the Other, Marion describes the face in both iconic and erotic terms. In encountering the Beloved or icon I am envisaged but I also open myself up to and envisage the Other. As in friendship, envisaging the Beloved gives rise to the phenomenon of the crossing of gazes.[111] Envisaging is an alternative to intending. To envisage the Other is to "admit that he or she expresses herself without signification [i.e., without uniquely determinate signification]" and to accept "an endless diversity of significations, all possible, all provisional, all insufficient."[112] To envisage is therefore to enter into an "endless hermeneutics" in which the lover commits to the ongoing project of interpreting the boundless givenness of the Beloved:

> Only someone who has lived with the life and the death of the other knows to what extent he or she does *not* know that other. Only such a person can hence recognize the other as the saturated phenomenon par excellence, and consequently also knows that it would take an eternity to envisage this saturated phenomenon as such—not constituting it as an object, but interpreting it in loving it.[113]

For Marion, the face saturates modality by exceeding any attempt to reduce its appearing to an object. The face of the Other is irregardable. The face's invisibility opens up to the possibility of love through "envisaging" rather than simply "looking at" the other. The crossing of gazes individuates beyond the ethical toward the erotic because it can only be experienced between the lovers who mutually envisage one another.[114] And to love is to love without end, to respond to the erotic call of the invisible Beloved by engaging in an endless hermeneutic that eternally interprets the meaning of her saturating givenness.

Individuation in *The Erotic Phenomenon*

How then for Marion does love emerge? How do givenness, saturation, and the endless hermeneutic relate and what do they have to do with love and individuation? How does Marion think *the* Other becomes *this* Other, the Beloved? We are now in a position to examine Marion's answer to these questions. Doing so sets the stage for both a critical and generative reading of his account of individuation and provides an opening to describe the role of the imagination in individuating the Beloved.

Marion's work on love culminates in *The Erotic Phenomenon*.[115] The book has three aims: to show that love (1) is univocal, (2) has its own rationality, and (3) is free from being.[116] Marion performs a series of "erotic reductions" in which he brackets the history and philosophy of love and—consistent with the phenomenological method—attempts to describe love as it appears. He moves through the different "stages" of love, analyzing the way in which the self emerges as lover and gives the gift of love without the expectation of reciprocity. The question of individuation pervades his discussion. The text can therefore be understood as a continuation of Marion's thematic encounter with Levinas (beginning with *Prolegomena to Charity*) and a fully articulated answer to the question of how the Other becomes the Beloved; that is, how the self and Other are individuated.

The Lover's Advance and The Crossing of Gazes

The first erotic reduction reveals a great desire; that is, the desire to be loved. By suspending metaphysical concerns and looking only at the self as engaged in the question of love we discover that we care more for love than anything else. We are all vain Hamlets, questioning the meaning of being absent love. We ask, "What's the use?" Another question follows: "Does anyone out there love me?"[117] I cannot resolve the question by demanding that another love me. And I cannot convert love into an exchange, although I try. I think to myself, "I will play the game of love, certainly, but I will only risk the least amount possible, and on condition that the other go first."[118] But this converts love into a transaction. It submits the gift of love to the economy of exchange. It destroys the possibility of love. I discover that love must be freely given. I cannot resolve the question by loving myself because I know myself too well. I know of my own shame and unworthiness. Self-love turns to self-hate. Love must come from elsewhere.

The second reduction reveals the lover's advance. To escape vanity (and its insufficiency), we realize that rather than asking, "Does anyone love me?" we must ask, "Can I love first?"[119] The lover's advance marks the first individuation: in stepping forward to love first, I individuate myself as lover. The lover's advance is an act of will; a decision: "I alone make the decision to love in advance and, as I love to love, I provoke through myself and by myself alone the intuition (in this case, the amorous affective tonality)."[120] But the second reduction reveals a difficulty. The lover's advance can only prepare the lover to receive the Beloved as a radical alterity. The lover cannot attempt to represent the other by fixing her intuition with a signification that would "degrade the other to the dishonorable rank of an object."[121] In stepping forward, "amorous lived experiences only confirm my status as lover, and that I make love; they do not render the other that I love visible or accessible to me (supposing that I really do love *one*)."[122]

Notably, in loving first I do not receive an assurance that I am loved. I am only assured of loving.[123] Nevertheless, "I become myself definitively each time and for as long as I, as lover, can love first."[124] Suspending reciprocity and acting without expectation of assurance allows the lover to appear as such and, in appearing, abolish the metaphysics of economy.[125] But this individuation poses a problem. While the lover is individuated, the Beloved is not. The lover loves "for the sake of love;" his intuition is filled with "the vague intuition of loving to love" but with no clear signification attributed to it.[126] The lover's advance risks replicating the idolater's gaze, endlessly wandering through the hazy landscape of amorous intuition according to the impulses of "desire, expectation, suffering, happiness, jealousy, hatred, etc."[127] The lover needs a Beloved. But no signification provided by the lover can ever reach the Other, because to do so would render the Other an object and deny the nature of the Other's givenness as a saturated phenomenon. The lover cannot know the Beloved. The lover's significations can only prepare the lover to receive alterity.

What does it mean to receive alterity with the kind of individuation Marion envisions? From whence comes the signification? According to Marion, the Other remains anonymous unless there is a countersignification—or more accurately, a counterintentionality—originating with and coming from the Other. "The signification in question will only arrive if it comes upon me from this alterity itself," as that which "affects me from out there, beginning with itself."[128] Echoing Levinas, Marion acknowledges that this first counterintentionality is the ethical injunction. The Other first enjoins me not to kill. The Other's counterintentionality delivers "exteriority's irrefutable shock," manifesting the Other as a whole phenomenon.[129] But in hearing "Thou shalt not kill," the lover "can and must, by virtue of being a lover, hear 'Do not touch me'—do not advance here, where I arise, for you would tread ground that, in order for me to appear, must remain intact."[130] The ethical injunction always signifies anonymously. It is universal, not a particular call, and love requires radical particularity. We must go beyond the ethical to the erotic in order to individuate fully. The erotic phenomenon appears not when the Other *enjoins* me, but when she *gives herself* to me, when she calls me forward in the promise of "Here I am!"[131]

As we have already seen, Marion argues that this counterintentionality takes its initial form as a unique phenomenon—"the crossing of the gazes"—and this marks the inaugural moment of individuation between lovers.[132] Love renders the Other unsubstitutable through the phenomenon of the crossing of the gazes, in which I expose myself to the gaze of the Other and she exposes herself to me. We disclose ourselves to each other, "uncovered, stripped bare, decentered."[133] I do not try to render the Other an object and she does not attempt to render me an object either. We are "unconscious" of each other in the sense that we cannot bring an intentionality to the gaze of the Other that is adequate to the intuition it provides. In the phenomenon of the crossing of gazes, the Lover and Beloved appear as neither subject nor object.

The crossing of gazes is only "visible" to the lover and the Beloved. They alone experience the crossing, which is its own, unique phenomenon (not two phenomena that co-occur). The lovers "feel the weight of a counter-aim" and "experience each other in the common lived experience of their two efforts."[134] Intentionality and the injunction are one-directional. The Other issues the injunction. The ego directs intention. But the crossing of gazes is mutual. They "come together in a lived experience which can only be experienced in common, since it consists in the balanced resistance of two intentional impetuses."[135] Marion compares this phenomenon to two dueling fencers, who when crossing swords feel the weight of each other's weapon, arm, and entire bodies in a crisscross moment of balance and equilibrium. Like the fencers, the lovers do not "see" each other in any phenomenological sense (as objects) but they do experience their encounter, "the lived experience of their tensions."[136] This phenomenon-in-common individuates the Other and me when I expose myself to the weight of the gaze of the Other and the Other advances, steps forward, throwing himself "madly into his alterity."[137] It is only in this movement that "the Other *as such* attains its final individuality because it moves ecstatically, through the *haecceitas,* into a gaze: the other passes completely into his gaze, and will never have a more complete manifestation."[138] The gaze of the Other gives me to myself and gives me the Other "without reserve or defense, the perfect operative of the unsubstitutable him."[139] The Other becomes this Other through or as his "uncontrollable gaze," which does not "passively reflect" my gaze but responds to it with his own."[140] In his later works Marion describes the result of the crossing of gazes not as a final individuation but as a moment on a continuum of individuation:

> The lover, and he alone, sees something else, a thing that nobody except him sees—precisely no longer a thing, but, *for the first time,* this other, unique, individualized, furthermore cut off from economy, disengaged from objectivity, unveiled by the initiative of love, surging up as a phenomenon so far unseen.[141]

Marion notes the limits of the crossing of gazes as well. The crossed phenomenon does not fully individuate the Other (although it does render her unique; without her the crossed phenomenon could not occur) because it too remains indeterminate. In being held in common the crossed phenomenon remains a formality. Like the ethical injunction, the declaration of a loving commitment *could* issue to *any* other. It "expresses no signification" and "any other love could just as well perform the same expression."[142] The lover's advance and the crossed phenomenon open onto love and invite individuation but by themselves are not enough to fully individuate the Beloved. Another crossing must be invoked: the crossing of flesh.

Before turning to his analysis of flesh, Marion highlights three ways the lover is individuated in the lover's advance. First, by desire. The lover's desire is his alone and is a desire for what he alone lacks: "[N]othing belongs to me more than that which I desire, for *that* is what I lack."[143] The self desires the Other because she lacks him and experiences this lack as a kind of deep mystery which "shows me my most secret center," revealing to me myself by "showing me what arouses me."[144] My gaze settles upon this Other and

> I confess *in petto* that "this time, this one's for me" . . . at this instant the other becomes for me a personal affair and appears to me different from all others, reserved for me and me for her; the other destines me for her and individualizes me through her.[145]

Second, by eternity. Each time the lover says "I love you," she expresses a conviction that "this time, it will be for good, that this time will be for good and forever."[146] It does not matter whether the love lasts. What matters is the moment of eternity expressed by the lover in the amorous vow. The vow can never be unsaid. It validates the lover's status as lover forever. This eternal moment marked in time belongs only to the lover, thus individuating him as lover once and for all. Third, by passivity. Passivity describes the impact the Other has on the lover who manifests as the oath she issues in the "Here I am!," the lover's advance himself, which "sets in motion an intuition all the more radically passive" (the vague loving to love that must receive signification from elsewhere), and the risk that opens up when the lover decides to love first without the expectation of return, leaving both lovers "like two castaways, holding onto the same piece of debris, treading water."[147] Thus, the lover is individuated of his own accord in his decision to love. As we will see in chapter 4, Marion's erotic phenomenology overemphasizes the lover's advance and does not sufficiently account for the saturating nature of the Beloved's givenness. While he does equate her appearance with the appearance of the face, which saturates according to modality, he does not fully explore her appearance in terms of a saturating event. If, as I argue, the Beloved saturates according to both modality and quantity then a phenomenology of love should include a description and analysis of the evental arrival of the Beloved in addition to the lover's advance.

The Crossing of Flesh

Marion describes the flesh as a saturated phenomenon given as a strict auto-affection. But he also recognizes the hetero-affectivity present in the erotic encounter: the Beloved gives me my flesh by making room for me, by allowing me to touch her flesh, by not resisting me as other objects do, and by welcoming me and not turning me away. Flesh exhibits a passivity akin to the passivity that emerges in the lover's advance because in receiving the flesh of the Other my flesh delivers me to myself. The lover gives the Other her flesh as well by eroticizing her flesh for her, and welcoming her flesh without resistance. The crossed phenomenon takes the form of the crossing of flesh. The eroticized Other is individuated when the flesh of the Other is phenomenalized in mine and mine in her flesh. The eroticized Other exceeds ethics by again rendering the Other radically unsubstitutable:

> We must recognize that the privilege of the face, supposing that it remains, no longer depends *here* on a distance, nor on an ethical height. Here, the face of the other . . . no longer says to me, "Thou shalt not kill!" . . . because she and I have left the universal, even the ethical universal, in order to strive toward particularity. . . . In the situation of mutual eroticization, where each gives to the other the flesh that he or she does not have, each only aims at being individualized in individualizing the other person, thus exactly piercing and transgressing the universal.[148]

Here, Marion boldly asserts his claim that love overcomes ethics insofar as it delivers radical particularity and individuation. There is nothing universal about the erotic phenomenon. Through the flesh the lovers experience each other not as objects in the world nor as ethical commands but as intimate, saturated phenomena that exceed any intentionality the ego might bring to them. The flesh delivers up to both the lover and the Beloved their own *haecceitas*. The lovers open their flesh to the touch of the other and in doing so receive their flesh, their own unsubstitutability, from the flesh of the other. But in this immanence, transcendence remains. The intimacy of the flesh preserves distance, although in the "here" of the erotic moment the "privilege of the face" no longer depends upon it.[149] The erotic phenomenon is not metaphysical merging. I can never experience the flesh of the Other as flesh of my own and so, paradoxically, in the erotic moment, "the other's transcendence, far from fading away, stands out like never before."[150]

For all its profundity, particularity, and saturation, the individuation delivered by eroticized flesh does not endure. After climax the flesh returns to body. "The phenomenon of the other appears in the white light of eroticization. But this light is ineluctably extinguished in the very moment of its flashing forth, and the other thus disappears in his or her very apparition."[151] The erotic encounter—and with it, the radical individuation present in the crossing of flesh—ends. Eros reveals to me my own finitude.[152] I recognize that I have only reached the Other through the medium of flesh, indirectly (though intimately). A paradox emerges: the erotic encounter both assures the lovers of their individuation and calls it into question. The lovers grow suspicious, asking, "Did the erotic phenomenon really take place?," "Did she feel anything?," and, "Did it change anything between the other and me?"[153] Moreover, the erotic phenomenon exposes a gap between the eroticized flesh and the person of the other. I never actually reach the lover through the flesh. My flesh appears only in its auto-affection (according to Marion). Each lover experiences climax alone. The erotic moment is therefore ultimately impersonal and anonymous. The gap opened up by the erotic encounter allows space for suspicion, which invites the possibility of lying, deceit, unfaithfulness, jealousy, and even hatred. Marion is no Romantic: "In the end, one could ask oneself if the enterprise of phenomenalizing the other does not owe as much, or even more, to hatred than to love itself."[154] To avoid the death of love stirring in the seed of suspicion the lovers must remain free and faithful to one another.[155] Only faith can enable the erotic phenomenon—and the individuation it engenders—to endure.[156]

The Adieu

Marion describes the oath of fidelity issued mutually and between the lovers as the key to temporalizing the erotic phenomenon and thus delivering up true individuation. Faithfulness assures the erotic phenomenon "a visibility that lasts and imposes itself."[157] Marion returns to his account of the lover's oath as a pledge that in a moment of time reaches eternity. To say, "I love you" is to say, "I love you now and for all time." But the oath must issue again and again. The mere annunciation of the oath is not enough to sustain love. Marion might add here that the oath of fidelity manifests according to different modalities. Lovers confess their love in more ways than the "I love you." Indeed, the oath itself is an expression of the endless hermeneutic Marion referenced earlier in his discussion of saturation. The lovers are faithful not only to the erotic phenomenon but to its endless interpretation. The oath of faithfulness issues as much as an imaginative and hermeneutic activity as a linguistic or spoken performance. In any event, Marion concludes that the oath does not issue once but over and over again, each time as a vow directed toward eternity. Full individuation emerges: "I thus receive myself, in the end, from the other. I will receive my ipseity from the other, just as I have already received my signification in her oath, my flesh in the eroticization of her flesh, and even my own faithfulness in her declaration, 'You truly love me!'"[158]

Marion is left with a final challenge: Can a third witness to the oath in a way that solidifies it more permanently than its performative repetition? Marion considers the child. The child renders visible the individuation given in the oath and erotic enjoyment.[159] But of course, the child is not merely a composite of lovers. She is her own flesh. The child grows up and leaves the lovers to their own world. The child receives the gift of life from the lovers but cannot return it in like fashion. Like eroticized flesh, the child leaves "too soon, and inevitably; for time takes back to its empire these two finitudes, which in fact form only one. Eroticization and the child thus quiet themselves with the same silence."[160]

Marion concludes *The Erotic Phenomenon* by considering God. The lover's oath is a moment of eternity. Each instantiation is an eschatological *as if*.[161] "The lovers do not promise one another eternity, they provoke it and give it to one another starting now."[162] In order to temporalize the erotic phenomenon the lovers must vow to each other toward God, in the *adieu*. The lovers summon God as their first and final witness, then, "[f]or the first time, they say "adieu" to one another: next year in Jerusalem—the next time in God. Thinking unto God [*penser à Dieu*] can be done, erotically, in this 'adieu.'"[163]

What are we to make of Marion's theological turn? Is it a mere reversion to ontotheology? Does the old God creep in the backdoor? For those familiar with Marion's distinction between theology and philosophy it is clear that the appeal to God is not a simple doubling-down on God as Being. The *adieu* should not be read metaphysically. Indeed, for Marion, God is without being. God is not simply givenness either.[164] Marion's *adieu* is more akin to Levinas or Derrida than Aquinas. It is a matter of supplication, not cognition.[165] The lovers hymn to each other in the *adieu,* abolishing repetition and signaling the eternal expressed as the yet-to-come. "Loving demands that the first time already coincide with the last time. The dawn and the evening make one single twilight."[166] Thus, the *adieu* signals toward God insofar as God is the eternal moment captured in the oath of fidelity issued by the lovers to each other in time. The lover's *adieu* is a sort of poetic signification, an amorous declaration of the experience of eternity piercing the veil of time. God is not "out there" witnessing to the lover's oath. God is another name for the oath itself. Vowing to God radicalizes the erotic phenomenon by "abolishing the difference even between the present instant and the final instance, between 'now' and 'again.'"[167] Unlike the oath that repeats, the *adieu* announces the "I love you" once and for all. "The *adieu* casts me into the accomplishment of my oath."[168]

Marion's Phenomenology, Individuation, and the Amorous Imagination

What is Marion's answer to the question of individuation? To summarize: we begin with the "erotic reduction," bracketing all other concerns and looking only at what appears in the erotic phenomenon. A self calls into question the meaning of her own existence, asking, "Am I loved?" Realizing that the answer cannot come from within, she asks, "Can I love first?," advances, and becomes a lover. The first individuation occurs: the self becomes a lover according to her own initiative, because of her decision to advance. But the lover's intuition is filled with love alone and lacks signification. It is not until the Beloved gazes back at the lover in a counterintentionality that the vague intuition of love manifests as a particular Beloved. The second individuation occurs: the lover and Beloved experience the phenomenon of the crossing of gazes. But this individuation falls short. It remains a formality. Individuation requires a fuller intimacy in the crossing of flesh. Here, the lovers individuate one another in the radical unsubstitutablility of the erotic moment. But the individuation of the flesh exposes finitude and calls into question the very individuation it reveals. The erotic moment ends. Individuation takes its final form in the oath of fidelity. The oath accomplishes individuation by touching eternity. "I at last see whom I love in the final instance—her face will arise and impose itself at the heart of the eschatological anticipation by passing into eternity."[169]

Does Marion's description of the erotic phenomenon explain individuation? It is quite compelling. It goes a long way toward explicating the appearance of the Other-as-Beloved and it is full of insights and generative openings. But in some ways, it also falls short, or at least remains incomplete. His emphasis on the lover's advance masks the way in which the Beloved saturates according to quantity and modality. While Marion is right to identify the importance of the lover's advance he underemphasizes the evental quality of the Beloved's givenness. Moreover, although he signals the need for an "endless hermeneutic" he does not sufficiently account for what that hermeneutic entails, or how it unfolds. Neither does he attempt to account for the creative-responsive interplay such a hermeneutic would involve as the lovers seek to understand but never know each other. Finally, Marion's discussion makes no mention of the role of the imagination generally, or the amorous imagination in particular, and its contribution to the process of individuation. Some of these gaps in Marion's descriptions make sense in light of the aim and scope of his project. Marion does not purport to provide a phenomenology of the amorous imagination nor does he claim to have developed a robust theory of the endless hermeneutic, although he does develop it somewhat at various places throughout his works. My identification of these gaps is not intended as a strong critique of Marion's project but instead to identify openings or invitations to develop the ideas he signals toward and unpack the implications of saturation, individuation, and the imagination for a phenomenology of love.

With all of this in mind, let us consider the conceptual tools Marion has developed through his phenomenology and their relevance to a study of the amorous imagination. Marion's phenomenology is a search for grounds, or "firsts." The reduction to givenness aims to reveal the fundamental structure of all phenomena; namely, that all phenomena are given according to the structure of a gift, freely appearing of their own accord. Marion's study of saturated phenomena exposes the structure of phenomenon-as-gift by showing that in giving themselves in excess of categories imposed upon them phenomena are not limited by the subject's intentionality. According to Marion, the fact of the saturated phenomenon reveals an underlying structure to the self. The self is *l'adonné,* the gifted who receives and bears up against the given, showing it in resisting it. Marion's theory of the self raises a number of interesting questions regarding how love shows itself. For example, if receptivity and resistance play instrumental roles in the given showing itself, and the nature of the resistance identifies the phenomenon as a certain kind of phenomenon or effects the way *l'adonné* understands it, then is not the very reception and resistance itself a hermeneutical enterprise? If, as Gschwandter points out, the "impact of the phenomenon functions indeed like a call or appeal, especially in the case of saturated phenomena, which each issue their own kind of claim," what kind of claim does each issue?[170] And what determines the type? How do the flesh, the face, the event, and the imagination conspire to render the Other-as-Beloved? More specifically, how does the hermeneutic response of *l'adonné* to the call of the Other convert the Other into the Beloved? Is the imagination a hermeneutic site or medium that brings together the various calls of the saturating Other? Or does the Beloved first give herself as an event which the lover resists (in the Marionian sense) and then imaginatively interprets? Both? Something else? Is the call of the Beloved shown in the imaginative response of the lover? How does the Beloved capture the lover's imagination? We turn to these questions in the remaining chapters of the book.

Let us next consider Marion's claim that love's emergence depends primarily upon the lover's advance. Several authors criticize Marion's emphasis on the lover's initiative in individuating both the lover and the Beloved. Gschwandtner argues that for Marion "it is always the 'lover' who phenomenalizes the 'beloved' and allows for her to appear."[171] Claude Romano reads Marion's insistence on the lover's initiative as the core of the erotic phenomenon, that love "boil[s] down to a single requirement from which all the others flow: to love first, to arrive ahead of the other in love."[172] Horner provides a more sympathetic interpretation, noting the serial structure of *The Erotic Phenomenon* and plotting the lover's advance as an early but ultimately inadequate stage in individuation.[173] All agree, however, that for Marion the lover's advance is an essential step in overcoming the problem of economy that emerges in conceiving love as reciprocity. As Stephen Lewis states, "The decision to advance in love discloses an infinite human will that is both passive and active, one that seeks to participate in the other through the gift of participation."[174] Love is indeed a gift. But why must a phenomenology of love focus primarily upon the *lover's* advance? Why does Marion not invoke the saturating qualities of the face and the event to describe the way in which the *Beloved* bursts onto the scene, disrupting the lover's solitude? He discusses the role of the Beloved in individuating the lover through the counterintentional gaze, the flesh, and the oath but he underemphasizes the Beloved's initiative in manifesting love. Indeed, one might argue that the saturating givenness of the Beloved does more to bring about the lover's individuation than his own advance. The idea of the saturating Beloved is not meant to imply a simple inversion of advances, replacing the lover's with the Beloved's (who is also a lover, of course), but highlights the evental way in which the Beloved is given in experience. While the lover's advance no doubt opens onto the landscape of love, it is the mutual and perhaps even simultaneous event of the Beloved that calls the lover into that landscape. A phenomenology of love should include a description of the Beloved as a saturated phenomenon.

Marion also draws criticism from his peers for failing to account for the role of hermeneutics in his phenomenology.[175] While I agree generally with these critiques I do think Marion's idea of the endless hermeneutic provides an opening to explore the way in which the Beloved is individuated beyond the advance, the flesh, and the *adieu*. If the Beloved is given as a phenomenon that saturates at least according to modality and quantity, then like any other saturated phenomenon he calls for an endless hermeneutic. It is precisely in the imaginative playing-out of this hermeneutic that the Beloved is individuated, over and over again, in an ongoing, interpretive project. Moreover, like Claude Romano, I argue that the event itself is structurally hermeneutical and so a description of the Beloved's givenness should include the way in which she arrives onto the scene of a preexisting horizon of meaning and how her arrival effects that horizon, what I call the "amorous event." In addition, a phenomenological description of love should explain how it is that the life-world of the lovers is reconstituted in light of the amorous event, according to a new horizon of meaning, and along a new temporal trajectory. Much of this can occur only because of and through the creative-responsive activity of the amorous imagination. But before looking specifically at the *amorous* imagination, let us examine closely the key features of the imagination-in-general, insofar as it operates as an individuating faculty.

3

From *The* Other to *This* Other

Individuation and Imagination

Key Features of the Imagination

The history of the idea of the imagination is defined by the "mirror or lamp debate." Is the imagination mimetic or productive? Does it simply *re-present* to the mind sense impressions, concepts, or whatever it is the mind "takes in"? Or does it *produce* the world of perception by shining its synthesizing light on all that appears? The answer is more complicated than the metaphor allows. As Kant argued in *Critique of Pure Reason*, the imagination is both, and as Husserl argued in *Ideas* and *Logical Investigations*, it is also much more. In this chapter, rather than providing a historical overview of the imagination I examine its role in individuating certain Others in order to explain how the imagination works to transform *the* Other into *this* Other: a radical particular. There are five key features of the imagination insofar as it operates as an individuating faculty: (1) its productive and reproductive capacities, (2) its hermeneutical structure, (3) its creative-responsive activity, (4) its embodied "location," and (5) its unique mode of consciousness. After explaining each feature, I relate them to the question of individuation and explain how they work in tandem to render certain Others unique. In the second section of this chapter, I connect the features to the central argument and, building on the previous discussion of Marion, provide a preliminary explanation of how the imagination individuates. In the final section, I narrow the discussion to the question of the amorous imagination as the site of the endless hermeneutic before going on in the next two chapters to provide a phenomenological account of the amorous imagination and its role in individuating the Beloved.

The Imagination's Productive and Reproductive Capacities

Most theories prior to Kant's analysis in *Critique of Pure Reason* endorse some variety of a mimetic view of the imagination. From Plato to Hume, philosophers concerned with the imagination focused on its ability to recreate sense impressions or ideas and represent them to the intellect. They viewed the imagination primarily as an image-making faculty: its power lay in its ability to reproduce. But with Kant, everything changed. Kant recognized the mimetic function of the imagination but he also discovered a deeper, more *productive* faculty at play. Kant argued that in order for experience to be possible, consciousness must bring to phenomena a conceptual apparatus that orders and makes sense of the sensible. Quality, quantity, modality, relation, time, and space all work together as ordering principles that "convert" phenomena into objects of experience.[1] Absent these forms and categories of understanding, phenomena would appear as chaos. The transcendental features of consciousness provide a pure synthesis out of the manifold of appearances by "acting on" our sensible intuitions, giving us access to a world and establishing the grounds for knowledge. But Kant recognized that something was still missing from this account. What, asked Kant, brings the categories and sensibility together? What power animates the synthesis? His answer was deceptively simple: the imagination, or, more specifically, the productive imagination. Kant argued that the imagination is not only a mirror but also (and more importantly) a lamp. It illuminates the world by bringing it into a synthetic unity.[2] Moreover, while the productive imagination constructs a unity of perception, it also plays a pivotal role in the experience of the unity of apperception. My consciousness of myself as the ultimate source of the unity of my perceptions is intimately related to the transcendental imagination.[3] Kant was aware of the radical implications of this account of the productive imagination. Grounding experience in the transcendental imagination implicitly suggests that existence is ultimately an act of creation, and that "I" am an imaginative projection.[4] But this implication carried with it significant consequences for Kant's system. In the second edition of *Critique of Pure Reason* Kant recalibrated his account and provided a more modest description of the power of the productive imagination.[5]

The first key feature of the imagination is its capacity to reproduce images and produce a synthesis of phenomena, converting them into experience. Both aspects of the imagination are relevant to a study of individuation in general, and love in particular. The productive and reproductive capacities of the imagination play an instrumental role in individuating the Other, because through them the self is able to "see" the Other uniquely, envisioning the Other as a particular Other accessible in some ways only to the self that envisions her. In other words, as a matter of reproduction, through the imagination we regard certain Others as holding a special place among the milieu of givenness. Only I see my wife the way I (imaginatively) "see" her. Dangers of narcissism notwithstanding, only I have access to the image of my wife, father, or friend that my imagination conjures. There is a privateness that marks my experience of certain Others, and this privateness helps to render them individuated. In secret the imagination holds certain others as standing out from all Others. While the stranger may move me to action he does not give himself to me as an unsubstituable Other, as an Other with the radical particularity akin to my child. Unlike the child, the stranger's appearance always remains in some way anonymous because it does not fully capture the imagination. Moreover, through the productive capacity of the imagination, the self is able to synthesize the world in light of the fact of *this* Other's givenness within it. In performing this synthesis, the imagination "embeds" certain Others into a construction of the world, into the very way my consciousness produces a world of experience. Phenomena appear and relate to one another against the backdrop of certain Others' givenness. As we will see in the following sections, not only does one "envision" certain Others in this unique way, one also imaginatively produces an entire world around the phenomenon of the envisioned Other. Indeed, through the imagination the self is able to synthesize phenomena according to a new horizon of meaning, one that only comes into view in light of the *event* of the Other's appearance in the field of the given.

The Imagination's Hermeneutical Structure

The imagination is hermeneutical "all the way down." In the very act of imagining we assemble, order, relate, oppose, connect, and generate meanings. By "meaning" I mean a cluster of ideas: the nest of significations in which we always already find ourselves (e.g., language), the significance we attach to phenomena as they appear (e.g., valuation), and the fundamental way in which we cannot but experience the world as a network of references, signs, signifiers, and symbols (e.g., configuration). Experience is itself an act of understanding, an interpretive enterprise. Paul Ricoeur taught us that. Writing in the wake of Heidegger's analysis of *Dasein*, Ricoeur re-posed the question of selfhood in terms of the ongoing human project of understanding. Questions such as, "Who am I?" and "How should I live?" require not only an ontological or ethical answer but also a phenomenological and hermeneutical account. Unlike Heidegger, Ricoeur did not see the various ways in which *Dasein* seeks to understand itself (anthropology, literature, psychology, etc.,) as detours on the way to Being but as keys to understanding how *Dasein* constructs itself through a plurality of methods, modes of inquiry, and investigations. For Ricoeur, there is no self, only selfhood, "an intersubjectively constituted capacity for agency and self-ascription that can be had by individual human beings."[6] Selfhood is a hermeneutical attestation, a taking-up of one's self as a self. We experience ourselves as something to be understood and "structured along the fault lines of the voluntary and involuntary."[7] Our minds and bodies are not distinct. They cannot be abstracted from one another. Ricoeur's insight into the constructed nature of the self (i.e., selfhood) leads him to an analysis of imagination, time, and narrative. Through the imagination's hermeneutical structure, we narrativize our actions by understanding them in terms of a plot, giving them meaning within a broader story. Self-certainty is a conviction rather than a clear and distinct idea.[8] Recall that Ricoeur describes narrativizing in three stages. The human field of action is always prefigured insofar as there are conditions set down for us (e.g., our ability to use symbols, follow a narrative, etc.). But that prefiguration is also configured according to narrative. We are free to bring together cosmological and phenomenological time by using narrative strategies (pace, order, etc.) so that experiences do not happen one *after* the other but *because* of the other.[9] They find meaning in relation to one another. And finally, the field of action is refigured in terms of imaginative possibility. Through narrative, we project and envision the type of world we want to inhabit and can act toward it in the here-and-now, constantly re-narrativizing our past in light of the present and future.[10]

Narrativity demonstrates the imagination's hermeneutical structure and highlights the role the imagination plays in individuating both the self and certain Others. Without the hermeneutical structure of the imagination I could not tell my own story, I could not attest to myself. Moreover, I am not only capable of self-individuation but I am also able to individuate certain Others who, like my own actions, take on meaning to me in their role or place in my narrative. For example, my ninth grade English teacher stands out against other Others because of the place my imagination assigns her in the development of my narrative self and my self's narrative. I find myself saying things such as, "Without Ms. Cavis I never would have learned to love literature." Narrativizing signals toward the more fundamental structure of the imagination as hermeneutical because it showcases the way in which the imagination takes inventory of available phenomena and configures them into a structural whole, a whole that quite literally makes sense to me. It also suggests that imagining is an innovative activity, one that is engaged in an ongoing project of refiguration, forming new assemblages of meanings in light of what is given. The imagination is not a pure, transcendental receptacle into which our sense impressions fall and out of which our minds pluck ideas. Quite the contrary. The imagination is fundamentally about meaning. It is structurally hermeneutical insofar as it is a site of signification and synthesis. To imagine is to mean. And through the imagination's meaning-making activity, the Other becomes this Other.

The Imagination's Creative-Responsive Activity

Charles Larmore argues in *The Romantic Legacy* that Romantic accounts of the imagination highlight its most important quality: the ability to create and respond at once to what is given in experience.

> There is, among the Romantics, a resistance to the idea that reality has a given structure, consisting in a tidy division of

realms and relevancies, which the mind has but to mirror and respect. The mind is instead understood in terms of its creative power, our notion of reality is seen as rooted in the imagination, so that our mission—that of the artist, but also the task of us all—is to transform what we are given in experience.[11]

It is through the imagination that we experience our fullest sense of reality.[12] In fact, the Romantic view puts at issue the distinction between "reality" and "imagination," asserting that we "all poeticize reality already, and that indeed our sense of reality, and of the claims it makes on us, is inseparable from the creative imagination."[13] The creative imagination is not make-believe, nor as Carl Schmitt argues does it amount to a substitution of what one imaginatively envisions for what is otherwise an objective reality.[14] The imagination is more complex than that. It is both and at the same time creative and responsive. It is responsive to what is given in experience. And what is given in experience "makes claims" on the imagination, to use Larmore's language, claims that cannot simply be dismissed. In Marionian terms, the given calls and *l'adonné* responds. In imaginatively responding to the given, *l'adonné* shows it in a certain light, articulating its meaning and constructing a world. The imagination's dual nature as both and at once creative and responsive shields it from Schmitt-like criticisms that all that is imagined is fancy, idolatry, or narcissism. Again, we see the imagination is both mirror and lamp. While receiving the given, it at the same time has the power to intensify, poeticize, and beautify it, but not transcend it. As Larmore puts it, "The essential work of the imagination lies . . . in the *enrichment of experience through expression*."[15] The imagination responds to the world by creating its own "forms of understanding," by engaging in a hermeneutical enterprise that seeks to receive what is given and to make sense of it through its interpretive and expressive projections. "Truth is at once made and found."[16]

Understanding the imagination's creative-responsive activity is key to understanding the role it plays in individuation. Without the creative aspect of the imagination, *l'adonné* is beholden to what is given and is not free to generate meaning from it, to see it as this or that. Without the responsive aspect of the imagination, *l'adonné* risks veering off into escapism or solipsism, replacing what is given with one's own projected conjurings. But because the imagination is at once both creative and responsive, *l'adonné* remains accountable to the given (responsive) while at the same time capable of enriching the given through expression (creative). As we saw in chapter 1, Romantics such as Novalis, Stendhal, and Shelley understood this double nature. With Stendhal, for example, the wintry bough left in the Salzburg mine is not simply decorated with the lover's imaginary idealizations, which amounts to self-delusion. Through the imagination, the lover creatively responds to the Beloved, receiving her hermeneutically within an imaginative space of possibility. Thus, to crystallize is not simply to fool one's self into believing that an object has qualities it does not actually possess. To crystallize is to interpret the Other in a way that remains accountable to the given while at the same time intensifying, enriching, and rendering the Other unique. Crystallization transforms or converts the very givenness of the Beloved as a phenomenon. Because of crystallization a new or different phenomenon appears, giving itself as a distinct phenomenon, one that appears of its own account, not as a delusional misrepresentation of some metaphysical thing lying "underneath" but as a new, shall we say (à la Ricoeur) "innovated," phenomenon that appears with its own dimensionality, qualities, affect, and inflection. The question of "real" versus "illusion" is no longer appropriate. We must describe the crystallized Beloved as she appears. This "form of understanding" deployed by the imagination shows the Other as an unsubstitutable Other, a radical particularity whose givenness is accompanied by a set of unique meanings that only make sense in reference to her. In doing so, in creatively responding to the Other through the imagination, she appears as *this* Other.

The Imagination is Embodied

Mind/body dualism haunts the history of the idea of the imagination. Many philosophers seem to imply that the imagination is fundamentally a mental activity that impacts the body indirectly, or as an aftereffect. But this view is misguided. Imagining happens in and to a body. The body, or, phenomenologically speaking, the flesh, is the site of the imagination's activity. There is no strict division between the two. As Merleau-Ponty points out, the flesh is the vinculum that connects me to the world and to myself. Touching, imagining, seeing, and sensing all happen together, informing one another within a rich, intertwining web that can never be pulled apart. To put it crudely, what happens in the imagination affects the body and what happens in the body affects the imagination. The flesh is the site of a complex hermeneutical negotiation between what is given, what is imagined, and what is expressed. The lover claims the Beloved has "captured" her imagination and her body is aroused. The widow recalls her life with her husband and feels the weight of his loss in her chest. My experience of the world is always a confluence of the demands of the body and the imaginings of the psyche. Or, as Merleau-Ponty puts it, there is a constant "descent of the invisible into the visible," an ongoing "commerce" between the world of the imagination and the world of the flesh.

In the next chapter, I provide a detailed account of the embodied imagination as a hermeneutical site that receives and responds to the Beloved as a saturated phenomenon. But for now, I will highlight more generally the role the embodied imagination plays in individuating certain Others with an eye toward the more nuanced discussion to come. The fact of the imagination's embodiment provides a condition for the possibility of radical intimacy between self and Other, and out of this intimacy the Other is individuated. If the world is always mediated through flesh, and the world includes the Other, then I encounter the Other in and through my flesh—and his flesh too—in an interplay that has the potential to deliver radical particularity. Indeed, when one touches or is touched the distance between self and Other is traversed (though not eliminated). Flesh-touching-flesh is a "diacritical" reading across distance, to use Merleau-Ponty's term, a mix of sensation and signification. As Marion describes in *The Erotic Phenomenon*, the crossing of flesh delivers radical particularity: the one who touches me stands out against all others as the one who traverses the distance between myself and Other and reaches me in my own *haecceitas*. This crossing is not purely biological. It is not simply stimulation. It invokes the imagination. When I receive the touch of another (or give him my touch) I do so within the context of meanings synthesized, projected, and enriched by my imagination. My hand and imagination touch together. And this bodily, hermeneutical, and imaginative confluence transforms what might otherwise be an anonymous encounter into a moment of radical intimacy. In other words, it individuates. The phenomenon of the flesh and the imagination implicates a complex interplay, but for now suffice it to say that the fact of the imagination's embodiment is a condition for the possibility of individuation because of the unique, carnal hermeneutic it implicates.

The Imagination as a Mode of Consciousness

Phenomenology's way of describing what appears while bracketing metaphysical questions casts the imagination's productive activity in a different light than what Kant originally envisioned. Rather than celebrating its hermeneutical and creative aspects, Edmund Husserl examined the imagination as a mode of consciousness. Husserl begins with the insight that all consciousness, whether perception, judgment, imagination, representation, or memory, is intentional. That is, it aims *at* something. We are always conscious *of something*. Rather than viewing imaginings as mimetic images of less-intense sense impressions, Husserl argues that imagination is itself a unique mode of consciousness. It is not just another kind of perception. The thing imagined (*noema*) and the act of imagining (*noesis*) should not be conflated. Bourgeois writes that, for Husserl,

> [w]hile both perception and imagination present an object in a "fulfilling" intuition as distinct from the empty intending of a sign, the object of imagination is somehow intuited in its absence, thus liberating us from the here-and-now limits of perception.[17]

And this liberation is for Husserl the key to knowing essences. Unmoored from presence, actuality, and the *as is,* imagination is free to intuit imaginings as a quasi-real absence, potentiality, and *as if*.[18] Imagined objects can be manipulated, varied, explored, and reduced. Consciousness can see beyond the normal mode of perception and intuit an "ideal, unvarying paradigm."[19] Husserl argues that the addition and (attempted) subtraction of qualities such as extension or time at play in free variation enabled by the imagination exposes an object's *eidos*.[20] Imaginative variation reveals what is necessary to an object. Perception cannot provide access to an essence because it does not present to consciousness the "test cases" required to distill an object to its essence. It only presents intuitions in the here and now. The imagination gives us access to knowledge. Where Hume saw in imaginings only a "collage of fictions," Husserl sees eidetic truths.[21]

The imagination as its own mode of consciousness carries with it a number of implications regarding the imagination's role in individuating the Other. Access to the *as if* opens a space for individuation that remains closed off in the mode of perception. It is a unique act, a unique way of intending objects. And this act has its own structural qualities. As Husserl claims, imagining can unmoor the imagined from the perceived and engage in the free play of variation. In terms of individuation, imagining as a mode of consciousness engaged in the *as if* rather than the *as is* invites creativity in a way that perception does not, and it is in part because of the possibility of creative play that the Other can be converted into a particular, unsubstituable Other. Through the imagination, the self can "see" or intend an Other in a way not limited by perception, memory, or judgment. The imagined given appears differently, under different conditions, in the *as if*. And this fact becomes a condition for the possibility of individuation because it allows the self to experience and to imbue the Other with meaning that need not be given in the mode of perception. Individuation occurs in the space of the *as if*. Consider the age-old riddle: Does the lover love the Beloved as such, or merely her qualities? The answer is neither. The lover loves the Beloved because of the way she appears to him, and the way she appears is contingent in part upon how he imagines her, how he intends her. To the extent that it needs justification, love finds recourse in the *as if,* not the *as is.*

Husserl does not set out to resolve the question of the ontological status of imaginings but he does suggest they appear in a form of "quasi-reality." Does this mean that the Other's individuation is also quasi-real insofar as it is imagined, that it is "made up" in someone's mind? I think not. To come to that conclusion is to fall back into the "real" (perceived) versus "unreal" (imagined) dichotomy and to fail to appreciate the phenomenological method. The question is not whether an Other is "really" individuated but how is it that an Other appears, is given, or shows herself *as* individuated. Recall that for Marion the given shows itself in being received by *l'adonné. L'adonné* "bears up against" or even "resists" the phenomenon and in so doing shows it, identifies it, and receives it. The given and the gifted work in tandem to allow a phenomenon to appear. Similarly, in individuation the Other is given as a saturated phenomenon but only shows herself when she is received by *l'adonné*. It is in the Other's reception that she appears, and it is in *l'adonné*'s *imaginative* reception and response that she appears as *this* Other, as a certain Other. The imagination as a mode of consciousness intends the Other as a radical particularity but the Other must first be given; the Other takes initiative. To receive the Other in the mode of consciousness of perception is to render her an object. But to receive her in the mode of consciousness of imagination is to acknowledge her saturation and respond to her in the *as if*, in the space of understanding, innovation, and hermeneutics. It is to receive her in a space of possibility, not adequation. The individuated Other appears, as such, in the mode of the *as if*, which says nothing about the "reality" of her qualities (that she truly is lovely; that she really is kind, etc.) but says much about the way *l'adonné* receives her. Through the imagination, the Other is received in a space of possibility, and in that space *l'adonné* is free to intend her as radically particular and unsubstitutable.

But Husserl's account can go too far. If the imagination becomes fully unmoored from the *as is* it ends up adrift in a sea of solipsism. That is precisely the charge issued by Husserl's critics.[22] When the imagination is no longer accountable to the given it wanders into flights of fancy, reveling in its own images rather than creatively responding to what appears. In terms of individuation, complete unmooring yields the undesirable result that there is no longer any Other to individuate: the imagination reaches only "inward," toward itself, not "outward," toward the Other. Thus, as a mode of consciousness the imagination is a double-edged sword. On the one hand, it opens up to the possibility of the given appearing as something other than perception, that is, the *as if*, which is the space of individuation. On the other hand, the *as if* invites self-love and solipsism when it no longer answers to what appears but instead turns its gaze toward its own imaginings. To avoid solipsism and engage in individuation, the imagination must be as responsive as it is creative. It must recognize that the *as if* is not "free" in the sense that it has no responsibility to the given, but that it is "free" from the confines of perception as a narrow mode of consciousness.

The Imagination and Individuation: A Preliminary Sketch

The key features of the imagination just outlined provide the preliminary answers to the question of amorous individuation. We have enough to begin to sketch an image, but only sketch. Chapters 4 and 5 provide a detailed account of amorous individuation and the endless hermeneutic. Note that while we have so far discussed the imagination as it contributes to the individuation of certain Others (friends, lovers, children, etc.), I will focus the remainder of this study on how the imagination individuates the Beloved, and how the features of the imagination outlined above are key to that process.

So how does the imagination contribute to the Other's individuation? Let us begin to lay out an answer. The Other arrives as an event, giving himself as a saturated phenomenon that lands upon the self, upending the self's preexisting horizon of meaning and calling for an endless hermeneutic that plays itself out through the ongoing, creative-responsive activity of the imagination, an imagination that is always and at all times embodied.[23] The imagination in its productive capacity constitutes the world according to a horizon of meanings that precede the given's arrival and accompany its appearance. But some phenomena leave a greater mark on the productive imagination's synthesis. Some phenomena saturate. Events, for example, upend, overturn, or disrupt our prefigured horizons of meaning such that their "happening" changes our sense of meaning forever. For example, as we saw with Montaigne and Boétie, the event of friendship interrupts and calls into question the world we've configured for ourselves. We are forced to restructure our world in light of the friend's arrival, and we do so by invoking the imagination's hermeneutical structure. The structure is twofold. The imagination provides (1) a preexisting nest of meaning onto or into which the given "lands" and (2) it provides the interpretive apparatus the self uses to make sense of the given after its arrival. This double hermeneutic allows for the Other's individuation by providing a landscape of significations and the possibility of its upheaval. It also provides the imagination's narrative capacity to reconfigure the horizon of meaning according to the saturated phenomenon; that is, the Other that has arrived and is now "folded into" the plot of my life. Moreover, through the creative-responsive activity of the imagination I am able to "see" this Other as radically unique and unsubstitutable. I respond to her saturating givenness by poeticizing it, enriching its meaning, and "crystallizing" her with "new proofs" of her significance. This imagined form of "seeing" is a form of seeing in the *as if,* made possible only in the unique mode of consciousness that is the imagination. Unmoored from the confines of perception, my imagination is free to imbue the Other with special significance, hold her out as fundamental to my own sense of self in a way that no other is, or appraise her value according to private and unspoken criteria that need make no reference to an "objective" reality. All of this happens in and to a body, my body and the body of the Other. When our bodies see, touch, and sense one another they do so while at the same time imagining one another. Indeed, what my flesh feels my imagination images, and vice versa. The gazes and the flesh cross at a nexus of bodies and imagination, at the confluence that is the embodied imagination. The radical intimacy delivered by the crossing of gazes and flesh ascends into the world of thought, affecting narrative and meaning. The world of thought descends into the world of bodies effecting their orientation and behavior. Out of this milieu of imaginative activity emerges *this* Other, unsubstituable, radically particular, and in her own *haecceitas.*

Love and the Endless Hermeneutic

In chapter 1, I made three core assertions intended to clarify my central argument. I revisit them now in order to remind the reader where we are in the overall trajectory of the analysis. The assertions: First, the amorous imagination is my answer to the question of how the Other becomes the Beloved. That phenomenon in many ways tracks the more general, preliminary process I've outlined in the above section but, as I argue in detail in the next two chapters, it takes on a particular inflection in the case of *amorous* individuation. My central concern regards individuating not just any Other, but individuating the Beloved. As we will see, this calls for a close analysis of the event of the Beloved as a saturated phenomenon and the hermeneutic response for which it calls. Second assertion: the amorous imagination highlights something that is missing in Marion's account of the erotic phenomenon; namely, that love emerges not only because of the lover's advance but also because of the saturating nature of the Beloved's givenness. Recall that in *The Erotic Phenomenon* Marion emphasizes (and takes criticism for) his description of the lover's initiative in inaugurating love. While Marion is right to identify the lover's advance as a critical moment in love's appearance he underemphasizes the role of the Beloved, who appears as a saturated phenomenon. And as we have seen, saturated phenomena call for an endless hermeneutic, which, in the case of love, is carried out by the amorous imagination. Third assertion: a phenomenology of the amorous imagination constitutes a substantive unpacking of the endless hermeneutic. As such, after describing the Beloved's saturating givenness in chapter 4, I provide a sketch of a phenomenology of the amorous imagination in chapter 5, in order to show how the endless hermeneutic unfolds and sustains the Beloved's individuation.

4

The Amorous Event and the Endless Hermeneutic

From the Lover's Advance to the Beloved's Givenness

Marion's erotic phenomenology goes a long way toward rethinking love, and his phenomenology of givenness provides the conceptual tools for an analysis of the Other's individuation. But while his phenomenological descriptions in *The Erotic Phenomenon* shed light on the lover's role in love's emergence, his account overemphasizes the lover's advance and underemphasizes the Beloved's saturation. Drawing upon my previous discussion of the imagination's power to individuate, in this chapter I argue that a phenomenology of love should describe the Beloved's givenness as a saturated phenomenon, or what I call "the amorous event," as well as the endless hermeneutic, both of which implicate the amorous imagination as an individuating faculty. More specifically, in dialogue with Marion's phenomenology of saturation and *l'adonné* (including his analysis of the self's interplay of receptivity and resistance when it comes to receiving the given), my question about how the Other becomes the Beloved focuses in on the question of whether the Beloved gives himself as an event which the gifted then interprets, or whether imagination is itself the hermeneutic site of the Other's disclosure. To that end, I examine the structure of the Beloved's givenness (focusing closely on the hermeneutical dimensions of event, flesh, and face) and the response he calls for in the endless hermeneutic in order to expose what I argue is an underlying hermeneutical process of individuation, the imaginative process by which the Other becomes the Beloved.

The Hermeneutical Structure of Events

Let us begin with a few general comments regarding Marion's concept of the event to highlight the need for a fuller description of the hermeneutical dimensions at play in the Beloved's givenness. Recall that, according to Marion, events saturate according to quantity. They provide too much data, too much information, too much givenness. They cannot be limited by a concept, divided or assembled together as a finite set of parts, or explained according to causality. Indeed, events invert causation, providing first their effects and then (only after hermeneutical engagement) their innumerable causes. And they disrupt. To use Ricoeur's language, they call for a narrative reconfiguration. Events are inexplicable in the truest sense. They cannot be known, but they can be understood; that is, they can be interpreted. Marion insightfully observes that it is the very nature of events as inexplicable that provides the grounds for the endless hermeneutic: we know that we can never explain an event in its fullness and so we must interpret it over and over again, making new meanings, seeing new insights, and reconfiguring our narrative according to its horizon.

Events implicate hermeneutics not only after the fact, in interpreting them, but before the fact, structurally, as a condition for their appearance. Marion scholars such as Claude Romano, John Greisch, Jean Grondin, Richard Kearney, Tasmin Jones, and Shane Mackinlay all argue to varying degrees that there is a structurally hermeneutic dimension of phenomenalization in which *l'adonné*'s reception of a phenomenon operates on an interpretive level as well as on a phenomenological level.[1] The given shows itself in being understood, in being received and responded to. Marion's account of structural hermeneutics is not always clear but he does at times discuss the dynamic between the given's priority in initiative and *l'adonné*'s receptive role in showing the given by receiving (or resisting) it. For Marion, *l'adonné* is not purely passive despite the fact that phenomena always give themselves first. There is a movement back and forth between the given and the gifted. The given takes initiative. It gives itself from itself, anonymously and freely, but it cannot show itself unless it is resisted by a self who is always already interpreting it. But Marion's insistence on the given's phenomenological priority creates (perhaps unresolvable) tensions in his phenomenology and he leaves underdeveloped an account of the relationship between *l'adonné*'s hermeneutical reception (or "gaze") and the given. The closest Marion comes to providing a full treatment of this relationship occurs in chapter V of *Negative Certainties*, although he discusses it elsewhere too.[2] In *Negative Certainties*, Marion argues that all phenomena share an "originary event-characteristic" insofar as they initially give themselves as an excess. But the self through its "gaze" can "mask" or even "suppress" primordial eventness, instituting a "phenomenal restriction" that can reduce the event to an object.[3] The self plays a hermeneutical role in what shows itself, perhaps even a constitutive role. Marion states that "the distinction between modes of phenomenality (for us, between the object and event) can be joined to the hermeneutical variations that . . . have (ontological) authority over the phenomenality of entities."[4] Thus, *l'adonné's* gaze plays a determinate role in what appears. But as we have already seen, Marion's emphasis on the given's priority seems to suggest that some phenomena like events appear *as saturated,* independent of the self's hermeneutical orientation. A tension emerges: Is Marion's theory of saturated phenomena intended to provide a more accurate description of the way phenomena appear (as essentially evental) or is it intended to provide a corrective in the way *l'adonné* receives phenomena in practice; that is, for example, recognizing a phenomenon as saturated rather than restricting it to objectness?[5] If the variation of *l'adonné's* gaze determines what appears according to its hermeneutical variation then it is unclear how the given maintains phenomenological initiative in terms of what appears. Despite these questions, one thing is for certain: much depends upon *l'adonné's* gaze.[6]

Shane Mackinlay provides a helpful analysis of the hermeneutical gap in Marion's account of the event. Drawing on Claude Romano's theory of the event, Mackinlay argues that rather than appearing as pure givenness, events always give themselves as personal, reconfiguring, inexplicable (that is, noncausal), and opening phenomena. Events constitute "[t]he fundamental phenomenological structure of our encounter with phenomena and of both the world and the 'subject' which are opened to it."[7] Like Marion, Mackinlay and Romano give events the phenomenological initiative: events first happen to the self but the self is in its very structure open to and opened by events. Romano calls this self the *advenant,* the one who has the "capacity to appropriate eventual possibilities articulated in a world that surface from an event, and to understand oneself from them."[8] This opening is fundamentally hermeneutical and allows for the possibility of individuation. Romano states,

> *Advenant* is the term for describing the event that is constantly underway of my own advent to myself from the events that happen to me [*m'adviennent*] and that, by addressing themselves to me, give me a destiny: adventure without return . . . the very opening to events in general[.][9]

The *advenant* comes to herself from an origin that is other than herself but is fundamentally related to the world and the event, which open her. Unlike *l'adonné,* who operates as a receptive screen or control panel that is lit up by the given, the *advenant* is a hermeneutic "nest" in which the event lands and upends a preexisting horizon of meanings.[10] The difference is subtle but is important with regard to the hermeneutical structure of receptivity. According to Mackinlay and Romano (and, as we will see, Richard Kearney), Marion is silent on the important point that the event is always a hermeneutical event in its very structure, and the preexisting horizon of meaning laid out before the self is a precondition for the evental nature of the event to occur. Moreover, Mackinlay's and Romano's accounts highlight the personal nature of events: they arrive and upend *ex aliquo,* not *ex nihilo.* The event overturns and reconfigures the self's hermeneutical horizon but it does not create out of nothing. The self recreates and reconfigures a new horizon out of what was already there. Events always address a particular entity who understands herself within a preexisting hermeneutical context. Events are more akin to Ricœur's concept of innovation than to pure creation. Events open a new world but only because a world already existed. And events are radically personal. They happen for and to a particular *advenant.* As Romano states, "I am myself at play in the possibilities which [the event] assigns to me."[11]

Romano's view of the event is relevant to our study of the Beloved's individuation for several reasons. First, it identifies an important dimension of the event missing in Marion's description. The event is structurally hermeneutical. Second, and perhaps more importantly, Romano's view raises the question as to what role the hermeneutical dimension of the event plays in the Other's appearance as the Beloved. In other words, the hermeneutical structure of the event forces us to consider how the Beloved appears with the kind of radical particularity we associate with love. If Romano is correct, then a phenomenology of love should include a description of the Beloved's givenness as an event insofar as it overturns, upends, and reconfigures the lover's personal horizon of meaning. It should account for how that upending and reconfiguration happens. I argue that it happens in and through the amorous imagination. Romano's emphasis on the personal nature of events further raises the question of individuation by highlighting the way our hermeneutical response to the event is not only an ongoing interpretive activity but one that brings the event "closer to home," personalizes it, and incorporates it into our sense of self. The hermeneutical act of folding the event into our selves is an intriguing idea when considering the question of individuation because (as we have seen) it is precisely through such an imaginative, hermeneutical act of narrative "absorption" that certain Others come to stand out against the milieu of all Others.[12] In the following section, I provide a phenomenological account of the amorous event, taking into consideration Mackinlay's and Romano's critique of Marion's theory of the event and highlighting the role the amorous imagination plays in individuating the Beloved as both the site of her reception and the lover's response.

The Amorous Event

Love first appears as an event. Its evental structure is implied in the language we use to describe it. We "fall" in love. We are "lovestruck." We are "enamored" with the Beloved. She comes out of nowhere and we find ourselves in love, but unable to say why. "I've met someone" is our only linguistic recourse. Even when love emerges slowly, over time, there is an evental quality to it: friendship develops into intimacy and once the possibility of love is whispered the world can never be the same. In each case, love is described as a "happening," an event that overturns and reconstitutes our horizon, rearranging the way in which we exist in the world.¹³ Despite his numerous insights in *The Erotic Phenomenon*, Marion misses this point. He overemphasizes the lover's initiative, concealing the evental nature of the Beloved's givenness. Like Montaigne and Boétie's friendship, the encounter with the Beloved constitutes a disruptive event that reconfigures the lover's (ontological and hermeneutical) horizons. This event marks the beginning of love's emergence and takes on a certain structure many of us know all too well.

The Encounter

First comes the encounter. Two selves appear to each other as saturated phenomena. In *The Erotic Phenomenon*, Marion describes the lovers' advance as the inaugural moment of love and the first individuation. But what he does not fully account for is the Beloved's appearance as an event that saturates according to quantity. Both Marion and Romano reference friendship as a paradigm event that gives itself as disruptive and intimate. Friendship carries a structural similarity to the amorous event.¹⁴ According to Marion, friendship's occurrence is both inexplicable and unforeseeable. Citing Montaigne and Boétie's initial encounter, Marion and Romano highlight the way in which neither Montaigne nor Boétie can describe what gave rise to their friendship. Its causes remain hidden. The friendship always exceeds the fact of the encounter. That Montaigne and Boétie attended a gala on such and such a night and that they spoke to one another about any given topic does not explain the phenomenon of their friendship, which "happened" *to them,* uniquely, and privately. Their friendship is not the effect of deliberate action or willful advance. It is, as Romano claims, the moment of new possibilities opened up by the very encounter with the Other-as-friend. And the event of their friendship is deeply personal. It is intimate. Their friendship takes on meaning because it happens *to them, between them,* and *for them.* The particularity of the Other-as-friend makes all the difference. As Montaigne states, there is only one explanation for their friendship: "because it was him, because it was me." Intimacy opens on to particularity, the preexisting horizon of meaning each friend brings to the encounter is a necessary condition for the event that upends it. The event of friendship wells up and disrupts the friends' hermeneutical nests, forcing a reconfiguration in light of the event. But to ask "What is it?" that caused the event of friendship to appear remains an unanswerable question. The best phenomenology can do is identify and describe its structure. Like all events, the cause of friendship eludes us.

The amorous event appears in a similar fashion. The Beloved's appearance is an event. Like the face of any Other, the Beloved is first encountered as a saturated phenomenon, an excess of givenness. The Beloved cannot be rendered an object by the lover's intentionality. She is invisible, resists reduction, and arrives onto the scene of the lover's horizon of meaning only to call it into question, to upend it and force its reconfiguration. Like a friend, the Beloved seems to come from nowhere, without cause or explanation. We see this phenomenon in any number of literary love affairs. In *Wuthering Heights*, Catherine and Heathcliff are not set up, they are not betrothed, they "happen" to each other. They beckon each other to come forth. Notably, however, the Beloved emerges from the milieu of Others by issuing not only an ethical injunction but also an erotic call. The lovers' gazes cross. They bear the weight of one another's appearance, giving rise to an initial individuation. But the event of the encounter is not reducible to the crossing of gazes. The givenness of the Beloved is itself an event. The first individuation of the Other-as-Beloved occurs not only when the gazes cross but when the crossing gazes land upon and call into question the preexisting horizon of meaning each lover brings to the encounter. The crossing of gazes and the hermeneutical upheaval conspire to bring about the amorous event. The encounter therefore constitutes an opening onto new possibilities for both lovers. It not only upends their sense of time, place, and meaning, it invites a new configuration and new assemblage of all three. The amorous event captures the lovers' imaginations from the moment of the encounter forward. It becomes their existential anchor, temporal compass, and hermeneutical wellspring.

The amorous event is inexplicable and unforeseeable. No causal explanation can account for the event, no litany of reasons can ever provide a sufficient description of the event's occurrence. The amorous event arrives as a *fait accompli*, it leaves the lovers no option, it is as if love was already decided for them.[15] Tristan and Isolde drink the love potion and their fate is sealed. The amorous event inverts causal relationships: the lovers first experience the effect of the event and then, upon reflection and interpretation, look for its causes. But of course, no single cause is sufficient to explain love's appearance. The event gives too much, it saturates with a quantity of givenness that no concept can fully capture. Because the amorous event inverts causation it remains unforeseeable. One cannot predict which Other will induce the amorous event. Failure to appreciate the evental nature of the amorous event has led philosophers of love to wrangle with questions such as, "Why does one person love another?" or, "Do you love *me*, or just my qualities?" But under a phenomenological lens we see that these questions miss the point by concealing the way in which love arrives in a noncausal manner. Once we realize that love's inauguration begins with the amorous event, questions like, "Why do I love you?" become affective expressions of the endless hermeneutic, not logical, philosophical problems.

Finally, the amorous event is irreversible. The lovers cannot go back, they cannot reconfigure their lives according to the horizons of meaning that preceded the event. The amorous event becomes the focal point, the ground, and the nucleus of the lovers' possibilities. Even if love dissolves, the lovers cannot undo the event. It remains an eruptive moment for the remainder of their lives.

Examining the evental structure of love reveals a number of hermeneutical insights about the nature of individuation. Consistent with Romano's and Mackinlay's observations regarding friendship, the amorous event has both a structural and an interpretive component. Structurally, the event cannot occur with the kind of radical individuality necessary for love unless the lovers bring with them to the event a preexisting hermeneutical horizon, which the event upends. Therefore, the amorous event is hermeneutical "all the way down," in its very structure. Indeed, the amorous event happens insofar as it disrupts and forces the lovers to reconfigure their horizon of meaning. Interpretively, the event calls for a response. As Marion argues, saturated phenomena call for an endless hermeneutic that acknowledges their irreducibility but still engages in the creative act of meaning making and interpretation which the excess of givenness demands. Thus, the amorous event happens insofar as it calls for a hermeneutic response. The hermeneutical dimensions of the amorous event are key to understanding the Beloved's individuation. The amorous event opens up to the possibility of the Beloved as a radically particular, unique, and unsubstitutable Other in a swirl of saturation, counterintentionality, and intimacy that comes from nowhere, happens to the lovers, and upends their preexisting horizons. Because of the hermeneutical structure of the amorous event, the lovers are capable of engaging in the imaginative, hermeneutical activity necessary to bring about individuation. But the Beloved is not fully individuated in the event of the amorous encounter. She remains a saturated phenomenon, an erotic call awaiting a response.

The Call

Evental structure aside, the amorous event includes a number of co-occurring phenomena that work together to constitute the amorous event as its own unique phenomenon. We begin with the face of the Other, which in love issues not only an ethical demand, but an erotic call. As we have seen, Marion relies heavily on Levinas's account of the face to describe the way in which it saturates. In Marion's language, the face saturates according to modality: its givenness calls into question categorical distinctions between possibility and impossibility, existence and nonexistence, and necessity and contingency. The face appears (if it "appears" at all) as an infinite excess, a transcendence that cannot be constituted in terms of modality. Strictly speaking, the face of the Other remains invisible. Marion describes the Other's face as an encounter that weighs upon me, that arrives with a force that cannot be denied and which calls me into question. But unlike Levinas, Marion insists that the ethical injunction always remains anonymous and must give way to an erotic call if the Other is to become fully individuated. For Marion, individuation occurs first as the crossing of gazes, the phenomenon of mutual envisaging between myself and the Other in which I am seen and see, and where I accept the surplus of significations given by the Other's face. Envisaging is the inaugural moment of the endless hermeneutic because it is the moment in which I accept the provisionality of any meaning I give to the Other and recognize her saturated givenness. The only appropriate response to her is to interpret her again and again, over and over in an endless act of understanding.

Although, as Levinas and Marion point out, the face of the Other is initially experienced as an ethical injunction, in the amorous event the Beloved's appearance gives an additional phenomenon: it calls to the lover, inciting his desire, beckoning his advance, and inviting his individuation. The Beloved lures the lover in a way the orphan, the stranger, and the widow do not. Unlike the injunction, the call identifies the lover out of the milieu of Others. The Other commands, "Thou shalt not kill," while the Beloved beckons, "Come to me." The call entices the lover to step forward and approach the Other-as-Beloved. But the Beloved recedes, or more properly, exceeds. The face of the Beloved is an icon. It saturates according to modality. At the same time that it calls the lover forward it exceeds the lover's advance, initially expressed as the lover's intentionality. The lover desires the Beloved but his excess resists knowledge. The lover is stunned, she cannot settle her gaze and render the Beloved an object but neither can she withdraw her gaze and look away. As with an idol, the lover's gaze roves around the Beloved's givenness searching for a place to land, but the excess and counterintentionality of the Beloved converts the idol into an icon which sees back and is seen through. Unlike Simone de Beauvoir's "male gaze," the lover's gaze responds appropriately to the saturated phenomenon. It recognizes the irreducible and nonobjective nature of the phenomenon and does not seek to render it a thing, object, or concept. When the lover does look away, her imagination conjures the Beloved for her and to her.[16] Paradoxically, the Beloved's givenness issuing as a call lures *and* resists the lover's gaze insofar as the lover cannot, strictly speaking, *look* at the Beloved and yet she *sees* him. The Beloved's call is an erotic call that arouses a desire for excess. In the amorous event, the erotic call does not promise to fill the lover's ontological lack; rather, it promises more: saturation, abundance, surplus.[17] And it is precisely in the interplay between call and response, saturation and desire, that the Beloved is individuated in the second sense: the lovers creatively respond to one another's call through an endless act of interpretation and in doing so personalize one another, rendering each unique and unsubstitutable.

The Response

Marion's concept of *l'adonné* is grounded in the self's receptivity. The given first gives itself but only shows itself when received by *l'adonné*. *L'adonné* bears the weight of the given and in doing so receives it and phenomenalizes it. Reception is therefore inherently hermeneutical.

It is not until *l'adonné* identifies the given that it shows itself as that which is phenomenalized. The Beloved is no exception. The Beloved gives herself freely but only shows herself in the lover's reception of her givenness, which bears up against the weight of her counter-gaze, the event, and the call. The Beloved can only be shown by a lover who receives her, by a lover who *responds*. The lover's response is hermeneutical. He resists the Beloved and in doing so phenomenalizes her *as* the Beloved. The lover's response is yet another moment of individuation. The Beloved is individuated in being received by the lover, in his response to her. And the lover is individuated by and through the Beloved's givenness, which gives the lover to himself by giving itself in the first place. While the Beloved cannot be shown without a lover who receives her, it is the lover's pleasure to hear and respond to the call of the Beloved, to become aroused by her impact and through an endless hermeneutic answer her call by engaging his imagination. He sees the world anew, declares his fidelity in the now, and reorients his selfhood according to a new horizon: the horizon of Her.

Proper reception of the saturated phenomenon of the Beloved involves the lover's recognition that the Beloved cannot be reduced to an object. This is how the lover avoids idolatry. Attempting to reduce the Beloved to objectness constitutes a form of phenomenological violence insofar as it reduces the Beloved to the Same, as Levinas eloquently points out with regard to the Other. Indeed, dangers lurk within the lover's gaze. The lover may phenomenalize the Beloved inappropriately. She may misidentify the call of the Beloved or hear a call where none has issued. She may fail to hear the call altogether. She may be blinded by the Beloved's excess, responding rashly, without constraint, or with an obsession that arises out of confusion. Like Goethe's Werther, the lover may become consumed by the abundance of the Beloved and suffer self-harm or unrestrained passion. Indeed, the Beloved never actually appears in such a case. Only an idol appears. If the self "responds" to a call that was never issued by an Other but was (mis)perceived by the self as a call, the Beloved never emerges. What shows itself is Narcissus, not Cupid. The self shows himself to himself in the improper response to the givenness of the Other, a response that reflects back to the self a desire for metaphysics rather than excess. The Beloved remains hidden and what shows itself is the lover's own obsession, his own desire, and his own ego.

Finally, the call captures the lover's imagination. It echoes even in the Beloved's absence. The amorous imagination, captivated by the Beloved's givenness, becomes the site of the endless hermeneutic. It is the creative space in which the lover responds to the call, interprets the amorous event, and reconfigures his horizon. The lover returns to the call and the event over and over again, like a painting or symphony, always reinterpreting it and never exhausting it. The lover becomes preoccupied by, even devoted to, the Beloved, and that devotion plays itself out in the amorous imagination. But more on this later (see "Love and the Endless Hermeneutic," below).

Distance and Separation

The amorous event is marked by distance and separation. There is a profound sense in which the Other "appears" as an absence, as an unreachable alterity that always remains in some way hidden. We need not go so far as Levinas and claim that the Other is *totally other* in order to appreciate the striking fact that the Other transcends and exceeds any intentionality we bring to him. But Western philosophy is characterized by a desire to know; viz., a desire to convert intuition into objects and to explain them within a totalizing system, to reduce them to the Same. Knowledge consumes. Levinas saw what the Romantics did not: when love is conflated with knowledge and becomes an urge for metaphysical merging it also becomes violent. If the Other is truly other and the task of love is to reduce the Other to the Same then the aim of love violates the very nature of the Other as alterity. There is a lesson for lovers here. Like the passionate youth in Keats's *Ode to a Grecian Urn*, lovers must forever remain at a distance in order to avoid idolatry, violence, and death.[18] Indeed, only in the space of distance can the Beloved appear as fully individuated.

Distance, separation, advance, and withdrawal are all at play in the amorous event. The lover is attracted to the Beloved, lured by his gaze, and drawn to his call, but the Beloved recedes, steps back, and remains other. The distance between lover and Beloved never collapses. The lover must choose. On the one hand, she can deny the Beloved's advance and withdrawal and try to overcome, insisting that the lovers merge into one. This converts love of the Other into love of death, as we will see in chapter 6. Here, the "lover" is no longer a lover at all insofar as she no longer appropriately responds to the saturated phenomenon of the Beloved. On the other hand, the lover can "stand still." She can acknowledge the distance between herself and the Beloved and respond to the call from afar, within the space that is the distance between them. It is a fecund space, a generative and creative space, an imaginative space. It is in this space that love grows and sustains itself, that it renews and reinvents itself, that it interprets and reconfigures, over and over again, the Beloved's infinite advance and withdrawal. It is the space of the endless hermeneutic. Of course, it is also a tragic space: the desire to merge is a strong one and it must be restrained in order to avoid violence. Distance can be as painful to endure as it is joyful to experience. But such is the nature of love.

Is this not the story of Tristan and Isolde? The two lovers decline to consummate in the woods of Morois not because it would be a breach of fidelity to their liege lord but because it would be a breach of fidelity to each other. They know that love requires distance. And not, as Denis de Rougemont argues, because theirs is a love of passion which is really a love of death, but because it is a love of life, a love that is played out through the endless hermeneutic of their constant advance and withdrawal. That is the phenomenology of love unfolding in the drama of the Tristan myth. The lovers are together and then apart, they experience both proximity and distance, indeed, they embrace it. And in that distance which is never to be collapsed but instead to be dwelled in, they think of each other, praise each other, long for each other, they *imagine* each other. Their imaginations are both productive and reproductive. They see the world anew because of and in light of each other. Light is the operative metaphor here: their imaginations are lamps that illuminate the world, that allow them to reconstitute the world according to the horizon of each other. A new world emerges because of their amorous imaginings. Their imaginations are also reproductive. They mirror back both the Beloved and themselves.

One might argue that Tristan and Isolde's imaginings are at best solipsistic and at worst narcissistic. But neither need be the case. Tristan avoids a reduction to solipsism because his imaginings find their root, their ground, their cause, or (better) their inspiration from outside. They are given to him by and as Isolde. Isolde captures Tristan's imagination. She comes to him from *without* (the given gives itself freely). Tristan's experience of Isolde as the Beloved is not solipsistic because his imaginings require an exteriority for their induction. They are at the mercy of what captures them. The imagination is accountable to the body, the Other, the Beloved that exceeds it. Here we might emphasize the responsive nature of the imagination. As a saturated phenomenon, the Beloved appears of her own accord, a gift that transcends and transgresses the lover's intentionality. The Beloved "captures" the imagination even before the imagination has a chance to respond. And what captures the amorous imagination enamors it. Like a gaze dazzled by an idol that gives too much intensity, the amorous imagination is filled to the brink with the Beloved's givenness. The imaginings themselves appear as a paradox. On the one hand they are my imaginings, only I "see" them. They are my own vision of the past, the present, and the future. But their inspiration comes from outside myself. The imagination must be fed, stimulated, and inspired by that which is outside of it. The amorous imagination cannot produce imaginings on its own. It must be enamored. It has no content without the gift of the Beloved who, like Isolde, comes from a distant land.

Tristan also avoids narcissism if he recognizes the hermeneutic project of love and does not reduce it to desire, impulse, or idealization. Love as amorous imagining is less about my vision of myself projected in my own imaginings of the Beloved (although it can devolve into that) and more about the free play of imaginings that constantly draw from their source, the wellspring of love that is the Beloved. On so many medieval caskets given between courtly lovers we see the motif of the fountain of youth: old folks crawling into a crystal-clear spring, playfully splashing about, and then leaving the fountain refreshed and young, their age literally dripping off their skin. Love is like that. Love avoids narcissism when it holds its imaginings lightly, when it understands the project of love as an endless hermeneutic that constantly rejuvenates itself and in so doing rejuvenates the lovers' love for each other. The imagination must not cling to its imaginings or it will fall into narcissism. Imaginings are not about naming or constructing or knowing. They are instead a kind of *hymning* toward the Beloved. They are a motion of praise that speaks out of the bedazzlement, saturation, and excess that is the Beloved. It is the response to the call, a response that calls back from the distance between the lovers that must remain a distance for the lovers to remain as lovers. Love of this kind is not love of self but love as *doing,* a gesturing toward, a praising response.

Indeed, this love can never be narcissistic because it is always directed *away* from the self toward the infinity of the Beloved. The imagination is the interpretive space in which all of this occurs. The amorous imagination is the site of love as an endless hermeneutic.

The Hermeneutical Nature of the Flesh

I now turn to an analysis of the flesh-as-hermeneutical-site in order to further demonstrate the hermeneutical structures of the Beloved's givenness that make possible her individuation. More specifically, it is (in part) due to the amorous imagination's embodiment that individuation can occur. The amorous event does not simply unfold in the minds of the lovers, in the world of thought. It happens to their bodies, in the world of flesh. The two are inseparable. The amorous event is received by *l'adonné,* an enfleshed self who always encounters phenomena in and through a body. The amorous imagination is a carnal site.

First, a few general comments. Marion hints at the idea of a "hermeneutical flesh" but he is generally more concerned with the flesh's autoaffection than its heteroaffection (although he does describe the flesh in terms of both). Marion argues that the flesh saturates according to relation because it is given with such immediacy and "mineness" that it is disanalogous to any other experience. For Marion, the flesh refers to nothing other than itself. But Marion's insistence on the flesh's autoaffection conceals the need to develop a more robust carnal hermeneutic arising out of the flesh's heteroaffectivity in order to show how the amorous event gives itself as a fundamentally hermeneutical event that opens up to the possibility of the Beloved's individuation. If, as Marion states, I am given to myself through the flesh of another then I am given to myself hermeneutically. I come to understand myself through the mediation of my flesh in contact with another's flesh. The flesh signifies me to myself and is itself the signified. Rather than as a strict autoaffection, the flesh always appears in and through the world in which it finds itself. Therefore, the flesh is not absolute. It is hermeneutic. It appears in and through its relation to the world. Moreover, it is through the mediation of the flesh that the Other accomplishes a form of individuation beyond the ethical because the crossing of flesh delivers intimacy. Touch signifies with radical particularity. As we will see, the "intertwinings" of flesh and flesh and flesh and sign call for what Richard Kearney describes as a "carnal hermeneutic," a hermeneutic that explains the way in which the imagination's embodiment contributes to the Beloved's individuation.

Flesh as a Hermeneutical Phenomenon

We begin with Edmund Husserl. Husserl introduced the key phenomenological distinction between body (*Körper*) and flesh (*Leib*) that opens up to carnal hermeneutics. In section two, chapter 3 of *Ideas II*, Husserl provides his famous example of the phenomenon of the left hand touching the right, which reveals a "double sensation" unique to the flesh.[19] In one sense, my body is like any other object in that it can be perceived by the senses. But unlike other objects, my body also senses. When I touch something, I sense not only the object that I touch but also the sensation of my hand sensing. The features of the object that I touch are sensed in my hand and belong to my hand. When I touch my hands together I experience both hands touching the other as an object but I also experience each of my hands experiencing the other hand. In sensing, my body becomes flesh. The sensations are double because both of them (my sense of the object and my sense of my sensing) belong to the flesh and yet refer to the features of the world that are being sensed. As Kearney states,

> In this bilateral gesture, one is no longer an isolated subject experiencing the body as mere object: one is flesh experiencing flesh, both active and passive, constitutive and receptive, spirit and matter—or to use Husserl's terms, *Empfindung* and *Emfindnis*.[20]

Unlike sight, which provides the ego control over objects, the flesh opens to a vulnerability and exposes me to the world. It is "the place where I enjoy my most primordial experience of the other."[21] The doubleness of my flesh reveals to me an interdependence that marks all of my being in the world. I experience myself experiencing and being experienced by others, as an embodied psyche, an enfleshed self that imagines, desires, and loves and that is imagined, desired, and loved by others. I project and am projected upon.

The "intertwining" of world and flesh provides the foundation for carnal hermeneutics. All sensations carry with them values, desires, repulsions, and attractions. Sensations carry meaning. Ricoeur states,

> Through need, values *emerge* without my having posited them in my act generating role: bread is good, wine is good. Before I will it, a value already appeals to me because I exist in flesh. . . . The first non-deductible is the body as existing, life as value.[22]

Following Husserl's initial phenomenological insights, the idea of carnal hermeneutics goes off in a number of directions. Jean-Paul Sartre describes the body as exposed to the gaze of the Other and opposed to it in space and time. The look of the Other expropriates me. "We resign ourselves to seeing ourselves through the Other's eyes."[23] And we become flesh for the Other (as in the erotic caress) "in order to appropriate the Other's flesh."[24] Bodies as flesh become enemies, mechanisms for control. Levinas describes the caress as sensibility that "transcends the sensible."[25] Like Marion's gaze roving about the idol, the caress forages for what is not yet, searches for a future never future enough, and reaches toward the impossible Other that lies beyond the flesh itself.[26] But it is in the works of Maurice Merleau-Ponty and Paul Ricœur that carnal hermeneutics is truly fleshed out and a space is opened up to examine the amorous imagination as an individuating, embodied phenomenon. We turn to their accounts now before tying together the threads of carnal hermeneutics and explaining how they contribute to the Beloved's individuation.

Imagining as an Embodied Phenomenon

While a full treatment of Merleau-Ponty's theory of the flesh is beyond the scope of this work, a summary of his insights regarding double-sensation, distance, and embodiment will illustrate his contributions to carnal hermeneutics and, more importantly, demonstrate how the very fact of the amorous imagination's embodiment provides for the possibility of the Beloved's individuation vis-à-vis the endless hermeneutic.

In *The Visible and the Invisible*, Merleau-Ponty introduces his idea of the flesh as a "chiasm" between the human being-in-the-world and the world itself. Flesh connects. It is a "mutual interweaving between perceiving and perceived."[27] Extending Husserl's theory of double-sensation, Merleau-Ponty argues that the flesh reveals a "reversibility" between and across all senses. The body touches and is touched, sees and is seen (Husserl) but also sees-by-touching or touches-by-speaking. This deep double-sensation marks all perception for Merleau-Ponty and reveals the fundamental truth that our primordial experience of the world is intertwined: flesh makes the world appear and flesh belongs to the world. Ontologically, I am first flesh. It is the layered vinculum that connects me to the lifeworld in which I always already find myself by virtue of being flesh. Language also carries a kind of "double sensation" within itself and with flesh. As Kearney puts it, "The I which speaks words is the I spoken in words."[28] And flesh has a language. Indeed, flesh and language are reversible.[29] The flesh signifies. Contrary to Marion's account of flesh, Merleau-Ponty argues for a radical heteroaffection of the flesh in which the self and the world are deeply interconnected by a chiasmic tissue that preexists, precedes, and preconditions any perception, subject/object dualism, or matter and form dichotomy.

But the flesh and the world are not reducible to one another. There is always a gap between the self and the world (and the Other). To use Merleau-Ponty's words, there is always an element of the invisible in the visible. While my visible body and visible things intermingle in the world there remain at least two "invisibles" that persist: the invisible on "this side" of perception (the world of thought), and the invisible on "that side" of perception (the world of transcendence). The invisible on "that side" of perception is given as an absence but also an excess. It is that which grounds, an "interior armature" that lies "behind" the visible.[30] The invisible on "this side" of perception is "the inner of what is outer," the mind, spirit, or soul that is attached to the visible but does not appear in it.[31] Merleau-Ponty makes the crucial point that the invisible world of thought arises from its interaction with the visible world of perception.[32] The "entities" and "domains" of the world of thought come to the self through its fleshy "commerce with the visible, to which they remain attached."[33] The world of thought is not disembodied. It is not unrelated or removed from the visible world. It is an "emergence of a life in its cradle."[34] Moreover, the visible "borrows from" and "intersects with" the world of thought.[35] Merleau-Ponty describes a "descent of the invisible into the visible," which manifests as culture, art, and history.³⁶ Thought gives flesh "its axes, its depth, its dimensions."³⁷ In a phenomenological move that echoes Hume's theory of the empirical imagination, Merleau-Ponty identifies and describes the deep interconnection between the world of thought and the world of things, the world of flesh and the invisible world of excess. One effects and affects the other. Indeed, they are co-constituted. These worlds do not create a subject/object dichotomy nor do they reduce the self to a mind/body dualism; rather, they capture the complexity of the world that arises from the ontology of flesh-in-the-world. For Merleau-Ponty, the chiasm of flesh is both a connective tissue and a membrane that preserves the "mineness" of my own experience and the "otherness" of the others without overemphasizing transcendence (Levinas) or insisting on metaphysical merging (Romanticism). The flesh and the world are intertwined but they do not fuse. The gap, distance, or separation between self and other invites interpretation and translation, but not reduction. The flesh provides for a diacritical reading across difference, that is, it is a condition for the possibility of the lovers' endless hermeneutic.³⁸

The flesh opens onto the world. Flesh is not just biological or subject to biological impulses. To live in and as a body, Merleau-Ponty argues, is to *express,* to take on a certain form of life in a particular kind of world. "The life of the flesh and the life of the psyche are involved in a relationship of reciprocal expression."³⁹ Expression is a hermeneutical activity that occurs because of and as part of existence-in-flesh. Speaking is a movement of the body. Touch is animated by desire. As Kearney puts it, "The body signifies meaning because it *is* that meaning."⁴⁰ This interwoven relationship between psyche and body that manifests as expression constitutes a kind of carnal hermeneutics that runs "all the way down," that penetrates all of human existence. Meaning and being are inseparable. Flesh and existence *are* each other.⁴¹ Embodiment in this robust sense marks a fundamental structure of human being. The flesh opens onto the world in an ever-expressing interplay of body and psyche, visible and invisible, self and alterity. My flesh allows the world to show itself. Like Marion, Merleau-Ponty describes the self as fundamentally receptive. One might say that *l'adonné* is enfleshed and in receiving the given shows it, allows it to appear, and imbues it with meaning. The interlacing of flesh and world, of self and the given, constitutes a natal pact where the world and self give birth to one another.[42]

Merleau-Ponty provides a compelling account of the flesh that has important implications for a phenomenology of the amorous imagination as the site of the Beloved's individuation. First, the flesh is hermeneutic, it is not absolute. Contrary to Marion's description, Merleau-Ponty convincingly demonstrates how the flesh operates as an expressive condition of existence. While Marion is correct to point out the unique "mineness" of my own flesh he fails to fully account for the heteroaffectivity and hermeneutics of the flesh. The flesh does give me myself but it does so through its contact with other things, with the world, and with others. It is unlike other things but it is given in relation to them. Thus, while the flesh may not provide the paradigm example of a phenomenon that saturates according to relation, it is a unique phenomenon and plays a fundamental role in love's emergence. Indeed, it is a condition for its possibility. Merleau-Ponty's account of the flesh illustrates the hermeneutical structure of phenomenality absent in Marion's account. While this does not undermine Marion's project, it does call into question the possibility of the "pure given" with regard to the flesh. In any event, the key for our purposes is that the flesh is hermeneutical and when it receives the given it does so in and through the process of interpretation. In this sense, the endless hermeneutic of which Marion speaks begins at the moment of reception, as soon as *l'adonné* bears up against the given, identifying it and responding to it *in the flesh*.

The amorous event is hermeneutical both before the fact, structurally, and after the fact, in the lover's response. The amorous event takes its hermeneutical structure from the flesh and the preexisting horizon of meaning it upends. Love happens to a person, and that person is embodied and makes meaning "along the way" of its existence. To put it in Heideggerian terms, *Dasein*'s fundamental openness to the world is marked by a hermeneutical engagement with it. While the amorous event does indeed saturate according to quantity, it does so through the hermeneutic upheaval of the self's horizon of being. The amorous event does not occur *ex nihilo* but *ex aliquo*. And the amorous event is hermeneutic after its occurrence, in the lover's response to the event, which seeks to interpret its inexhaustible causes over and over again, meaning without end. As I argue in the next section, the amorous imagination is the site in which the endless hermeneutic unfolds as well as the condition for its possibility. As such, it is, in short, the condition for the possibility of the Beloved's individuation. Here, we might distinguish between the subject's *knowing* and the lover's *understanding*. Phenomenologically speaking, the transcendental subject is a knowing subject: it renders a phenomenon an object by intending it, bringing a concept adequate to the intuition. It constitutes a world that it can manipulate, master, and describe. The lover is an understanding self: she engages the saturated phenomenon of the amorous event and the Beloved, recognizing that no concept is adequate to the phenomenon, it cannot be rendered an object, and instead must be interpreted through an ongoing hermeneutic process. The lover seeks to understand, not to know. Understanding is the never-ending process of hermeneutic engagement with the saturated phenomenon. The amorous event is hermeneutic after the fact insofar as the lover seeks to understand it. Indeed, it is this hermeneutic orientation that sustains the lover *as* lover and opens the space for the Beloved's individuation. For the lover to lose this orientation is for the lover to revert to a subject, to "fall out of love," and to (attempt to) reduce the Beloved to a (substitutable) thing.

Finally, Merleau-Ponty's description of the flesh signals toward a fundamental quality of the amorous imagination: the amorous imagination is an embodied phenomenon, and its embodiment contributes to its ability to individuate. If the amorous imagination is the site of both the structural and endless hermeneutic, a complete account of the amorous imagination should include a description of its relationship to embodiment, the flesh, and the world in order to show how through the hermeneutical activity of the amorous imagination the Other becomes the Beloved. The imagination is not a floating mind. It is not a world of illusion disconnected to the world of things. Imagination "happens" in and to a body and a world. As Merleau-Ponty suggests in his analysis of the expressive flesh, the visible and the invisible are always at play with one another. They are not two separate domains—thought and things—but a single, intertwining phenomenon that includes experiences of both presence and absence. The interconnected relationship between the visible and the invisible characterizes the amorous imagination's relationship to the hermeneutical structure of the flesh. And these hermeneutical structures set the stage for individuation

Imaginings emerge in the cradle of the flesh. The world gives rise to imaginings and imaginings descend into the visible world, effecting it by taking the form of culture, art, and signification. They help me make the world my own, and they provide me the ability to "see" the Other as radically unsubstitutable, to interpret her excess as such. The hermeneutical relationship between world, self, and imagination is a condition for the possibility of love.

Flesh, Imagination, and the Hermeneutical Response

While Merleau-Ponty's description of the flesh highlights the hermeneutic *structure* of the amorous event as a markedly carnal hermeneutic, Paul Ricoeur's account of embodiment highlights the carnality of the hermeneutic *response* to the event. In his early work, *Freedom and Nature: The Voluntary and the Involuntary*, Ricoeur examines the life of the "incarnate cogito" as a "dialectical rapport between the voluntary and the involuntary."[43] Like Merleau-Ponty, Ricoeur argues that "incarnation" is experienced through the phenomenon of affectivity, which mediates between our existence-in-flesh and the order of thought.[44] Affectivity is at its root a mixing of the two. For example, my experience of need is a confluence of the demands of the body and the values that animate it. Values emerge from the phenomenon of embodiment itself. Ricoeur describes the imagination in a similar fashion: it is a carnal imagination that "takes place" in a body, projecting out and taking in the world of bodies, reading the affective signs of the sensible world, and "mobilizing our desires and discerning between good and bad ways of realizing them [so] that our life can be *evaluated*."[45]

Ricoeur returns to the body and carnal hermeneutics later in his career, after his so-called linguistic turn. In *Oneself as Another*, Ricoeur argues (in a vein similar to Merleau-Ponty) that the flesh mediates and opens the self to the world. The flesh is the point of hermeneutical negotiation between the immanent transcendental ego and the transcendent face of the Other. Like Marion and Merleau-Ponty, Ricoeur recognizes the phenomenological receptivity of the self-in-flesh, which gives to us our sense of belonging in the world while also maintaining a distance between "me" and "the world." The paradox of the flesh is the paradox of proximity and distance, intimacy and separation. It is the touch that never touches. In a move that beckons toward what

Marion will later describe as the flesh which "gives me myself," Ricoeur insists that the flesh reveals to me both myself and the Other. The gap between myself and the Other which is traversed across flesh but never eliminated gives to me the phenomenon of the Other as an intimate absence. Indeed, the gap between what I experience and what you experience, what I am and what you are, can never be closed. Nor should it be. The distance makes all the difference. Like Tristan's sword in the woods of Morois, in creating a boundary and preserving distance the phenomenological gap between self and Other opens a space for hermeneutical mediation. The Beloved calls and the lover responds but there is no consummation, no merging, no fusion. Unlike the Romantic vision of metaphysical union, the phenomenological account of the flesh reveals a space between us: the appearance of distance and separation that in conjunction allow for love's possibility. And it is precisely because of this gap that amorous individuation is possible. The call of the Beloved beckons as the lovers read across the space that separates them, rather than trying to dissolve into sameness.[46] In doing so, they give love expression and voice.

The Amorous Imagination as the Site of the Endless Hermeneutic

Let us recap. Marion's description of the erotic phenomenon provides a number of insights regarding the way in which the Other is individuated and becomes the Beloved. But his description fails to fully account for the role hermeneutics plays in individuating the Beloved. Building on Marion's theory of the self, I argued that his concept of *l'adonné* suggests a hermeneutical dimension to phenomenalizing the given, one that must be unpacked in order to understand the Beloved's individuation. *L'adonné* receives the given and in doing so shows it. Reception is neither passive nor active but a combination of the two: it "bears up" against the given, converting the anonymous call into an identifiable phenomenon. *L'adonné*'s resistance to the Other as a saturated phenomenon is the first step toward individuation because it suggests that *l'adonné* in some way "converts" the given into a phenomenon. Shane Mackinlay and Claude Romano (among others) recognize this hermeneutic dimension of Marion's phenomenology. They describe phenomena as structurally hermeneutical "all the way down." While Marion says little of the hermeneutic structure of phenomena, he does suggest that an endless hermeneutic is the appropriate response to a saturated phenomenon. Because saturated phenomena exceed all intentionality they call for endless interpretation. They are inexplicable. Combining the insights of Mackinlay, Romano, and Marion, I argued that love first emerges within the context of an amorous event. The amorous event is hermeneutically structured and calls for an endless hermeneutic in response to its excessive givenness. The amorous event is characterized phenomenologically as an encounter, a call, a response, and distance and separation. The amorous event's hermeneutical structure implicates the imagination as a meaning-making faculty. Through this imaginative, hermeneutical activity the Other is able to become the Beloved. The amorous event is not abstract. It happens to an embodied self. The lover receives the amorous event and responds to it in and through the embodied imagination as a site of interpretive activity. Therefore, a proper account of love requires attention not only to the amorous event but also to carnal hermeneutics. Examining the phenomenology of the flesh in Husserl, Merleau-Ponty, and Marion, I highlighted the deep intertwining between flesh and world. The flesh is not absolute. Like the event, it is structurally hermeneutical. It is given in relation to a world. The flesh opens the self to the world with an intimacy and distance that invites a reading across gaps. Again, this "reading" requires imaginative engagement. But it does not collapse the gap between self and Other. Carnal hermeneutics strikes an interpretive balance, a negotiation and navigation along the membrane of flesh and the world. The endless hermeneutic takes place in the affective, embodied, amorous imagination, an imagination that reads from and into the world of meaning all the while preserving the distance between lover and Beloved.

How do these ideas contribute to an understanding of phenomenological individuation? In short: through the amorous imagination the self-as-lover creatively responds to the saturating givenness of the Other-as-Beloved, acknowledging that the lover can never know the Beloved and choosing instead to individuate the Beloved, by "seeing" her as radically particular and imbuing the world with meanings generated though the lover's endless hermeneutic and the Beloved's appearance. The amorous imagination is the embodied site of the endless hermeneutic. It is the nest in which the amorous event lands and the innovative activity that interprets it. It is a condition for the possibility of love.

We are now in a position to make a number of observations about the nature of amorous individuation. First, recall that the amorous event saturates according to quantity, upending the lover's preexisting horizon of meaning. The amorous event is radical in the truest sense: it overturns a preexisting order and re-roots the lover's orientation in the world. The first individuation occurs not only when the lover advances, as Marion posits in *The Erotic Phenomenon*, but when the Beloved calls. The call and response individuate the lovers for the first time. The call and response are not reciprocal. They are an event, not a transaction. Marion is right to point out the noneconomic, nonmetaphysical nature of love. But they do constitute a phenomenological moment in which the Other appears to the lover with a particularity that sets him apart from all Others. The lover experiences the Beloved not only as an injunction but as an erotic call. For Levinas, the injunction is a command that places one's being into question. It is a phenomenon that implicates the *ontological status* of the self as separated from the *il y a*. But in love, the call places one's *hermeneutical horizon* into question. It is a phenomenological moment that calls into question the significance of the self and the Other, radically denying the appearance of the Other as substitutable, indistinct, or one-among-many-others. The endless hermeneutic plays out according to the amorous event insofar as it is a moment of hermeneutical upheaval and reorientation. To put it in terms of Ricoeurian narrativity, the amorous event happens to a self whose constitution is prefigured and configured but must then be reconfigured in light of the event. Or to put it in Marionian terms, the amorous event must be *received* by the lover who in responding to its call identifies it as such. Reconfiguration, response, and reception work in concert to individuate the Other as the Beloved.

The imagination's embodiment is a necessary condition for individuation. The amorous event always gives itself in and to embodied selves, selves-in-the-flesh. The signifying flesh is a condition for the possibility of love because love requires a hermeneutical response and the flesh provides for that possibility. It is the site or nest of meaning in which the event lands and is taken up as a new orientation or disposition—a new series of significations—expressed through the enfleshed self's being-in-the-world. The amorous event happens as much to a body as to a psyche. Their intertwining means that the amorous event is not reducible to some psychological disposition or biological impulse. It is ontological insofar as it gives to the lovers a new horizon of being that is lived out in the flesh. It marks their being in the world as lovers who experience the world with a new affect, a new significance, and a new grounding, all as a result of the amorous event. The call of the Beloved touches our bodies. It arouses the flesh both literally and metaphorically. It invokes desire. It lures. The amorous event is felt, heard, and seen in and through the flesh. The desire for excess appears in the body. And the lover responds to the call through the body. The lover's caress is not a transcendental ego intending the Beloved's body in search of an adequate intuition. The lover does not grope about in the dark looking for some object she can identify. She signifies differently with her flesh. In love, the lover responds to the Beloved's call through the hermeneutical caress that seeks to understand but not to know. In the intimacy of the flesh the lovers are individuated vis-à-vis a carnal and hermeneutical encounter. The caress signifies "you and only you." The Beloved cannot be substituted within the context of the amorous event and the carnal hermeneutic for which it calls.

The amorous event opens to the possibility of individuation not only in the flesh it arouses, but in the way in which it captures the imagination. The lover's imagination is snared by the amorous event. As we have already seen, the imagination is (in part) a productive faculty. It does not merely reflect sense impressions or conjure fanciful ideas. It provides a unity to perception and apperception (Kant) or even the possibility of our experience of Being (Heidegger) by allowing the possibility of projecting presence over time. Understood in this manner, the individuating capacity of the imagination becomes clear: the lover sees himself and the world anew when his imagination is captured by the Beloved. His experience of Being is contingent upon his imaginative synthesis and projections, which now take on an amorous inflection because his horizon is constituted in light of the Beloved's abiding presence within it. In other words, the captured imagination sees the self and the world differently, in light of love's emergence. It cannot be any other way. The captured imagination arouses, enamors, and kindles the desires of the flesh. Lovers often feel "aflame" in their passions. In the hermeneutical phenomenon of touch the lovers imagine each other's satisfaction as much as they feel it. And in this touch the Beloved is given as unsubstitutable: there is no other like him, none other but him. The truth delivered in intimacy is the truth—at once made and found—of the Other's radical particularity. The amorous event sets the lovers off on a passionate path marked by imaginative and carnal engagement, hermeneutic interpretation, individuation, and diacritical reading across distance. The endless hermeneutic is the lover's conversation. It reifies the Beloved's uniqueness. It is amorous expression said again and again, for now as if for all time. And no saying could happen without the amorous imagination.

Love "says" through the endless hermeneutic, but love never "sees." Love is blind. In other words, amorous expressions are always marked by what B. Keith Putt calls an "agnosticism." To love properly means to acknowledge one's inability to "see the other with total transparency."[47] In engaging in the endless hermeneutic, the lover must "make decisions as to the identity of the other, constantly interpreting whom I love when I love the other and accepting no termination to the process of discovery inherent in love."[48] This inherent unknowing is what Putt means when he describes love as blind or agnostic. And because love is blind, it requires faith, "a trusting that the future holds further disclosures of meaning[.]"[49] But of course, faith carries with it the seeds of doubt because it does not deliver cognitive certainty as to who the Beloved is or whether the lover loves sufficiently. The logic of love does not "grant enlightening assurances;" rather, it operates according to the structures of risk, wager, and undecidability.[50] As it is said: the heart has its reasons, which reason does not know. According to Marion, the excessive nature of the saturated phenomenon (here, the Beloved), which calls for an endless hermeneutic, may actually result in a sense of disappointment because the lover has no adequate concept to bring to the Beloved, she must encounter him without having the possibility of ever knowing or fully understanding him.[51] Amorous imagining as the loving activity of the endless hermeneutic is not a romantic enterprise full of flowery assurances. It both affirms and defers, it says but does not see, and thus resides in a space of desire and doubt.

How might we account for the various ways in which love is expressed in different cultures? Is all love the same? Yes and no. The amorous event is a universal phenomenon but the endless hermeneutic renders it a particular manifestation in place and time. Through the endless hermeneutic, the amorous event is expressed culturally, linguistically, and aesthetically. The event happens to situated, enfleshed selves who despite their common hermeneutical structure express and respond to the amorous event from their own specific historical locations. The playful, courtly poetry of Bernart de Ventadorn is different from John Donne's honorific verse in "A Valediction: Forbidding Mourning" or Edna St. Vincent Millay's lament in "What lips my lips have kissed and where and why." But the underlying phenomenon is the same. The endless hermeneutic is the birthplace of individuation expressed through creative variation. The lover and her amorous imagination are always embedded in a historical and cultural location and she must draw from the inventory of significations available to her within that location in order to engage in the endless hermeneutic. Love is expressed differently in different cultures, according to that culture's norms, values, signs, and symbols, but it carries a common structure across cultures insofar as it implicates the amorous imagination. The Beloved is shown as such in the lover's hermeneutical response to him, which is always historically and culturally situated.

One final comment regarding the "co-occurring" nature of the amorous phenomenon: the face, event, and flesh "happen" together in a convergence of phenomena that constitute their own, unique phenomenon. The whole of love is greater than the sum of its parts. The erotic and the ethical are caught up in what we might call *amour*. Like streams merging together to form a river, the various phenomena constitute a confluence that joins into a single current, taking on a force of its own. The phenomena do not layer, unfold chronologically, or cancel each other out like a sound wave; rather, they merge, magnify, and intensify in their co-occurrence such that the weight of their pull takes on a new life and appearance not reducible to any one phenomenon that makes it up. Love appears as its own, unique phenomenon.

At the confluence of all these hermeneutical phenomena lies the imagination. The Beloved gives himself in and to the gifted's imagination, which is so much more than an image-making faculty. It fashions a world of meaning out of myriad phenomena. It creatively responds to the given, able to intend it in the *as if*. Through its receptive and responsive hermeneutical activity, the amorous imagination transforms the Other into this Other, into the Beloved. The hermeneutical structure of phenomena provides the imagination the capacity to allow the Beloved to show herself as individuated, radically particular, and unsubstituable. And it is the amorous imagination's hermeneutical reception and response to the Other that allows for the endless hermeneutic to unfold, and the imaginative, hermeneutical activity of the lover renders the Beloved unique. In the next chapter I turn to a phenomenological study of the amorous imagination. While in this chapter I argued *that* the amorous imagination is a condition for the possibility of love because of its power to individuate, in the next chapter I provide a phenomenological sketch of the amorous imagination in order to show *how* it individuates.

5

Toward a Phenomenology of the Amorous Imagination

A Preliminary Note on Time and Culture

The imagination plays a fundamental role in individuating the Other-as-Beloved. In its productive capacity it lays out a new horizon, a new world that the lover inhabits as a result of the amorous event. In its reproductive capacity it conjures amorous imaginings that work together to constitute the lover's new way of "seeing" the Beloved. Operating in the *as if*, the amorous imagination opens to creative-responsive interpretations of the Beloved, interpretations that are not constrained by the mode of perception. The amorous imagination is the site of the endless hermeneutic that, rather than individuating the Beloved once and for all, continuously individuates though an ongoing process of innovation, of seeing and re-seeing, of providing assurances of the Beloved's meaning through the act of understanding. The Beloved is shown in the lover's response to his call. And the response manifests in and through the lover's enfleshed, amorous imagination. But how precisely does all of this happen? How does the productive activity of the amorous imagination operate? How do amorous imaginings appear? We turn now to a phenomenological sketch of the amorous imagination's activities in order to illustrate the different ways in which the Beloved appears as such; that is, how she *appears* individuated.

But first, two notes, one on time and one on culture. We take them in turn. The amorous event and the activities of the amorous imagination (production, reproduction, creation, response, etc.) do not operate on a timeline. They "happen" together, or in various amalgamations and in different combinations. Sometimes the creative aspect of the imagination operates in the forefront. At other times the lover's imaginings dwell on the distance and separation marking the Beloved's appearance. Different combinations of phenomena occur together, synchronously, and with different emphases. Recall that the amorous imagination is both a hermeneutical site of reception and a hermeneutical faculty of interpretation. This double nature complicates the question of time because the Beloved is given, received, and interpreted at the speed of thought; or, more precisely, at the speed of imagination. The amorous imagination is at work whenever the Beloved appears, whether he is given "in the flesh" or in his absence; that is, as "an image" conjured by the lover in her own consciousness. In fact, phenomenologically speaking, the Beloved is always given as both a presence and absence, regardless of whether or not he actually stands before the lover. The amorous imagination is always in some way receiving the Beloved, responding to him hermeneutically, reconfiguring the lover's horizon of meaning, and reaching out to the Beloved through both the visible and invisible worlds. There is a kind of "swirling instantaneousness" to the amorous imagination's activity. The horizon of meanings in which the Beloved appears, which indeed allows the Beloved *to* appear, precedes the Beloved's arrival. Therefore, the amorous event and the amorous imagination's activities are not a series of events that happen as love progresses. That's not the picture. Love arrives on the scene within and as a milieu of imaginative activity where the whole is greater than the sum of its parts. Love is a confluence of phenomena that flow together, not a march of moments along a developmental timeline. And the confluence makes up its own phenomenon, one that is not reducible to any of its constituent components.

In the last chapter we touched briefly on the question of cultural variations in the expression of love. While it is obvious that amorous expressions differ across the world and throughout history, it is less obvious that there is a difference in the role the imagination plays in manifesting those expressions. Each culture expresses love in its own language. Of this, we can have no doubt. Linguistic or symbolic expression—even thought itself—always occurs within a cultural context and takes on the values, inflections, and senses of meaning coded into that culture. But cultural variation is not evidence of structural variation. A phenomenological description of the amorous imagination reveals an underlying framework that brings the lover and Beloved together, one that (I am suggesting) might be present across cultures. All lovers imagine. All Beloveds appear. They do so as an event, as a saturated phenomenon that calls for an endless hermeneutic. Out of this hermeneutic comes the wondrous and beautiful variety of amorous expressions, from Keats's sonnets, to Vallana's stanzas, to Hemingway's short stories. Love finds its articulation in and through culture, but the imagination makes possible that articulation.

Amorous Illumination

Recall that for Kant the imagination is both a mirror and a lamp. It brings together the categories and sensibility, forming a unity of perception and apperception. But the imagination's productive power in many ways exposes the limits of Kant's project because, as Kant readily admits, the productive imagination does not show itself as an intuition. It operates "in the background," synthesizing our experience into a unity. And yet, without it, knowledge would not be possible. Heidegger saw the radical implications of Kant's observations. Heidegger argued that Kant's insight revealed a deeper truth: the imagination operates according to the horizon of time and through its projections provides the experience of abiding presence. In other words, the imagination conjures Being.[1] Through the imagination's productive and projective faculty *Dasein* experiences a world of beings. Indeed, *Dasein*'s experience of itself as a being is constituted by the imagination. Whether or not one finds Kant's or Heidegger's account convincing, it is hard to disagree with their fundamental observation that the imagination plays a productive role in the self's experience of the world. Without its ordering capacity our experiences would not be experiences at all. They would be chaos. And its projective capacity is no less obvious. As beings-in-time, we constantly experience ourselves as having been, being, and yet-to-be. Time, the self, and the imagination are intimately related. Kant and Heidegger were right to emphasize the imagination's power to illuminate existence.

The amorous imagination in its transcendental form exhibits at least three features. First, as Kant and Heidegger observed, the amorous imagination is productive.[2] The amorous event upends the self's horizon of meaning and world and the amorous imagination reconstitutes it according to the horizon of the Beloved. After the amorous event the world is never the same. Our experience of time becomes contingent upon its having happened. We experience the past, present, and future *in light of* the amorous event. It becomes the beacon or anchor of both chronological and existential time. Our entire experience of our temporal landscape orbits around the amorous event, and the Beloved becomes the unmoving arm of a compass. And it is the amorous imagination that produces this new world, that synthesizes it according to the horizon of the Beloved. Like Kant's transcendental imagination, the amorous imagination brings the world into a unity that is penetrated by the presence of love. As Marion points out in the first erotic reduction, before love we experience life as meaningless, aimless, or empty. We ask, "What's the use?" Even before the amorous event we find ourselves in search of love, or at least in search of the assurance of our own meaning, which we suspect love can provide. The amorous imagination brings together a world framed by love, imbued with a desire for *amour,* and built upon the possibilities opened up by the amorous event. The amorous imagination sets boundaries for the lover's world according to the Beloved's givenness. One might say that the Beloved operates like a "fifth Category" according to which experience is given. The amorous imagination produces a synthesis of meaning, a world of possibility, and an experience of experience that at all times carries with it the trace of love.

The amorous imagination's productive function opens its hermeneutical function. While the amorous imagination's productive capacity synthesizes being according to the horizon of the Beloved, in its narrative capacity the amorous imagination operates by reconfiguring the lover's sense of self in terms of a new story, a new plot. The amorous imagination folds the fact of the Beloved's givenness into the narrative self. In the wake of the amorous event, the lover is no longer constituted by her autonomous existence as One, *tout seul,* but as a "Two scene," as Alain Badiou calls it.[3] In this "Two scene," the lover engages in an ongoing, narrativizing project of constituting and reconstituting selfhood in terms of the Beloved's appearance through the amorous event, which serves as an anchoring point around which her new narrative revolves. The narrativizing feature of the amorous imagination is innovative in the double sense of the term: it draws from the inventory of meaning that precedes the amorous event in order to invent meaning by reconfiguring the hermeneutical nest into a new arrangement which has as its existential node the Beloved. We see here again the structurally hermeneutical quality of the amorous event and imagination that leads to the Beloved's individuation. The lover attests to her new sense of self in and through her imaginative projections, which always carry with them the touch of love. When the lover imaginatively envisions her past, it is a past that was before her encounter with the Beloved. When she attests to herself in the present, she does so as a lover to the Beloved, as linked to him in a way that cannot be undone. And when she projects into her future she does so with the secret presence of the Beloved always in mind. It is a future that is no future unless he is there, even unto his death. "What will be the meaning of my life," she asks, "if he is no longer here with me?" Both cosmologically and phenomenologically the lover's sense of time is experienced in terms of the Beloved, given as amorous event. Without him—and him alone: unsubstitutable, unique, irreplaceable—the story of her life would not be the same.

The amorous imagination also has an ontological function that is related to the narrative function and contributes to individuation. The ontological function of the amorous imagination affects the lover's experience of time, but with a particular focus on the enigmatic relationship between love and death. The lover no longer experiences time according only to his own death but according to the death of the Beloved. Being-toward-death becomes being-toward-love, but only by way of the amorous event. Love is not more primordial than time, but it reconfigures it. It also anticipates separation, which haunts the lovers, lurking phenomenologically in the distance they experience between each other. Paradoxically, however, the distance of love must be preserved. Tristan's sword must separate him from Isolde. There is tragedy here. Distance and separation open to the anxiety of death. Indeed, death finds its abode in the amorous imagination, like an unwelcome guest. Perhaps we can make use of Sartre's description of imaginings as a kind of negation: our imaginative projections of the Beloved always carry with them the taint of naught and a sense of inescapable finitude. But the amorous imagination does not acquiesce to the unwelcome guest. The actual death of the Other-as-Beloved, or simply the fact of her impending death intensifies her singularity and unsubstitutability. She cannot be replaced. Her death changes the world forever. As Wordsworth wrote, "she lived unknown, and few could know / when Lucy ceased to be; / But she is in her grave, and, oh,/ The difference to me!" The possibility of the Beloved's death is "taken up" in the imaginative projections of the amorous imagination. The Beloved alone can give the lover an assurance of meaning. The lover cannot give it to himself without falling into vanity. But the Beloved's impending death radically calls this assurance into question. Moreso, even, the Beloved's impending death is itself an event that the lovers know will again reconfigure existence. It always threatens to undo the world created by love. And here we find the ontological function of the amorous imagination: Being-toward-death issues a radical call to transform the self into Being-toward-love. The lovers can never reverse the trajectory upon which the amorous event has set them. The lovers are always being-toward-(the) death of the Beloved, which intensifies the lover's project of being-toward-love. The phenomenon of the Beloved's death in some ways is always already happening, and does so over and over again, because there is a trace of her finitude in every amorous imagining that appears. But her ultimate disappearance is an event that only arrives for the lover. The phenomenon of death never gives itself to the dead. The lover must carry with his love the impending event of the Beloved's death, which is phenomenologically given as both a presence and an absence, a death that is yet to come. No other death is like the death of the Beloved.

Amorous Intention

The amorous imagination is for the lover a lamp that illuminates the world in light of the amorous event. It synthesizes the world according to the category of love, lays down a new plot or narrative self to which the lover attests through his ongoing innovation, and imbues existence with an experience of distance and separation that reorients the lover's being-in-the-world toward love and death. But the amorous imagination is not only productive, it is also a way of "seeing." It is a variation on the imaginative mode of consciousness, to use Husserl's term. Insofar as the amorous imagination is precisely that—an act of imagination—it intends in its own unique way. It "sees" phenomena according to its own mode, a mode distinguishable from other modes of consciousness such as memory, perception, or judgment. Recall that, unlike perception, the imagination unmoors what it intends from the *as is* and leaves the subject free to intuit imaginings in the *as if*. According to Husserl, the free play of the imagination allows for creative activity (and access to eidetic truth). Unlike memory, which relives past perceptions over again in the present (albeit in a peculiar, absent way) accompanied by a belief that they really happened, the imagination conjures a sort of "nowhere" that is unbound by belief grounded in past perception. While the imagination's *as if* mode of intending allows for innovation, it also displaces the self and feeds anticipation. The self that imagines finds itself in another time and place (memory does this too), it experiences itself as both here and there.[4] And imaginative activity allows the self to project itself into another place and anticipate a future that has not yet come, as we have seen in the amorous imagination's ontological function. These distinctions are not trivial. They reveal a fundamental activity of consciousness that is at play in the amorous imagination. As we will see in the next section, an imagination animated by love beautifies, builds, responds to, and individuates the Beloved through its creative-responsive activity. The amorous imagination is a kind of imaginative intending that exhibits the qualities of imagination as a unique mode of consciousness.

Despite talk of the imagination's projective capacities, one must not lose site of the fact that the imagination is an embodied phenomenon. The imagination may conjure a "nowhere," but it does so "from here," within a material body. For Merleau-Ponty and Ricoeur, the invisible world of thought and the imagination both have a distinctly carnal dimension. For Merleau-Ponty, the invisible world of thought is always engaged in "commerce" with the visible. It is never an abstract mind afloat in a transcendent realm. The world of thought is "attached" to the visible world of things (and the invisible world of things too). Thought penetrates into the visible and the visible penetrates into thought. For Ricoeur, the imagination is both semantical and carnal. It innovates through language but always in an enfleshed self. In both cases the fundamental point is the same: the world effects and affects the imagination and the imagination effects and affects the world. Marion's concept of the given adds another layer. The given always takes initiative, it always comes from "without," landing upon *l'adonné* like light upon a screen. Cartesian mind/body dualism is untenable when one looks closely at the structures of consciousness and experience. Imaginings appear in experience in concert, because of the given. The implications of this on the imagination are clear: the imagination is not solipsistic. Its content is not made up. They are not fancy or fantasy. The imagination draws its content from the world of things, from what is given to it from "without," from what lands upon it anonymously and of its own accord. The imagination remains accountable to the given.

Not only does the imagination receive what it can imagine from outside itself, it also produces, projects, and conjures imaginings that "descend into the visible," to use Merleau-Ponty's language. What the lover imagines is not limited to what the lover perceives. The imagination has the capacity to create a new world and it does so in a way that responds to what is given, enriching it through creative expression. Through her imagination, the lover "crystallizes" the Beloved with layers of meaning. She sees the world anew in light of what she sees through the creative lens of imagination. The mode of consciousness of the imagination is the mode of *as if*, which is not a mode of delusion or illusion but a mode that employs its own epistemology, axiology, and ontology. The *as if* invites possibility and creation. It is not moored to correspondence theories of truth (perception) that operate as a norm for belief. Like Husserl's eidetic imagination, the amorous imagination is free from the limits of perception (the *as is*) and is free to imbue the lover's experience of the Beloved with truths more akin to mythology, poetry, and art. That the lover "sees" the Beloved in a way that no one else sees her makes complete sense according to this description, for it is he alone that receives her call and imaginatively responds to it and, in doing so, shows her in her unique individuation as Beloved (to him). The lover experiences the Beloved in and through the enfleshed, amorous imagination. The flesh mediates the imagination's reception of the given and its expression of meaning, giving shape to the Beloved as such.

The carnal mediation of the flesh affects the way the Beloved appears to the lover and the way the lover experiences the world.

The Beloved is given as a saturated phenomenon that captures the lover's imagination and in so doing captures her flesh. The experience of love is in many ways a "total experience" insofar as it affects the lover "all the way down": she is "taken" by the event and enamored of the Beloved. When he is present his givenness calls her imagination to respond, and the call and the response are felt in the body. In his absence she imagines him. She feels his absence. The lover takes on the *as if* mode of consciousness, wondering what the Beloved might think, say, or do in any particular scenario in which she finds herself. As Stendhal noted in *Love*, the lover projects and renders present the Beloved through her amorous imagination. She feels his presence and absence, not in a disembodied way, as a thought projection, but in an embodied way, as an impressional experience of his physical presence or absence. Her body longs for him. *Would that the Beloved be here beside me in the cool orange groves beside the sea at Genoa!* The embodied, amorous imagination produces a lived impression of the Beloved that is "there" all the time, permeating the lover's body and psyche and giving a new phenomenological texture to even everyday experiences.

But where Stendhal in some ways trivializes these imaginings as mental fictions or delusions, we now see that they are actually quite profound. Stendhal's pseudo-scientific method conceals the truth of the imagination as a creative-responsive, hermeneutical faculty. Husserl is more helpful here. Understood in the *as is* mode of perception the lover's imagination does indeed seem to be fancy or even obsession. She does not "see clearly." She "idealizes" the Beloved, adorning him with imagined "crystals" that aren't really there. But understood in the *as if* mode of imagination the lover's imaginings become a hermeneutical enterprise. They amount to her interpretive response to a saturated phenomenon. She sees the world anew and always in light of the amorous event, an event that has affected her completely, through to her flesh. Her entire disposition and orientation toward the world and herself have changed. She physically feels different because the Beloved is given. She experiences the world anew and others experience her differently too (the invisible descends into the visible). Her imaginings do indeed crystallize "around" the Beloved but they do not amount to an illusion or delusion. They are a new way of "seeing" the Beloved and being in the world, of receiving him as a saturated phenomenon, and responding to him hermeneutically. The amorous imagination intends the Beloved in a nonobjectifying way that opens up to understanding and interpretation; that is, to possibility, creation, and individuation.

Amorous Imaginings

We now turn to amorous imaginings themselves. Traditionally, when one thinks of the imagination one thinks of its content: the images it conjures. Think of a yellow canary, and there in your mind's eye you have an imagining. But as we have seen, the imagination is not reducible to its content, to the images it produces. Nevertheless, the amorous imagination's images are an important part of its individuating capacity, and so a detailed description of how these images appear will round out our discussion of the amorous imagination as an individuating faculty. Note first that imaginings are themselves phenomena. They are given. They appear (albeit with a peculiar kind of presence and absence, a sort of quasi-reality). Imaginings have their own nature, their own inflections, their own way of showing themselves. And amorous imaginings in particular, that is, the images the lover conjures when imagining the Beloved, have their own sort of "presentation" or manifestation too. As we will see, amorous imaginings are marked by a whole host of unique qualities that contribute significantly to the way in which the Other becomes the Beloved.

Romantic Envisioning

For Novalis, Romantic philosophy involves a double movement: "alternating elevation and lowering."[5] To "romanticize" the world is to "give the commonplace a higher meaning, the ordinary a mysterious countenance, the known the dignity of the unknown, the finite an appearance of infinity."[6] Poetic "making" is not an illusion, delusion, or self-deception. As Kneller points out, "To make the familiar unfamiliar is not to seek cognitive oblivion, but simply to look at the world again with wonder."[7] Imaginative creation is the expression of a living power.[8] But Novalis also recognized the inverse: to romanticize is to demystify the mysterious. The imagination moves from the extraordinary to the ordinary at the same time that it creates the world anew. This latter movement is seldom emphasized in Novalis studies and runs counter to the traditional interpretation of "romanticizing" articulated by Abrams in *The Mirror and the Lamp*, but it constitutes an important aspect of Novalis's theory of the imagination, one relevant to understanding the imagination's creative-responsive ability to individuate. Romantic "lowering" provides a counterbalance to romantic "elevation" and restrains its impulse to "seek the undetermined—a child of fantasy—an ideal."[9] Novalis recognized that "[a]n unknown lover of course has a magical charm. Striving for the unknown, the undetermined, is extremely dangerous and disadvantageous. Revelation must not be forced."[10] While the imagination is the power to create a new reality by drawing out of the world what is there and making it appear magical, it is also the power to naturalize the mysterious and see in the world an order, structure, or form that is in no way mysterious. The Romantic imagination does both at one and the same time, resisting any simple reduction or distinction between reality and fantasy. [11]

Amorous imaginings operate in a similar fashion and constitute a new way of "seeing" the Beloved, which I term *envisioning*. In responding to the Beloved through the amorous imagination the lover engages in the endless hermeneutic. She interprets, understands, and creatively answers the call of the saturated phenomenon. She "sees" the Beloved differently than she sees anyone else in part because of what the Beloved gives but also in part because of what the lover creates. Amorous imaginings are a creative-responsive activity that calls into question any simple distinction between the imaginary and the real. In phenomenological terms, recognizing that the Beloved cannot be reduced to an object, that the Beloved resists intentionality and yet calls to be shown in the lover's response, the lover imagines the Beloved as extraordinary and expresses her love for the Beloved through her amorous imaginings. Amorous imaginings are akin to romantic imaginings in that they express the truth of the Beloved, which is at once made and found. When the lover envisions the Beloved she sees and experiences the unsubstitutable Other. The Beloved is more beautiful than any Other not simply because he has an attractive figure, charming smile, or humorous wit. The Beloved is more beautiful than any Other because the lover imagines him to be so and because she experiences him through creative expression. She sees him in a different light, a light illuminated by the amorous imagination. Any single quality he might display ultimately signals to his excessive givenness. The lover's amorous imaginings are not delusions or deceptions. They are a way of seeing the Beloved with wonder but they remain responsive to what gives itself. As any long-time lover knows, the Beloved is not perfect. He is not without his flaws, idiosyncrasies, and failures. Amorous imaginings do not wash over the ordinary. They respond to it. They understand it. They envision it as much as they envision the extraordinary. In "romanticizing" the Beloved the lover does not idealize him, but she does imbue him with significance that goes beyond the significance of any other given. Amorous imaginings "elevate" and "lower" the Beloved, render him both mysterious and ordinary, all the while signifying his unsubstitutability. Amorous imaginings are the lover's way of envisioning the Beloved, of seeing him as this Other, as other than any Other, as radically unique.[12]

Reading across Distance

As we have seen, amorous imaginings happen in and to the flesh. But they also happen across flesh. They are the activity of reading across the distance and separation that marks the Beloved's givenness. Paradoxically, the Beloved is given as both a radical intimacy and alterity. She is nearer to the lover than any Other can ever be, and yet each time the lover advances she recedes, like the pool of Tantalus. Intimacy and distance, proximity and separation, characterize the saturated phenomenon that is the Other-as-Beloved. What is a lover to do in the face of this narrow, carnal chasm?

The lover understands, interprets, translates, transmits, mediates, discerns, recognizes, envisions. In short, he imagines. Amorous imaginings are the lover's hermeneutical activity offered in response to the Beloved's amorous call. Through them the lover reads across the distance that separates him from the Beloved. As we have seen, the flesh mediates but it also marks a boundary and border. It is a threshold the lover can never cross or escape. But it is not a prison. It is a possibility. It is a messenger. It signifies. It opens us up to the world. The gaps between the lovers are both traversed and preserved through their enfleshed imaginings. Like the gaps in texts and in language (e.g., between plot points, *différance*, translations, the saying and the said, *parole* and *langue,* speech and silence, etc.) the gaps between bodies offer a surplus of meaning.[13] Who is the Beloved? The lover can never know. Instead, from moment to moment or perhaps all at once, he reads the Beloved as this way and now that; eroticized and mundane; counselor or muse; mother, friend, sometimes even enemy; a violent storm, a placid ocean; a victor; a partner; an obstacle or a cause. Each time the lover imagines the Beloved he expresses her and enriches the experience of her. The imaginings descend into the visible world and affect the Beloved as well. She sees the way she is seen. She hears the lover's words, sees his body speak, and moves within the same shared milieu of meaning. The Beloved speaks too. She reads across distance. The at times artful play of interpretation that is the amorous imagination crosses the phenomenological chasm that exists between lovers, but it never collapses it.

The distance between lovers can be dangerous, too. Idolatry, narcissism, and solipsism lurk in the dark corners of the amorous imagination. The lover's imaginings can, as Novalis warns, become "forced revelation." They can provide too much elevation without the counterbalance of lowering. They can render an ideal or idol of the Beloved. Or worse, they can become the lover's own reflections, mirroring back to himself an image of his own desires (though, properly speaking, he is no longer a lover at this point). The amorous imagination becomes solipsistic when it does not respond to the call of the Beloved (which gives itself from "without") and instead becomes infatuated with its own visions, unmooring them completely from what gives itself. In each case the lover betrays the endless hermeneutic by failing to answer the call and address the Beloved as alterity. Love is not merging. It is marked by a distance and separation that can be traversed but never collapsed.

Belief, Presence, and Absence

In "Amorous Intention," I argued that, generally, the imagination is as much an act of consciousness as its imaginings are objects of its intentionality. But, unlike perceptions, imaginings are not tethered to the *as is* and are given in the *as if*. And unlike memories, which rely on past perceptions and a certain kind of belief, imaginings arise in a liminal sort of "nowhere" and do not require belief in the same sense as memory. But amorous imaginings are a special case of imaging.

They do not appear in exactly the same way as generic imaginings. In love, the lover's amorous imaginings are accountable to the Beloved's givenness and remain rooted in the flesh. Contrary to Husserl's account, amorous imaginings are not disembodied acts of consciousness that allow for free variation of objects but are instead ways of envisioning the Beloved anew and, drawing on and from her givenness, interpreting that which exceeds objectness. Moreover, amorous imaginings carry with them an element of belief, although not the sort of belief present in memory. In memory, the self recalls and relives past perceptions on the belief that what is remembered actually happened. But in amorous imaginings, the Beloved happens to the lover and the lover responds to his saturating givenness by interpreting it in the endless hermeneutic. The lover's imaginings are accompanied by a belief that the Beloved is actually given as a phenomenon and that the imaginings are an appropriate response to his saturating nature. In other words, memories appear accompanied by a belief that they happened in the past and amorous imaginings appear accompanied by a belief that they are responding to what is happening now and has happened since the amorous event (and, as we will see, what may happen in the future). The presence of belief in amorous imaginings demonstrates the way in which amorous imaginings remain tied to the given and, unlike Husserl's eidetic account, are always accountable to what gives itself. When they become untied from the Beloved's givenness the lover's imaginings are no longer amorous and become narcissistic, idolatrous, and solipsistic, as we will see in detail in the next chapter. Amorous imaginings contribute to individuation only so long as they remain accountable to the Beloved as given.

Amorous imaginings appear in a peculiar mix of presence and absence. When the Beloved is "present" (given in experience), the lover imagines him by envisioning him. But her romantic envisionings are accompanied by another set of impressional amorous imaginings that, while perhaps less specific and clear than what the lover envisions of the Beloved, are nonetheless present in her reception of the Beloved. For example, when the lover receives and imagines the Beloved, she "sees" in him qualities that beautify and crystallize around him. Her experience of the Beloved is enriched by her creative-responsive expression of him. But she also experiences a sense or has an impression of time and a world with and without him. Always accompanying the lover's encounter with the Beloved is an imaginative impression that the world and the lover's experience of time are different because the Beloved is in it. The lover not only imagines the Beloved before her but also the world reconstituted as a result of the amorous encounter. I call this an "impressional amorous imagining," because it is not given as an object but rather as a prereflexive, originary experience of time and the world that co-occurs with the Beloved's givenness. It operates as an impression, somewhat vague and in the background of life. But it is there. It is part of the lover's amorous imaginings. Consider the lover who sees before her the Beloved. She envisions him, but she also experiences the "unthought" impression that she will be with him in the future, that her world will include him in some way, that her past is what it is only in relation to his presence in her present. This impression manifests as an imaginative "sense," a way of experiencing the world that is qualitatively different than the way the lover experienced the world prior to the amorous encounter.[14]

Amorous imaginings appear somewhat differently when the Beloved is no longer given directly in experience. When the Beloved leaves, the lover still "sees" her, still envisions her. While he may not conjure images of her, he moves about the world with the same impressional sense of her presence, which is given to him as both a presence and absence. The lover is alone but faced with a decision. In his quiet deliberations he asks, "What would my Beloved say?" He is viewing a piece of art and wonders, "What would my Beloved think?" He meets someone new and considers—perhaps not cognitively, "Who is this person in relation to my Beloved?" In the Beloved's absence the lover imagines the Beloved's presence. And this sort of imagining is not limited to mundane occurrences. Indeed, the lover carries with him an impressional imagining of the Beloved's perpetual absence, which can manifest as a fear of her death. Because she is absent, he wonders when she will once again be present. He wonders when she will return. He anticipates her presence in light of her absence. He imagines her present, but his imaginings are marked with an absence insofar as their ontological status is called into question. In this limited sense, the Beloved imagined is not the Beloved given. Despite their creative force, amorous imaginings cannot replace the Beloved's givenness. A tension therefore emerges between presence and absence which pervades every aspect of the amorous imagination. The Beloved is not an object and is never fully present before the intending ego. The Beloved is irreducible and so her ultimate meaning is never fully disclosed. Distance and separation keep the lovers apart. The Beloved withdraws as much as she advances. She is present when she is absent and absent when she is present. The lover attempts to navigate this tension through the amorous imagination, but amorous imaginings themselves manifest the very tension they try to address. Love is indeed a paradox.

Impossibility and Insufficiency

According to John Caputo, the "Enlightenment imposed certain restraints upon our thinking, certain 'conditions of the possibility,' to use Kant's expression, which, like border police, mark off the boundaries and patrol the limits of possible experience."[15] He goes on,

> [T]he *new* Enlightenment would constitute a second childhood which is given over to dreaming to the *impossible,* arising from a deep desire for what, given the constraints and conditions imposed by modernity, is precisely not possible, which for that reason is precisely what we most deeply desire.[16]

Descartes constrained knowledge to rationalism and the *cogito*. Kant set out the limits of the possibility of experience in his first *Critique*. And Husserl limited phenomena to the constituting acts of the transcendental ego. But thinkers such as Derrida and Marion contest these limits. They question the authority of reason; examine its underlying assumptions and its own limitations; challenge the self-grounding self; invite a discourse on language, narrative, and excess; and ask: What do we make of our desire for the impossible that persists even in the face of the constraints laid down by modernity?

Derrida and Marion answer these questions from two different angles. For Derrida, Husserl discovered the fact that signifiers can be empty of intuition and therefore are free to play and defer endlessly. In other words, Husserl discovered the possibility for the impossible fulfillment of intentionality (a kind of intentional emptiness or "blindness"). Impossibility is emptiness, a signifier without intuition. This liberation of the signifier allowed Derrida to develop the program of deconstruction, which at its best takes seriously the desire we have for the impossible intuition that is yet to come: justice, messiah, love, etc. This represents for deconstruction a kind of theological turn of its own. Marion took the other route: there arises at times too much intuition, there is givenness that exceeds our intentions, appearing as invisible or impossible. The given can saturate the very conditions for experience. Saturated phenomena call into question Western philosophy's obsession with ontotheology and open the door to the impossible in both phenomenology and theology.

From a deconstructive point of view, amorous imaginings operate like "empty" signifiers. They do not adequately correspond to any specific intuition. The imagination's power lies in its freedom from the *as is*, from perception or intuition. The lover can transform the world. But the imagination's freedom can also be its limitation. Unrestrained imaginings can drift away, taken by the current of endlessly streaming reflections. They can mirror themselves and transform into an infinite play of parody rather than a hermeneutic response to a saturated phenomenon. And yet, amorous imaginings do reference the impossible. They signal to what is always yet to come. The Beloved is given as separate, distant, other. She is never fully "here" in the same way an object is "here" because intentionality cannot reach her, cannot constitute her. The Beloved exceeds the lover's concepts. The lover imagines the Beloved's presence but, as we have seen and as Caputo points out, love is always marked by absence. Therefore, the structure of love includes a desire for the impossible that is the Beloved, and the lover responds to the Beloved's impossibility through the endless hermeneutic. All amorous significations remain insufficient because of impossibility. Amorous imaginings signal a desire for the Beloved's arrival, a yet-to-come that is never fully here.

From a phenomenological perspective, amorous imaginings can be seen as the only adequate response to the excess of intuition given by the Beloved. The Beloved is impossible in a second sense: he gives too much. He exceeds the limits for the possibility of experience set down by Descartes, Kant, Husserl, and Heidegger. The Beloved's saturating givenness saves amorous imaginings from endless deferral and empty signification because the Beloved *does* appear, he gives himself. In Marion's terms, the Beloved "arrives," but his arrival is too much, so much in fact that any signification or hermeneutic response is shown to be insufficient. No amount of amorous imagining can ever capture the Beloved as such. The Beloved cannot be said. He cannot be known. He cannot be fully described. The endless hermeneutic is never complete. The lover can never receive enough assurance of her own meaning expressed through love, nor can she ever provide enough assurance to the Beloved. Love is characterized by an excessiveness and an incomplete-ability. This excessiveness induces both anxiety and the call for more assurance. The "I love you" is a pledge of eternity given in the present that is never fully realized and so must recur. The lover must repeatedly "love first." The pledge takes shape in and through the creative space of the amorous imagination: the lover orbits around the grounding principle that is the Beloved, saying to him over and over again, "It is you. It always has been you and always will be you." The lover's amorous imaginings appear with a trace of insufficiency, with a sense of "not enough," or, as the Upanishads say, "*neti, neti.*"[17]

One should not mistake a desire for the impossible or the insufficiency of amorous imaginings as the lover's desire to know the Beloved or to merge with him. The desire for the impossible—both deconstructive or phenomenological—is an expression of love, not an epistemic impulse. In other words, the desire for the impossible is a characteristic of the experience of love expressed through the endless hermeneutic. It is a structure of love revealed by a close examination of the amorous imagination. The amorous imagination's activity demonstrates a desire for the impossible that animates or gives rise to amorous imaginings. But the lover's desire for the impossible is not something the lover overcomes, nor does she desire to overcome it. Rather, to desire the Beloved, to view love as the impossible, is to admit its dangers, risks, and ruses and yet plunge in, wholeheartedly. It is to long for the Beloved that never appears and to respond to his saturating appearance with an endless hermeneutic.

Castle-Building

In his 1729 *Hibernicus's Letters*, James Arbuckle discusses the free play of the imagination and its ability to construct a world that contributes to the happiness of both the self and society.[18] Through the imagination, philosophers, artists, and historians explore the range of human possibility and sympathetically reach out to one another. Arbuckle calls this imaginative activity "castle-building" because of its ability to construct a world out of a milieu of experiences, and to produce artistic compositions that delight and fascinate. Although Arbuckle's theory of the imagination focuses mainly on sympathy and aesthetics, his somewhat Husserlian suggestion that the free play of the imagination can produce new worlds or significations "around" a phenomenon is a useful way of thinking about how the lover and Beloved construct for themselves a bower of meanings arising out of and responding to the amorous event, a bower that frames their lives in relationship to other Others.

As we have already seen, the Other-as-Beloved is always advancing toward and retreating from the self-as-lover. Because the Other can never be known, through the creative, amorous imagination the lovers construct a "castle" of meaning around each other and engage in an ongoing hermeneutic, providing assurances to each other that each is meaningful to the other. A world of meanings emerges as a result of the Beloved's givenness, a world of meanings that goes beyond understanding the Other-as-Beloved and constitutes a reconfiguration of the lovers' lifeworld *in toto*. "Things" take their meaning in reference to the Beloved. Time is oriented around the Beloved's appearance (and potential and eventual absence vis-à-vis death). The lovers themselves become embodied symbols whose meaning is created though the play of the amorous imagination. The world references the Beloved, and the Beloved gives rise to a new world. In other words, the amorous imagination works "on" the Beloved through romantic envisioning, but it also works "on" the world by constructing a "castle" of signification that surrounds the lives of the lovers, fortifying the Beloved's place within the milieu of meaning and creating a hermeneutic enclosure, which the lovers inhabit.

The castle metaphor is appropriate because it inflects the exclusionary nature of the lovers' hermeneutic enclosure. It is a protected space shared by its inhabitants. Like a medieval stronghold, the lovers' world appears to them as deeply private, a world unto itself. They experience love as a living intimacy shared between them alone. It produces a lifeworld set apart from the lives of others The lovers guard its gates and are selective as to who may enter, and to what degree. They raise offspring within its ramparts. They sense that the world is operating around and outside them, but the center of the universe is the castle of meaning they have constructed in relationship to each other. Of course, all castles have cracks and may crumble. But the point here is to express in a metaphorical sense the phenomenological experience of love appearing as a universe within a universe, imbued with meaning that arises because of the Beloved's appearance, meaning that is not shared with the entire world but that is constructed through and between the lovers.

The kind of hermeneutic enclosure generated through amorous signification runs the risk of going too far, of closing the lovers off to a world to which they have obligations and which offers new alternatives and possibilities. Such an enclosure takes the form of a defensive fortification rather than a castle, which in truth is a hub of life that remains open to the world while at the same time configuring a world of its own. In forming the life of Two, the lovers create for themselves a new orientation and truth procedure, a new structure to inhabit and dwell within. But when lovers truly "forsake all Others" and withdraw to the keep of their own significations they alienate themselves and limit the possibilities present in sociability. They may in the name of intimacy disregard or even deny their ethical obligations to other Others. Their bower can become an echo chamber and stifle the kind of hermeneutic innovation that is the joy of love sustained. The lovers can come to see the world as a threat, and their significations a fastness to guard against it. They become unable to maintain their own world while at the same time welcoming-in society, which carries its own risk and requires a dangerous vulnerability (who will enter? Stepanitch or the Trojans?) The temptation for castle-building is exclusion to a dangerous degree, which in its most extreme form manifests as death, though more insidiously as denial or disregard of other Others.

Hidden Away

There is more to say about the privacy of love. The lovers appear as such only to each other. They receive and respond to each other through the intimacy of their amorous imaginations and in so doing create a distance between themselves and the world of others, of community. Love occurs between lovers, not lovers and others. The interplay of the lovers' amorous imaginings is "hidden away" and there is an aspect of the phenomenon of love that is always secret and withdrawn from all Others save *this* Other. Of course, love is not *completely* private. The expression of love is carried out in relationship with an Other who is in the world. Love is sanctioned by public ceremony and events. Philosophers such as Heidegger and Nancy point out that being-in-the-world is being-with-others. The lovers demonstrate their love before a community in their interactivity, their speech, their expressions, their shared flesh. And yet love is radically intimate. It is a society of Two. Amorous imaginings lie "in the eye of the beholder," so to speak. The amorous imagination constructs as part of the experience of love a hidden world shared only between the lovers. The lover cannot explain to his friend what draws him to the Beloved. He cannot do justice to the givenness of the Beloved. He babbles endlessly about her "qualities," or perhaps simply remains silent. Echoing Montaigne, the best explanation he can give regarding the cause of his love is simply, "because it is her, because it is me."

Other philosophers have acknowledged the hidden nature of love. Alain Badiou, for example, notes that intimacy is a structure of the truth procedure of love: the lovers become militant with regard to their love. Their truth takes shape in the "Two scene" that inaugurates a new truth and testifies to an event. Love's privacy is more problematic for Levinas. According to him, erotic intimacy precludes justice precisely because it closes off society, it neglects all Others in favor of the Beloved. The introversion of intimacy distracts us from the ethical obligation we have to the widow and the orphan. Regardless of the ethical or procedural aspects of intimacy, from a phenomenological perspective the hidden nature of amorous imaginings suggests that love is not a phenomenon given communally. Amorous imaginings do not appear for non-lovers. The lover's conduct might publicly signal their love but these signals are in some sense always derivative of a more private intercourse between the lover and the Beloved.

Fidelity, Assurance, and Meaning

Amorous imaginings are attestations of fidelity to the Beloved. As we have seen, in *The Erotic Phenomenon*, Marion argues that final individuation comes in the form of the mutual oath issued between the lovers. Marion's insight into the relationship between fidelity and time is important here. The pledge of fidelity temporalizes the erotic phenomenon and individuates the other-as-Beloved because it delivers an assurance of the erotic phenomenon that "lasts and imposes itself." It signifies the unsubstitutability of the Beloved and invokes a moment of eternity. It is the *adieu*. And the *adieu* is itself an amorous imagining, a saying that marks the moment when eternity pierces the veil of time. The oath of fidelity does not signify according to the boundaries of chronological time. The moment of love's arrival is an enchanting one, one that calls upon the eternal. The oath and amorous imaginings pay homage to that moment. The truth of love is not contingent upon its duration in the field of time. Its truth is that it appears, and the oath, assurance, fidelity, and imaginings testify to that appearance in the language of the eternal. Love need not endure over (chronological) time to be true. Love can end, and it often does. But the lover cannot claim to love provisionally; she must attest to the eternal. She must hymn rather than predict. She must proclaim rather than promise. The oath must be repeated again and again. No single expression is sufficient to assure the Beloved of his individuation. "I love you" makes its meaning in its saying.

Amorous imaginings expand the various ways the lovers express the oath. Because no single expression can provide the lover enough assurance, the lover's amorous imaginings reveal a second fidelity: a faithfulness not to the abiding presence of love but to the creative project of love. The lover promises to engage the Beloved in the endless hermeneutic, to be faithful to the call of the saturating phenomenon. Lovers do fail, however. They are at times unfaithful. But infidelity is not erasure. It does not by necessity render love inauthentic or negate prior affirmations. It is taken up as a part of the project of love that is riddled with failures and creativity. In this way love is more akin to Derridean impossibility than to the phenomenological given. Enduring love is always yet-to-come. Loving and the activity of the amorous imagination signals toward an impossible love that endures over time, the love that can never be. But there's the rub: the signaling *is* the love. It is Rumi's *Love Dogs*. The lover must give her life to be one of them, to howl and long, to assure and whisper "you alone." She must creatively respond to the excess of the Beloved that never fully arrives, that can never be known. Each moment of hermeneutic response, each amorous imagining is a moment of love. Love expressed through the amorous imagination is the now, the present gesture, the erotic caress, the shared "look and see," the romantic envisioning, the child.

Haunted by Death

Love is always accompanied by death. Structurally speaking, death is a part of the experience of love. Although death never fully "appears" on its own, as a phenomenon, it does appear as an impression of an impending inevitability, of a future destined to come. Death is present phenomenologically as a part of love in the sense that the lovers always carry with them the impression of a coming finality, of an event that will once again upend the lovers' world. In this sense, love is haunted by death. Death poses the ultimate dilemma: it threatens to negate the lovers' amorous enterprise while at the same time heightening the lovers' experience of love. Death imbues love with intensity and gives it a "charge" that would not otherwise be there. Mortality demands the lovers attend to their love with an immediacy, delicacy, and care that would not be required if life was unending. As Todd May writes in his essay, "Love and Death," in love the "scarcity of our moments together confers on them a preciousness that might otherwise go missing or at least be diminished," that is to say, "the threads that bind us in romantic love . . . are more taut because of our mortality."[19] Love appears then as a wager, and we experience it as such: the amorous imagination individuates the Beloved, imbuing life with meaning, while at the same time reminding us that one day love will end and charging love with a distinctive intensity.

This sense of tautness, wager, risk, and fragility is an important part of the phenomenon of love. It is a hallmark of love's appearance. The lover experiences both euphoria and anxiety through the Beloved's individuation. Amorous imaginings often take the form of imaginative projections. Lovers "see" their life together. They envision growing old. They recall past memories and relive them through the intimacy of conversation. They mark out a path together. But all the while an impression of death is present, sometimes vague and sometimes clear. It calls into question the power of individuation to give meaning. Amorous imaginings appear with a trace of mortality, of finality, and of finitude. They present as fragile possibilities as well as adventurous projections. The lovers know that their love is a risk that carries with it the ultimate loss: the loss of meaning; the loss of assurance; the loss of the unsubstitutable Other. Of course, in one sense, the death of the Beloved is not an end to love, because in the oath the lover has proclaimed for eternity the unsubstitutability of the Beloved. She can express fidelity through the amorous imagination, even after his death. But in another sense the creative project of love as a *shared* and *ongoing* project does come to an end. Life after death is lonely. The widow wonders what meaning existence can provide after the death of the Beloved. She does not know. She cannot provide her own meaning; it must come from without. Only the Beloved can provide it, but he is gone. She may search for meaning in other activities, other people, or other concerns. Indeed, she may find it. But nothing will replace the Beloved because he has been individuated, because he is, once and for all, unsubstitutable. Moreover, nothing can replace his ability to imagine *her* as a Beloved, for her to experience life as another's Beloved, as *his* Beloved. All of this is felt deeply in and through the activities of the amorous imagination.

Amorous Individuation

We return now to our original set of questions: How does *the* Other become *this* Other? How does the Other become the Beloved? How does love emerge? Through the encounter, the call, the response, and the endless hermeneutic. In short, through the amorous imagination. As Marion claims of all saturated phenomena, the Beloved is shown in the lover's response. The Other becomes the Beloved through a process of individuation that originates with the amorous encounter and is expressed in the ongoing activity of the lovers' interpretation. The lover receives the Beloved and shows her as such. The lover's interpretation is an embodied phenomenon and an imaginative one. It arises in the world of thought and the world of flesh. It is affected by the world of things and imparts its own affect upon the world. Through the amorous imagination the lover renders the Beloved unsubstitutable. But the hermeneutic is truly endless. The Beloved is *never fully individuated*. She is *always being individuated* through the hermeneutical activity of the amorous imagination. The amorous imagination is active at all times. We can see it at play in the lover's passing glance, in the pleasure of the erotic moment, and in the anticipation of the Beloved's death. The amorous imagination produces a new unity of experience. It "crystallizes" the Beloved through romantic envisioning. It projects across a new timescape and horizon, reconstituting the self as lover and issuing a new wager of life-as-love, all the while accepting the risk and vulnerability that emerges as a result of that exposure (hurt, betrayal, death, suffering, disharmony, resentment, frailty, etc.). It reinterprets the meaning of any subsequent event in light of the amorous event and the Beloved. It eroticizes and gives meaning to the Beloved by reading across the thin veil of flesh. Marion is right to suggest that the crossing of gazes, the lover's advance, the flesh, the oath, and the *adieu* all contribute to the Beloved's individuation. But he only hints at the evental nature of the Beloved and never mentions the role of the lover's imagination in rendering the Beloved unsubstitutable. The amorous imagination is an essential aspect of how the Other becomes the Beloved. Without it, love cannot appear.

6

The Dark Side of Love

The Dangers of the Amorous Imagination

Critics of Romanticism claim that its zealous faith in the imagination's power to reinvent the world goes too far. They claim a generative theory of the imagination overemphasizes its creative aspects and papers over the harsh realities of the world. But it is important not to dismiss Romantic ideas out of hand. It is true: some Romantics deified the imagination, or viewed it as a way to reach (achieve?) divinity. These Romantics thought that through the imagination we could fuse with the Absolute and reach human perfection. Critics claim the "perfectibility thesis" amounts to a "confusion of orders" that fails to appreciate the objective distinctions between nature and "the standards of relevance that govern reality."[1] Romantics are also criticized for the political indecisiveness that accompanied their primary concern with subjective expression. Carl Schmitt argued in *Politische Romantik* that the "root of romantic sublimity is the inability to make a decision."[2] Citing Novalis's claim that reality is but "the start of an unending novel," Schmitt concluded that political Romanticism was a contradiction in terms and that Romanticism's so-called obsession with the imagination resulted in unprincipled commitments and a lot of chatter.[3]

Like their Romantic adversaries, these critics may be overly zealous in their criticism. They fail to appreciate the subtlety of Romantic ideas of the imagination. Sadly, Schmitt-style critiques still hold purchase today and many postmodern thinkers (in an age "after" God) banish

Romantic theory to the backwaters of metaphysics or trivialize its contributions by historicizing and dismissing Romantic claims. But we must not move from one extreme to another. We can take seriously the dark side of the imagination—its limits, delusions, and obsessions—without relegating it to fancy or rejecting the fundamental idea of the imagination as a creative-responsive faculty. It is no secret that love under the sway of the imagination can take an ugly turn. Even before the Romantic movement was in full swing, novels such as *The Sorrows of Young Werther* explored the dangers of the unmoored imagination. Indeed, literature is replete with mad lovers lost in the tempestuous seas of their own passions. But where does it all go wrong? At what point does the amorous imagination become solipsistic, narcissistic, or delusional? We turn again to phenomenology for the answers.

Solipsism

Husserl's phenomenology is marked by a trace of Cartesianism. On his account, the transcendental ego aims its intentionality at intuition, constituting objects in the world. The mind is the primary agent. Through it the subject comes to know the world. While it is true that Husserl paid close attention to the flesh and its relationship to the mind, his emphasis was on the transcendental ego's structure and the role it plays in allowing for the possibility of scientific knowledge. To that end, Husserl has been accused of solipsism, or at least an inability to fully escape critiques of solipsism in light of his account to the transcendental ego. The problem of solipsism arises any time there is a categorical distinction between mind and body or subject and object.[4] Although I have tried to demonstrate throughout this work that such a distinction is misplaced and mischaracterizes the way the amorous imagination operates, the danger of solipsism lurks in the background for the lover who fails to see that amorous imaginings are only amorous insofar as they are accountable to the Beloved *as given*.

Amorous imaginings become solipsistic when they become completely untethered from the Beloved as he appears, as he "arrives," in the Marionian sense. This "untethering" poses for the lover the greatest risk of solipsism. The imagination finds both its greatest strength and greatest weakness in its ability to engage in the *as if,* to creatively respond to the *as is.* Structurally, the amorous imagination is untethered from but still accountable to perception (or more accurately, the given). According to Husserl, once the imagination has its content it does not need perception to engage in the free play of images, to access eidetic truths. But amorous imaginings are never *completely* unmoored from perception insofar as they draw their content from what the self first perceives—or *receives*—and all reception occurs within a hermeneutical nest of preexisting meanings assembled by the imagination. In love, the *as if* is a creative response to the *as is,* and both are made possible by the imagination. To maintain their amorous quality, amorous imaginings must receive and respond to the Beloved given as alterity. Only in remaining accountable to the given do they retain their amorous character.

To untether amorous imaginings from the Beloved-as-given is to convert the amorous into the egotistical, the solipsistic. Recall that imaginings are themselves phenomena. They appear. And when they appear, they appear in relation to a world. But they can become untethered fancy when they become disengaged from the Beloved's givenness (to use Marion's term) and draw their reference only from *other imaginings.* Consider works such as Goethe's *The Sorrows of Young Werther,* sections of Dante's *La Vita Nuova,* or even the medieval legend of *Lancelot and Elaine,* all of which dramatize the excessive passions that can emerge when the lover no longer responds to the Beloved-as-given but instead responds to her own imaginings. Elaine laments Lancelot's disinterest to the point of self-destruction. Prior to her death, in order to preserve his anonymity at a tournament she hides his shield for him under her bed. The shield symbolizes his true identity: if he were seen with it the spectators at the tournament would know the knight who carries it is Lancelot. Rather than the actual Lancelot, with whom love is impossible, Elaine takes in and protects the shield, making it the object of her affection and a symbol of false hope for amorous requite. After he is wounded in a joust, Elaine nurses Lancelot back to health, mistaking his vulnerability and physical need for germinating love. But Elaine is lost. Lancelot does not call. Her amorous gaze fixates upon the images of the shield and his wounds rather than that which gives itself as Lancelot-the-Beloved. Lost in a labyrinth of mirrors, her amorous imaginings confuse and excite in their self-referential solipsism. She looks to other imaginings to find meaning and is adrift in their own free play. She mistakes his sporting her token at the tournament for the call of love because she imagines it to be so, not because he has appeared as such. Her imaginings become fantasies: receiving and responding to other imaginings. Lancelot's shield, token, and wound come to symbolize her amorous imaginings themselves, swirling in a torrent of their own, unmoored from what gives itself. She turns away from the givenness of the Other, which comes from "without," and becomes instead infatuated with her own romantic imaginings that churn about "within." This "detachment" from the given, which always appears as an alterity (the Beloved), transforms into a concern only with that which now appears as similitude. Although initially prompted by the appearance of the Other, the "lover" (for she is no longer truly a lover at this point) draws her amorous inspirations from her own imaginings and no longer looks to the Other-as-Beloved as the source of her creative response.

In the case of solipsism, the Beloved is no longer a participant in the call and response of the amorous event. The lover responds only to herself. She is no longer accountable to the Beloved as a saturated phenomenon. She no longer engages in the endless hermeneutic. She no longer envisions romantically. Her "love" exists on its own, in its own world of self-referential mimesis. To avoid solipsism, the lover must always *respond* to the given, to the Beloved as a saturated phenomenon. She must remain accountable to it. Recall that the amorous imagination is a creative-responsive power. It creates in the *as if* but it responds to the *as is*. The two are interconnected. Like Merleau-Ponty's idea of the visible and the invisible, amorous imaginings must interact with the visible, they must draw from and descend into the world as it appears. And the world of things moves into the world of thought through the imagination, influencing it, animating it, and inspiring it. The same intertwining that marks the psyche's relationship to the flesh marks the lover's relationship to the Beloved. In order to become a lover, one must imagine the Beloved from what appears and not become lost in one's own imaginings.

Delusion and Misapprehension

Recall that, for Marion, the endless hermeneutic is the proper interpretive response to the saturated phenomenon. Because the saturated phenomenon is given with an excess of intuition it resists reduction to objectness. Saturated phenomena reveal knowledge as a 'negative certainty;" that is, knowledge without an object, or the discovery that the thing we desire to know is unknowable. However, *l'adonné* can misinterpret the saturated phenomenon, mistaking it for a common phenomenon. *L'adonné* can attempt to know it by bringing an intention adequate to the intuition, although ultimately the adequation will fail. Recall also that the given gives itself anonymously. It is only in the given's reception that it is identified as God, Being, Other, or Beloved. In phenomenalizing the given, *l'adonné* identifies it. The call of the given is shown in *l'adonné*'s response. The self bears up against the given and in resisting it phenomenalizes it. The lover shows the Beloved by receiving him and responding to him through the endless hermeneutic. The Beloved appears as a saturated phenomenon. He exceeds all intention. The proper response to the Beloved is not knowledge but understanding. It is the endless hermeneutic. By receiving and responding to the Beloved, the lover shows him as such, and love emerges. But as *l'adonné,* the lover can misapprehend the Beloved. She can mistake him for a common law phenomenon and try to render him an object (of desire). She can seek mastery over him. She can deny her negative certainty and impose a phenomenological restriction upon the Beloved, suppressing or masking his excess. Her attempts lead only to delusion and destruction. She either persists in her phenomenological futility or else convinces herself that she has indeed captured the Beloved in objectness. Neither amounts to love.

We see this phenomenon dramatized in the myth of Cupid and Psyche. Taken up in the amorous event, Psyche finds herself immersed in a shadowland of darkness, a place of unknowing and negative certainty, where she enjoys the caress of Cupid's flesh. The lovers cannot see each other. They remain at an intimate distance, engaged in erotic understanding that does not attempt to reduce the Other to an object but that celebrates the excess of the other's givenness. Cupid, the Beloved, recedes each dawn, each time the light arrives and threatens to reveal his identity, which would render him an object of knowledge. It is only when the lovers approach each other at night, in darkness, that their love appears as hermeneutical play, creative and responsive. But the Beloved's excess is too much. Psyche desires to *see* him, to expose him to the light, to know him, and in knowing him establish his identity and fix his givenness through adequation. When the lamp light falls on the Beloved, he is wounded. He flees, vanishes. Psyche is left to wander the world in search of a lover that—in order to retain his status *as lover*—must always evade the restricting gaze of her knowledge.

Delusion threatens in a second way. Not all Others issue the erotic call. Because the amorous event itself arrives as a saturated phenomenon, it escapes causal explanation. But it is nevertheless true that some Others are silent while some Others beckon. We cannot say why, only that it is the case. When the would-be lover misidentifies the injunction for the call, she misapprehends the given for an amorous phenomenon that does not actually appear. The would-be lover is wrong. The Other is not the Beloved. He does not beckon her to step forward, and yet in her delusion she advances anyway. The lover responds to the injunction as though it is a call and in interpreting it as such fails to appropriately respond to the saturated phenomenon. She is faced with a choice: insist that the injunction is the call and engage her imagination hermeneutically with the hopes that the Beloved emerges, or accept the injunction and await the call from another Other. In the first case, the would-be lover's advance may never identify a Beloved. It may either dissolve or persist. If it persists, delusion appears in the form of the self-in-denial: the would-be lover strains in the silence, listening for a call that never comes. She imaginatively projects onto Others a call which they do not issue. She deludes herself into thinking—through her own imaginings—that the call can be heard without reference to the phenomenon itself. Again, we see the ontological function of the imagination at play: absent love, the self is being-toward-death, its own death, and yet it yearns to orient itself around the life of another, around the life of the Beloved.

This is the tragedy of Hermaphroditus and Salmacis. Salmacis, the water nymph, gazes upon Hermaphroditus and mistakes his appearance for the amorous call. She advances, asking whether he is indeed Cupid (again, a desire to know defeats love), and offers herself to him. He resists. Salmacis's misapprehension of the injunction-as-amorous-call escalates. Hermaphroditus continues his rebuffs. He never appears as the Beloved. Indeed, he does not even comprehend the effect his appearance has on her. He is blind to her attraction because it is she who misapprehends through her own imagination. But Salmacis cannot resist the desire to possess, to know, and to merge with Hermaphroditus. She follows him into a pool and wraps her arms around his naked body, calling out, "Oh, may the gods thus keep us ever join'd!"[5] Her wish is granted, and the two bodies combine in a "single body mix."[6] Salmacis's imaginative delusions conceal the Other through a misapprehension of his givenness, swallowing him up in a violent act of reduction. The Other becomes the Same. She mistakes the ethical injunction for the amorous event. He appears, but not as the Beloved. Her delusions result in a kind of death: both identities are destroyed when the deluded "lover" insists that the Other appear otherwise, which is not for her to decide.

Idolatry and Narcissism

In *In Excess*, Jean-Luc Marion describes the way in which what he calls "idols" saturate according to quality. Marion's uses the term *idol* with different inflections throughout the course of his thinking. In some works, idols refer to ideas or concepts caught up in metaphysics. To create an idol of an idea is to claim that it serves an ontotheological purpose, that it is a grounding principle. Marion's use of the term in these cases strikes a critical tone. But in other works, such as *Idol and Distance*, Marion develops his idea of the idol to a fuller degree, nuancing it in order to demonstrate the way idols (and icons) function as their own mode of seeing. Idols are not inauthentic or false; rather, they reflect the desires of the devotee in all their fullness. As always, Marion's descriptions are phenomenological. The viewer's gaze roves about the given looking for something that interests it. When it encounters the idol, the idol saturates the gaze completely. It dazzles the viewer, capturing her attention. It provides "an exact measure of what the gaze can bear and functions as an invisible mirror."[7] The idol corresponds precisely to the viewer's vision of the divine and, in doing so, reflects the viewer's desires back at her. Idolatry occurs because it makes a god of the idolater.[3]

The beautiful youth Narcissus loves no one, but all who gaze upon him fall in love. One day he spurns a would-be lover. In a prayer of vengeance, the lover cries out to the gods to make Narcissus know what it is to love Narcissus in vain. The wish is granted, and when Narcissus sees his own reflection in a pool he falls in love with himself. Before his encounter with the image his gaze roamed the world, unsatisfied and unsettled. Once his gaze becomes enamored with what dazzles it, what fills its horizon to the limit, he cannot look away. But Narcissus sees only his own gaze turned back on himself. He becomes his own idol. Like Narcissus's gaze, amorous imaginings can become idolatrous and convert what might have been an endless hermeneutic into narcissism. When the lover becomes fascinated by his own imaginings rather than what is given in excess, he runs the risk of becoming an idolater. He mistakes his own imaginings for the Beloved. Disconnected from what appears, the imaginings no longer reflect the Beloved but the lover's own desires. He "sees" only what he wants to see, the Beloved appears only on the lover's terms, according to what his gaze can bear. The Beloved is in a sense "constrained" or even masked over insofar as the lover's imaginings take the place of her givenness. Indeed, it is not the Beloved that becomes the idol, but the lover's image of her. The lover imagines her to be something that she is not: she is not only what he desires but more, and yet rather than her givenness his imaginings capture his gaze and limit her to his own desires. In reflecting the lover's gaze back to himself, amorous imaginings are no longer amorous. They are narcissistic. They are vivid, dazzling, and captivating images, but they are not accountable to the given. The amorous imagination avoids narcissism when it remains both creative and responsive to the Beloved's givenness and does not become completely unmoored and set adrift in the *as if*.

Violence

Romantics championed the sympathetic power of the imagination. Through the imagination the poet represents to himself the feelings of another. He imaginatively transforms himself into the Other, in what Novalis called an act of "spiritual mimesis." But sympathy carried to its extreme manifests as a desire to merge.[9] According to many Romantics, not only can the poet imaginatively recreate the Other's experiences, he can metaphysically unify with the Other through the imagination's capacity to dissolve distinctions. According to Samuel Taylor Coleridge, "Love is a desire of the whole being to be united to some thing, or some being, felt necessary to its completeness, by the most perfect means that nature permits, and reason dictates."[10] Coleridge argued that all ideals, even religious ones, issue from a search for union between male and female.[11] The goal of philosophy was the idealization of ever-increasing totalities: "[I]n everything the blending of the similar with the dissimilar is the secret of all pure delight."[12] The ecstasy of oneness runs throughout the grand corpus of Romantic literature. For many Romantics, the quest for the Absolute, a quest made possible by the power of the imagination, culminated in a collapse of difference, in a union of the Other with the Same.

The desire for oneness expressed by the Romantics is an old mythology. It originates with Plato and still dominates modern concepts of love. Popular culture is replete with references to "two becoming one" and lovers uniting under the stars or before a congregation. But the Romantic ideal of metaphysical merging is not without its critiques. A desire to collapse the distance and separation between self and Other—between lover and Beloved—can become a sort of ontological violence, and in actuality render love impossible. As Levinas warns and I have reiterated, reducing the Other to the Same, totalizing all difference, amounts to a denial of the alterity that marks the Other *as such*. While I have advanced a relative alterity (as opposed to the hyperbolic alterity of Levinas), I still maintain that distance is a condition for the possibility of love. To insist that the Other merge with me, that he fit into a totalizing system, that he cease enjoining me and instead assimilate into me violates the nature of the Other given as difference. Or, to put it in Marionian terms, to mistake the saturated phenomenon for a common phenomenon and (attempt to) reduce her to an object is to misapprehend the Beloved and construct an idol, subsuming her into my phenomenological horizon. When the lover demands that the Beloved join with him and deny the distance and separation that is the *requisite* space for the endless hermeneutic he in effect demands the dissolution of love itself. Distance and separation must remain precisely because the Beloved is an Other, and the space of alterity is the space of possibility: it is the site of the free play of love as the lovers seek to understand (hermeneutics) but never to know (epistemology) one another. The desire for merging betrays the conditions that make love possible.

But not all sympathy is violent. There is a balance to strike. The amorous imagination need not go so far as to insist on unity in the lover's attempt to understand the Beloved. The lover can through her imaginative projections mirror or attempt to simulate in herself the

Beloved's experiences without totalizing him. We need not overstate the critique of the Romantics. Moreover, the lover can sympathetically "reach out" to the Beloved in a gentle act of concern rather than a violent act of conflation. After all, she cares about him. The point is that the amorous imagination is not always violent when through it the lovers attempt to share an experience. It only becomes so when the lover uses it as a medium to close the very distance that enables love to appear in the first place.

Death

But what if the desire to merge is mutual? What if it is not just the lover's desire to merge with the Beloved? What if, as in the Tristan myth, both lovers seek union? In *Love in the Western World*, Denis de Rougemont asks this very question, and provides a chilling answer:

> The love of love itself has concealed a far more awful passion, a desire altogether unavowable, something that could only be "betrayed" by means of symbols such as that of the drawn sword and that of perilous chastity. Unawares and in spite of themselves, the lovers have never had but one desire—the desire for death! . . . In the innermost recesses of their hearts they have been obeying the fatal dictates of a wish of death; they have been in the throes of *the active passion of Darkness*.[13]

Although in this passage Rougemont describes courtly love as ultimately a desire for desire itself ("the love of love"), his observation is germane to the broader idea of love as a desire for metaphysical merging. Phenomenologically speaking, the lovers' mutual desire to merge into one phenomenon can constitute a sort of "death wish" insofar as the desire is a desire for the annihilation of a separate self. The death wish of mutual desire is a variation on Levinasian violence: the lovers seek the experience of union, which is itself an experience of dissolution. To the extent the amorous imagination plays a part in the lovers' "active passion of Darkness," it is a mechanism of death. The imagination's creative and sympathetic capacity can manifest as a desire to dissolve into oneness in such a way that it carries the mark of death, if not literally, at least metaphorically. Whether this experience of oneness ever occurs in life or appears as a phenomenon is a conversation for another day. But the presence of the desire for oneness does indeed at times accompany the presence of love. "Two become one" is a modern trope, and we have the Romantics to thank for magnifying the idea that love is fundamentally about metaphysical merging. In any case, as we have seen, this desire to merge is only one aspect of love. Phenomenology reveals that love also appears as distance and separation, as a space between flesh that calls for an endless hermeneutic, a reading across difference without a need to collapse it.

The power of the amorous imagination to foment the death wish is intensified and more dangerous when the desire is experienced only by one of the lovers.[14] Take Werther, for example. In *The Sorrows of Young Werther*, Goethe explores the tragedy of the lover lost in the throes of the death wish. The novel is composed of a series of letters written by the young artist Werther recounting his growing passion for Charlotte, a beautiful woman engaged to a suitor eleven years her elder. While Charlotte's feelings for Werther remain ambivalent throughout the novel (we only ever get Werther's side of the story), Werther's desire to be with Charlotte overwhelms him with suffering and he sees only one solution to his dilemma: he must die. In a pathetic scene of romantic excess, Werther attempts suicide but botches the job, causing a slow and painful death. Charlotte does not attend his funeral. Throughout the text we see Werther's passions escalate, gaining more and more momentum as they drive him toward his fated end. But what kind of end? Werther's sad story exemplifies the dangers of the amorous imagination when it is taken by all of its darker aspects: solipsism, delusion, narcissism, idolatry, and violence. This is no trivial thing. The imagination can indeed, as David Hume warned, "interfuse and combine passions with ideas," leaving us at the whim of imaginative impressions that seem to carry more force than the original sense impressions from which they were derived. The Beloved can capture the imagination, but the imagination can also capture the lover.

One could spend an entire career exploring the relationship between love and death, but we end our discussion here, with a final observation and paradox. Death is the phenomenon that never appears. Death never gives itself to the self. The self never experiences its nonbeing. Death is beyond experience because, as Epicurus reminds us, when I am here, death is not; and when death is here, I am not. And yet death is always present in its absence. To the extent that it does appear, it appears as a haunting, to use Derrida's term, a phantom that lurks in the background of Being. But the death of the Beloved does appear for the lover, or at least it *can* appear. Unlike my own death, the death of the Beloved is a possible given. I can experience the world without her. As we have seen, the possibility of the appearance of the Beloved's death reorients the lover's sense of time and ontology. But for Werther neither love nor death would appear. Like his own death, love would not give itself to him. Love appears only as an absence, as a haunting. Love and death are given as the same phenomenon in their nonappearance. And so Werther, or the lover for whom the amorous call never issues, experiences a world without meaning, a world that can only resolve itself in one way. Werther's life is reduced to a paradox. He must make appear what can never appear: his own death.

The Dissolution and Disillusion of Love

Modern romances depict love as an idealized state, a relationship of ultimate importance that delivers existential meaning in its fullest sense. But as we have seen, there is a dark side to love. Caught up in the throes of an imagination, unmoored from the Beloved-as-given, love can dissolve into idolatry, delusion, and death. Although the word *imagination* has an almost playful connotation in our popular discourse, in the case of the amorous imagination, it can be both creative and destructive. Not all love is romantic. No love is pure. When we remove naive assumptions about the fanciful nature of love and recognize the power of the imagination as an image-making faculty we begin to appreciate the depths to which the imagination goes in shaping our experience of what appears. We see that love requires caution as well as creation. It requires attention to amorous imaginings, what gives rise to those imaginings, and the way in which those imaginings operate in orienting our experience of the Other. Over-romanticizing the amorous imagination or failing to appreciate its dangers can lead to disillusionment. What at first appears as a thrilling encounter can degrade into a labyrinth of mirrors. Lovers preserve love insofar as they engage in the endless hermeneutic, which is an imaginative and interpretive project that goes on forever and ever. But love dissolves and disenchants when the lovers attempt to fix their gazes on one another, reducing the Other-as-Beloved to an object or identity. As Cupid and Psyche reveal: to love best is to love in the dark.

Conclusion

Love's Univocity and What's Left Unsaid

Love's Univocity?

Love has always been a mystery. Perhaps it will remain so, and that is why we find it fascinating. But one thing is for certain: love matters. It is among the most important experiences we can have. Like other objects of philosophical inquiry such as reality, truth, beauty, or justice, love seems to evade totalizing systemization, and yet it calls for rigorous analysis. There is a "there, there" but it is hard to put a finger on. Historically, philosophy has treated this enigmatic quality as something in need of dissection, classification, and clarification. Love is something we should try to know. With good reason: knowing is one of philosophy's calls, its aims. This study is no exception. But philosophy can obscure what it seeks to illuminate. The traditional typology of *eros, agape,* and *philia* provide useful categories to help us analyze the many voices of love, but these same categories distort love's appearance by insisting that it is essentially multivocal, that there are indeed several different kinds of love. Are there? Or, as Marion argues in *The Erotic Phenomenon*, does love speak with one voice—the voice of the gift—manifesting in different domains but always with the same, nonreciprocal structure? The question of love's univocity is complicated, and a meaningful treatment of the question would require a sustained analysis outside the scope of this book. But a few exploratory comments may prove useful in setting out possible lines of inquiry to investigate the question of love's "voice."

Whether love speaks univocally remains for me an open question. What I have attempted to show is that when love does speak, it speaks *imaginatively*. Love is not reducible to imagination but the imagination plays a central role in love's appearance. I have argued that through the amorous imagination the self-as-lover creatively responds to the saturating givenness of the Other-as-Beloved, individuating her and affirming the Beloved's meaning by engaging in an endless hermeneutic. But the imagination is not only at play in love of the Beloved; it also operates in a parent's love for his child, or a friend's love of her friend. In these two cases specifically, we can see that in ways structurally similar to love of the Beloved the imagination plays an important role in both receiving and phenomenalizing the Other. The Other appears as an alterity but is individuated as child or friend, in part due to the creative play of the self's imagination. The Other-as-child appears as a radical *responsibility* in the Levinasian sense, but perhaps more so as a radical *possibility*. The Other-as-child gives herself to the parent as a call, but a call that must be answered by the co-creative activity of the parent and the child, together. Through the imagination the parent individuates the child by engaging in an endless hermeneutic with regard to the Other-as-child, and the parent also imaginatively projects for the child and for himself a world of possibility laid out before them. The importance of this inflection (and whether it endures a sustained critique) remains to be seen, but what does seem important is that in a parent's love for his child the amorous imagination plays an integral role in phenomenalizing not only the Other-as-child but also the child-as-possibility. Both love of the Beloved and love of the child implicate the amorous imagination.

As we have already seen with Montaigne and Boétie, the phenomenon of friendship shares a common (although not identical) structure with love of the Beloved. Both involve the phenomenon of the crossing of gazes and appear as an event. Both call for an endless hermeneutic. But there are differences too. Love of the Beloved seems to go beyond love of the friend in the radicality of its individuation. The crossing of flesh, the oath, and the child make space for and are more pressing expressions of the *haccaeitas* of the Beloved. Friendship may not achieve the same level of "atomistic particularity" achieved in love of the Beloved, at least phenomenologically. Still, the love of the friend, like the love of the child and the Beloved, requires imaginative engagement in order to achieve the kind of individuation that marks the Other-as-child, Other-as-friend, or Other-as-Beloved. It is through the creative-responsive activity of the amorous imagination that the friend is called out from the milieu of other Others. What seems to distinguish the friend from the stranger is precisely this "calling out," this sustained imaginative engagement with the Other as one who both anchors me in a world of meaning and also lures me toward a horizon. Unlike the stranger, widow, or orphan, the friend does not remain an ethical injunction, universal and anonymous. The friend demands responsibility but also calls for intimacy. In this way, love of the friend and love of the Beloved seem to appear in a similar fashion, but perhaps with varying degrees of individuation.

Love of God complicates the question of love's univocity even further. God does not appear in the same way as the Beloved, friend, or child. In a traditional theological register, there is a self-evident phenomenological difference between the Beloved that stands before me and the God that does not. But in a different theological register, however, one more informed by phenomenology, we might say that God's appearance is marked by both a presence and an absence (among many other things). In either case, the phenomenon of God must be treated with respect and sensitivity, and an openness to new meanings, experiences, and possibilities regarding what it means for God "to appear." To think of God ontotheologically unnecessarily limits the phenomenological inquiry into the nature of the love of God. Perhaps Richard Kearney's suggestion that we consider God manifest in the arrival of the Stranger provides an opening into an exploration of the structure of the love of God and what it has in common with love of the Beloved. Indeed, one is tempted to say that love of God is in some way *more imaginative* than love of the Beloved, in the sense that an experience of God (in Kearney's sense) appears as and within an entire milieu of religious poetics. Where the Beloved stands before the lover and issues the call, God swirls about, a spirit in our midst never fully appearing but always beckoning for a response. Needless to say, the question of whether the love of God speaks with the same voice as the love of the Beloved requires a serious and sustained study.

The degree to which love is univocal therefore remains unclear. For Marion, love's univocity is demonstrated by the structure of the gift, which is the structure of love. On my (less ambitious) account, the amorous imagination is a condition for the possibility of love, but identification of that condition does not yield the conclusion that love is univocal, only that the possibility of love is predicated upon the fact of the amorous imagination as both a hermeneutical structure and hermeneutical activity. While I do think the amorous imagination underlies all amorous experiences, I remain open to the question of whether love speaks with one voice.

Synopsis

I began with a discussion on method. While acknowledging the limitations of all method I also recognized the need to determine a method before engaging in this study. I provided a thumbnail critique of empirical methods (i.e., psychology, biology, and cultural theory) before settling on phenomenology. Phenomenology, I argued, is best suited for a philosophical analysis of love because it allows love to "speak for itself." Phenomenology insists on rigorous descriptions of phenomena as they appear without limiting them to predetermined categories. Of course, phenomenology is beholden to language, consciousness, and description and so like any other method it is not free from limitations. Still, it presents the best methodological option for an analysis of love and the imagination because it avoids reductionism and begins with the lived experience of love. It does not insist that love is the byproduct of some underlying structure, drive, or complex chemical reaction. I critiqued love's traditional typology and identified Romanticism as a watershed moment that opens onto new possibilities because of the way in which the Romantics took seriously the power of the imagination. I then discussed different types of phenomenology, starting with Husserl and working through Heidegger, Levinas, Ricœur, and Marion. I concluded my discussion on method by demonstrating how when Romanticism and phenomenology cross they provide fertile ground to examine the relationship between love, individuation, and the imagination.

I explicated Jean-Luc Marion's phenomenology before turning to a close reading of *The Erotic Phenomenon*. I used the debate between Marion and Levinas regarding individuation as an entry point into the broader question of love. While I agreed with most scholars that

Marion's critique of Levinas on individuation is a misreading of Levinas, I maintained that Marion's deeper question about the emergence of love and the Other's conversion into the Beloved is quite significant and worth examining. I then turned to Marion's phenomenology of givenness and the saturated phenomenon, analyzing their implications for a phenomenology of love and the imagination. Tracing the theme of individuation through Marion's *The Erotic Phenomenon*, I argued that, while compelling, his description of love does not fully explain the role of hermeneutics and imagination in individuating the Other-as-Beloved. Marion's phenomenology emphasizes the lover's advance as the inaugural moment of love rather than the Beloved's saturating givenness. While this emphasis preserves the idea that love has a nonreciprocal structure (because the lover must step forward first, without the expectation of return), it conceals the evental nature of the amorous encounter and the Beloved's appearance as a saturated phenomenon. I then traced Marion's individuation argument through the flesh to its ultimate expression in the *adieu*. I concluded that Marion's phenomenology of love demonstrates the deep insights a phenomenology of love can yield. And yet, *The Erotic Phenomenon* is missing some key descriptions, particularly regarding hermeneutics and the imagination's role in individuating the Beloved.

Next, I analyzed five key features of the imagination to show how it functions as an individuating faculty. Drawing on Kant, I described its productive and reproductive capacities, emphasizing the imagination's ability to synthesize not only our experiences but an entire lifeworld of meaning. I then discussed the imagination's hermeneutical structure. The imagination functions as both a "nest" of meaning within which phenomena "land" and a meaning-making activity that generates understanding through its interpretive activities. Next, I explored the imagination's creative-responsive capacity. I examined the way the imagination enriches experience by imbuing it with meaning that goes beyond what is given but focused on its accountability to the given. The imagination in its creative-responsive capacity is in an important sense beholden to what appears. I then discussed the embodied nature of the imagination, analyzing its relationship to the flesh. Finally, drawing on Husserl, I examined the imagination as a unique mode of consciousness, the *as if*, which is distinct from other modes of consciousness, especially perception and its tie to the *as is*.

Tying these threads together, I offered a preliminary answer to the question of individuation, arguing that because of these five qualities the imagination plays a central role in the way in which *the* Other appears as *this* Other.

My argument then took a generative turn. I provided a phenomenological account of love that takes seriously its imaginative and hermeneutical dimensions. Drawing from Marion's theory of *l'adonné* and Romantic theories of the creative imagination, I argued that love begins with an amorous event, which gives itself as a saturated phenomenon and happens to the lover. The amorous event emphasizes the Beloved's givenness rather than the lover's advance, as well as the evental nature of love as a phenomenon. The amorous event is marked by an encounter, a call, a response, and distance and separation. It is also an embodied phenomenon that happens in and to the flesh. The encounter is an event that upends the lover's preexisting world. The event has a hermeneutic structure insofar as the event "lands" upon the lover who already has a preconstructed "nest" of meanings which the event overturns. Moreover, the lover must then reconfigure her world in light of the amorous event, revealing another hermeneutic dimension to love. Like any Other, the Beloved appears as an ethical injunction but the injunction is accompanied by something more: the erotic call. The call shows itself in the lover's response to the call, which is hermeneutical through and through. The lover identifies the saturated phenomenon as the Beloved and in doing so interprets her. A third hermeneutic dimension emerges: the Beloved's alterity brings with it an experience of distance and separation that must be "read across" but not collapsed. Through the embodied imagination, the lovers seek to understand (but not to know) each other and engage in an endless hermeneutic.

I concluded my study by sketching out the contours of a phenomenology of the amorous imagination. While my description was far from exhaustive, I tried to provide a detailed enough account to unpack the way in which the amorous imagination functions in individuating the Other-as-Beloved. I observed three aspects of the amorous imagination. First, I described its transcendental activities; that is, the ways in which the imagination functions as a lamp that "illuminates" the world through its synthetic power. The amorous imagination has a productive dimension insofar as it produces a new world from the inventory of meanings that are upended by the amorous event. The amorous imagination has a narrative dimension evidenced by the lover's ability to reconstitute her self through her imaginative projections that always in some way signal toward the amorous event. She attests to her self through a new plot, a new story that finds its meaning in relation to the Beloved's givenness. The amorous imagination has an ontological dimension. Through it, the lover's experiences of being and time become grounded in the Beloved's life and death. In light of the amorous event, the lover moves from being-toward-death to being-toward-love. The amorous imagination reconfigures time according to the horizon of the Beloved. I then argued that the amorous imagination is a special case of the imagination's unique mode of consciousness. The amorous imagination intends in the *as if* but is not completely untethered from the *as is*. The amorous imagination responds to the Beloved and is therefore tied to her appearance. Moreover, the amorous imagination is an embodied activity. Its projections, synthesis, and images occur in the flesh of the lovers, affecting and effecting the world in which they live. This intertwining between the world of imagination and the world of flesh reveals another phenomenological dimension of the amorous imagination: it produces an impressional affectivity in the lover such that she is aware of her intended imagining, that she is imaging, and that her imagining happens in the flesh. What captures the imagination captures the flesh. The two cannot be abstracted apart. The border between the *as is* and the *as if* begins to blur. Finally, I looked at amorous imaginings themselves as phenomena that call for detailed description. I looked at a number of features of amorous imaginings, such as envisioning, reading across distance, presence and absence, insufficiency, etc., to explain the way in which amorous imaginings give themselves in such a way that they contribute to the Beloved's individuation in their very appearance. I concluded my argument by answering the original question: How does the Other become the Beloved? My answer, in short, is that individuation happens in large part through the on-going activity of the amorous imagination.

The Hermeneutic Continues

Like the Beloved, the philosophy of love seems inexhaustible. I will therefore conclude by highlighting a few lines of inquiry others might pursue in light of the current study, and by offering a personal note discussing briefly why I think the phenomenology of love is philosophically and existentially important.

Thanks to the groundbreaking work of Richard Kearney, there remains much more to be said about carnal hermeneutics and the relationship between flesh, imagination, and meaning making as love "plays itself out" over time. How do the lovers negotiate the balance that must be maintained between distance and separation, between Other and Same? How does the lovers' dialogue, which speaks in and through flesh, provide not only hermeneutical understanding but also existential orientation to their world? Theological questions abound: How does a phenomenology of human love contribute to our understanding of divine love? If God is love, and love implicates the amorous imagination, what does it mean to seek God, envision God, or imagine God? Historical and literary questions emerge as well. If there are indeed universal conditions for the possibility of love, one of which is the amorous imagination, how can we make sense of the incredible variety of amorous expressions we find throughout the world and throughout history? Any number of historical or literary epochs invite a more specialized study of the amorous imagination. What images of the Beloved emerge in contemporary literature and what do they have to do with the imagination? How do the songs and poems of twelfth century troubadours express the lovers' movement between distance and separation? How does the postmodern idea of imagination-as-mimetic parody challenge our experience of love as a fundamentally imaginative and hermeneutical enterprise? How can we reclaim the imagination without deifying it (Romanticism) or becoming cynical toward it (Postmodernism)? Can we recover the power of the imagination in a world that always seems void of meaning? Can the imagination guide us to an enchanted world "this side" of secularity? Can the amorous imagination avoid the pitfalls of both radical idealism and radical materialism? The questions seem endless. There is much more to be said about love.

But why pursue any of these questions? What makes the philosophy of love worthwhile? Part of the answer, for me, lies in love's ubiquity. We live in an age of cynicism and insincerity. Market capitalism, scientism, and postmodernism have formed an unlikely alliance that in many ways leaves us feeling disenchanted, as Max Weber and Charles Taylor put it. The ideals that once served as a beacon for human aspiration are reduced to brain states, commodities, or fraying fictions. In our popular discourse, love is often trivialized as mere sentimentality. It amounts to a socially codified sexual desire or the psychological reaction to a deep-seeded fear of being alone. Even when it is not treated harshly, discussions about love still seem to carry a trace of cynicism. Those who insist on love as a source of meaning risk being labeled "hopeless romantics," judged negatively for their immature insistence on a juvenile attachment to a long-dead ideal. Perhaps ideals such as love, heroism, and beauty need deconstruction. Perhaps they need to be dethroned and interrogated, especially given the way so many Western ideals have been co-opted by forces of oppression and domination. Too often, such ideals serve to justify empire and reify the politics of power. But in reducing, commodifying, and deconstructing human ideals we can also lose touch with the deep, existential desires they express, desires for something more, something beyond ourselves, something transcendent. Contemporary philosophers such as John Caputo, Richard Kearney, and Julia Kristeva have written extensively on this impulse and are keen to observe that even in the face of the Death of God, our sense of something else compels us to live at the fringes of ourselves, to remain open to excess. The philosophy of love, and especially the phenomenology of love, provide me both a subject matter and a method to investigate at least one of these ideals without rendering it a cultural relic or trivializing it by explaining it away. Love is philosophically important because, despite attempts to dislodge it from our cluster of centering ideals, it continues to offer a wealth of meaning and truth. It remains a grounding force and a radical opening. Love's ubiquity testifies to its importance in human meaning making and human understanding. It has much to teach us about joy, sorrow, creation, and loss. Through love we are in some way able to experience moments of eternity piercing the veil of time, as Czech philosopher Erazim Kohák puts it. But, as Marion states, like modern culture, philosophy has not always treated love fairly. Philosophy must find new ways to reveal love's truths. In order to take seriously love's continuous pull, we must find new methods to explore and express it. My hope is that this study contributes some small insight into the nature of love and adds to our understanding of how it appears and infuses our lives with meaning. Others will no doubt discover more profound ideas and insights, and I look forward to experiencing for myself the joy of their discoveries, which is the joy of *eros*.

Notes

Introduction

1. Jean-Luc Marion, *The Erotic Phenomenon*, trans. Stephen E. Lewis (Chicago: University of Chicago Press, 2007), 1.

2. While we experience many kinds of "unsubsititutable Others" (friend, spouse, parent, child, etc.), my concern here is with the Beloved.

3. Not all philosophers agree imagining is a good thing. Plato viewed the imagination's mimetic capacity as dangerous and deceptive, whereas for Kearney the imagination's productive capacity is a source of innovation and possibility. But more on that later.

Chapter 1

1. See, e.g., Irving Singer, *The Nature of Love*, vol. 1, *Plato to Luther* (Chicago: University of Chicago Press, 1966), 316–19; Anders Nygren, *Agape and Eros*, trans. Philip S. Watson (Chicago: University of Chicago Press, 1982), 210. Luther argued that *agape* is the sole source of salvation. God's bestowal of love is an unmerited act of divine grace and the sinner's only chance at redemption. Nygren agrees that *eros* and *agape* are irreconcilable, but for analytical reasons. Aquinas and Augustine both argue in favor of the *caritas-synthesis*: humankind's striving up toward God (*eros*) and God mercifully reaching down toward humankind (*agape*) accomplishes salvation.

2. See, e.g., Ronald de Sousa, "Chapter 1: Puzzles," in *Love: A Very Short Introduction* (Oxford: Oxford University Press, 2015).

3. See, e.g., Denis De Rougemont, *Love in the Western World* (Princeton: Princeton University Press, 1983).

4. Plato, "Symposium," in *Complete Works*, ed. John M. Cooper (Indi-

anapolis: Hackett, 2009), 206a.

5. See, e.g., Friedrich Schlegel, *Lucinde and the Fragments*, trans. Peter Firchow (Minneapolis: University of Minnesota, 1971).

6. Adam Smith, *Theory of Moral Sentiments*, 2nd ed. (1761), 2–3.

7. James Engell, *The Creative Imagination: Enlightenment to Romantic* (Cambridge: Harvard University Press, 1981), 150.

8. Ibid., 241.

9. Ibid., 239.

10. Rüdiger Safranski, *Romanticism: A German Affair*, trans. Robert E. Goodwin (Evanston: Northwestern University Press, 2014), 70.

11. Ibid., 71; emphasis added.

12. Ibid., quoting *Hymns to the Night*, "Christendom or Europe."

13. Ibid., 72, quoting Novalis, *Schriften* (1837), III.189.

14. Ibid., 73.

15. Ibid.; emphasis added.

16. Ibid., quoting Novalis, "Letter to Caroline Just of March 24, 1797."

17. Safranski, *Romanticism*, 73.

18. Ibid., quoting Novalis, *Hymns to the Night*, 1st hymn.

19. Ibid., quoting Novalis, *Hymns to the Night*, 4th hymn.

20. Stenhdal, *Love*, trans. Gilbert and Suzanne Sale (London: Penguin Books, 1975), 45.

21. Ibid.

22. Ibid., 60.

23. Ibid., 45–46.

24. In deference to modesty the original publisher deleted the more erotic third stanza, which reads: "Follow to the deep wood's weeds / Follow to the wild-briar dingle, / Where we seek to intermingle, / And the violet tells her tale / To the odour-scented gale, / For they two have enough to do / Of such work as I and you." Percy Bysshe Shelley, *The Complete Poetical Works of Percy Bysshe Shelley*, ed. Thomas Hutchinson (London: Oxford University Press, 1909), 579.

25. Irving Singer, *The Nature of Love*, vol. 2, *Courtly and Romantic* (Cambridge: MIT Press, 2009), 415.

26. Ibid., 422.

27. Percy Bysshe Shelley, "On Love," *The Keepsake for 1829*, ed. M. W. Shelley et al. (London: Hurst, Chance, 1829).

28. Ibid.

29. Ibid.

30. Singer, *The Nature of Love: Courtly and Romantic*, 416.

31. Ibid., quoting Shelley.

32. Shelley, "On Love."

33. Ibid.

34. Jere Paul Surber, *Culture and Critique: An Introduction to the Critical Discourses of Cultural Studies* (Boulder: Westview, 1998), 55.

35. Edmund Husserl, *The Crisis of European Sciences and Transcendental Phenomenology: An Introduction to Phenomenological Philosophy*, trans. David Carr (Evanston: Northwestern University Press, 1970), 69.

36. Richard Polt, *Heidegger: An Introduction* (Ithaca: Cornell University Press, 1951), 2–5.

37. Levinas himself seemed to acknowledge that the anonymity of ethics may give way to the individuation of the erotic. See, e.g., Emmanuel Levinas, "Beyond the Face," in *Totality and Infinity*, trans. Alphonso Lingis (Pittsburgh: Duquesne University Press, 1969); Jean-Luc Marion, "From the Other to the Individual," *Transcendence: Philosophy, Literature, and Theology Approach the Beyond* (New York: Routledge, 2004), 52; Christina Gschwandtner, "Ethics, Eros, or Caritas: Levinas and Marion on Individuation of the Other," *Philosophy Today* 49, no. 1 (2005): 74.

38. Don Ihde, *Hermeneutic Phenomenology: The Philosophy of Paul Ricoeur* (Evanston: Northwestern University Press, 1971), 95.

39. Henry Isaac Venema, *Identifying Selfhood: Imagination, Narrative, and Hermeneutics in the Thought of Paul Ricoeur* (Albany: State University of New York Press, 2000), 93–95.

40. Ibid.

Chapter 2

1. "It goes without saying that we owe it to Emmanuel Levinas to have ingeniously reconfigured phenomenology so as to let it finally reach the Other as saturated phenomenon." Jean-Luc Marion, *Being Given: Toward a Phenomenology of Givenness*, trans. Jeffrey L. Kosky (Stanford: Stanford University Press, 2002), 233, n. 88.

2. Jean-Luc Marion, "The Intentionality of Love," *Prolegomena to Charity* (New York: Fordham, 2002), 71–101; "From Other to the Individual," *Levinas Studies* 1 (2005): 99–117. See also, Christina M. Gschwandtner, "Ethics, Eros, or Caritas?: Levinas and Marion on Individuation of the Other," *Philosophy Today* 49, no. 1 (2005): 70–87.

3. For a detailed and thoughtful analysis of the limits of Marion's critique, see Gschwandtner, "Ethics, Eros, or Caritas?"

4. Marion, "The Intentionality of Love," 74, 75.

5. Ibid., 76–77.

6. Ibid., 75.

7. Ibid., 83.
8. Ibid.
9. Ibid., 92.
10. Gschwandtner, "Ethics, Eros, or Caritas?," 71.
11. Marion, "The Intentionality of Love," 92.
12. Ibid.
13. Ibid.
14. Ibid., 93.
15. Marion, "From the Other to the Individual," 105–11; see also, Gschwandtner, "Ethics, Eros, or Caritas?," 71.
16. Marion, "From the Other to the Individual," 108.
17. Ibid., 109.
18. Of course, Levinas does discuss love in a number of his works. See, for example, Levinas, *Totality and Infinity*, or Levinas, "The Ego and Totality," *Collected Philosophical Papers: Emmanuel Levinas*, trans. Alphonso Lingis (Pittsburgh: Duquesne University Press, 1987), 25–45.
19. Marion, "The Intentionality of Love," 95.
20. Ibid., 95–96.
21. Brian Treanor, "Absence Makes the Heart Grow Fonder," in *Transforming Philosophy and Religion: Love's Wisdom*, ed. Norman Wirzba and Bruce Ellis Benson (Bloomington: Indiana University Press, 2008), 148–51.
22. Ibid., 146.
23. Ibid., 147.
24. Ibid.
25. Ibid., 149.
26. Ibid., 159–61.
27. Ibid., 150–51.
28. Ibid., 150.
29. Marion, "The Intentionality of Love," 87; emphasis added.
30. Marion, *Being Given*, 5; emphasis in original.
31. Ibid., 119.
32. Gschwandtner, *Marion & Theology*, 58.
33. Marion, *Being Given*, 222–25.
34. Ibid., 225–28.
35. Gschwandtner, *Marion and Theology*, 83–84.
36. Marion, *In Excess*, 48.
37. Marion, *Reduction and Givenness*, 199.
38. Gschwandtner, *Marion and Theology*, 86.
39. Marion, *Being Given*, 264.
40. Ibid., 217–18.
41. Ibid., 282; Marion, *In Excess*, 49–53.

42. Gschwandtner, *Marion and Theology*, 87.

43. Marion, *In Excess*, 123–27.

44. "This danger [of solipsism], while no doubt undeniable, results less from the saturated phenomenon itself than from the misapprehension of it. When this type of phenomenon arises, it is most often treated like a common-law phenomenon, indeed a poor phenomenon, one that is therefore forced to be included in a phenomenological situation that by definition it refuses, and it is finally misapprehended. If, by contrast, its specificity is recognized, the bedazzlement it provokes would become phenomenologically acceptable, indeed desirable, and the passage from one horizon to another would become a rational task for the hermeneutic. The saturated phenomenon safeguards its absoluteness and at the same time dissolves its dangers when it is recognized as such, without confusing it with other phenomena." Marion, *Being Given*, 211.

45. Jean-Luc Marion, *Negative Certainties*, trans. Stephen E. Lewis (Chicago: The University of Chicago Press, 2015), 192.

46. Ibid., 193.

47. Ibid.

48. See, e.g., Shane Mackinlay, *Interpreting Excess: Jean-Luc Marion, Saturated Phenomenon, and Hermeneutics* (New York: Fordham University Press, 2010), 108–12.

49. Ibid., 198.

50. Ibid., 199.

51. Jean-Luc Marion, "Le phénomène saturé," in *Phénoménologie et théologie*, ed. Jean-François Courtine (Paris: Criterion, 1992), 79–128; "The Saturated Phenomenon." trans. Thomas A. Carlson, in Dominique Janicaud et al., *Phenomenology and the "Theological Turn": The French Debate* (New York: Fordham University Press, 2000), 176–216.

52. Shane Mackinlay, *Interpreting Excess*, 57.

53. Jean-Luc Marion, *The Visible and the Revealed* (New York: Fordham University Press, 2008), 119–44.

54. Ibid., 130.

55. Marion, *Being Given*, 227.

56. Ibid.

57. Ibid., 199–212; Marion, *In Excess*, ch. 2–5.

58. Not everyone is thrilled about this turn. See, e.g., Dominque Janicaud, "The Theological Turn of French Phenomenology," in *Phenomenology and the "Theological Turn:" The French Debate* (New York: Fordham University Press, 2000), 16–103.

59. Marion, *Being Given*, 199–202.

60. Ibid., 200.

61. Ibid.

62. Ibid.
63. Ibid.
64. Gschwandtner, *Degrees of Givenness*, 7.
65. Marion, *Being Given*, 200.
66. Mackinlay, *Interpreting Excess*, 91.
67. In *Being Given*, Book IV, Marion first cites Descartes's idea of amazement and cubist paintings as "privileged examples" of saturation by quantity. But for our purposes Marion's account of events in the later sections of *Being Given* and in *In Excess* provide a more relevant and insightful example as it relates to the phenomenology of love and, more specifically, the amorous event. See Marion, *Being Given*, 200–202; Marion, *In Excess*, 30–53.
68. Marion, *Being Given*, 228.
69. Ibid., 165–73.
70. This observation will also have important implications for Marion's theory of the self, *l'adonné,* as we will see.
71. Marion, *In Excess*, 37.
72. Ibid., quoting Montaigne.
73. Ibid.
74. Neither does love. Failure to recognize this has led to many metaphysical and logical "problems" to be resolved in the history of the idea of love. But love always seems to resist causal explanation.
75. Michel de Montaigne, *Essais,* I, 28, *Les Essais,* ed. Pierre Villey and Verdun-Louis Saulnier, vol. 1(Paris: Presses Universitaires de France, 1965), 188ff.
76. Marion, *In Excess*, 36.
77. Although less important for our purposes, it is worth noting that Marion uses the term *event* to describe not only saturation according to quantity but also as a determinate of each type of saturated phenomenon. Indeed, he goes farther to argue that eventness "governs all phenomena" insofar as eventness is a characteristic of phenomenality per se. Marion, *In Excess*, 38. As we will see in chapter 4, hermeneutical variation (i.e., *l'adonné*'s "gaze") plays a crucial role for Marion in determining whether what appears does so as an event or an object, or something in between. For a clear and nuanced account of Marion's different senses of "event," see Mackinlay, *Interpreting Excess*, 75–116.
78. Marion's use of the term *idol* is complicated. In his earlier theological writings, he employs the term to critique ontotheology. In his phenomenological works he refers to idols as both false images but also a real experience of seeing that merits phenomenological analysis in its own right. Marion shifts later in his writings and describes both the idol and icon as "different but essentially equivalent instances of saturated phenomena." Gschwandtner, *Degrees of Givenness*, 52–53.
79. Gschwandtner, *Degrees of Givenness*, 53.

80. Marion, *Being Given*, 229.
81. Mackinlay, *Interpreting Excess*, 119.
82. Immanuel Kant, *Critique of Pure Reason*, ed. and trans. Paul Guyer and Allen W. Wood (Cambridge: Cambridge University Press, 1998), 290, A 166/B 208.
83. Ibid., 291–92, A169/B 211.
84. Ibid.; Mackinlay, *Interpreting Excess*, 118.
85. Marion, *Being Given*, 229–31.
86. Ibid., 203–204.
87. Mackinlay, *Interpreting Excess*, 131.
88. Marion, *Being Given*, 206–12, 231–32.
89. Marion follows Husserl's distinction between body and flesh. The body is a knowable object, given as a common phenomenon. The flesh is unknowable, given as a saturated phenomenon.
90. Marion, *Being Given*, 206.
91. Ibid., 231.
92. Marion, *In Excess*, 86.
93. Ibid., 87.
94. "The individuation of the *ego* is thus made neither by form (the too universal understanding) nor by matter (the too undifferentiated physical body) but by the 'unanimous white conflict' of the one with the other—precisely by the taking of flesh." Marion, *In Excess*, 97–98.
95. Ibid., 98.
96. Ibid., 99.
97. Marion, *The Erotic Phenomenon*, 106–40; Mackinlay, *Interpreting Excess*, 139.
98. Marion, *The Erotic Phenomenon*, 113.
99. Ibid., 114.
100. Ibid., 117–18; Mackinlay, *Interpreting Excess*, 141.
101. Ibid., 118.
102. Ibid.
103. Ibid.
104. Ibid., 119.
105. Mackinlay raises this question in his analysis of flesh in *Interpreting Excess*, 140–41.
106. Mackinlay, *Interpreting Excess*, 141.
107. Marion, *The Erotic Phenomenon*, 117.
108. Marion does describe a fifth category of saturation, what he calls "revelation," but that is for another day.
109. Marion, *Being Given*, 214.
110. Marion, "The Intentionality of Love," 71–101; Marion. "From

Other to the Individual," 99–117; see also, Gschwandtner, "Ethics, Eros, or Caritas," 70–87.

111. In the next section, "Individuation in *The Erotic Phenomenon*," I explain in detail the phenomenon of the crossing of gazes as it relates to love.

112. Marion, *In Excess*, 117, 122–23.

113. Ibid., 126–27.

114. "Mutuality" is key to understanding Marion's treatment of love. The crossing of gazes is mutual, not reciprocal. Reciprocity occurs in the domain of economy but love according to Marion is a gift and therefore exceeds the metaphysics of transaction.

115. Marion, *The Erotic Phenomenon*, 10. "All of my books . . . have been just so many steps toward the question of the erotic phenomenon."

116. Ibid., 4–6.

117. Ibid., 40.

118. Ibid., 69.

119. Ibid., 71. "Puis-je aimer, moi le premier." Jean-Luc Marion, *Le phénomène érotique: Six méditations* (Paris: Grasset, 2003), 116.

120. Marion, *The Erotic Phenomenon*, 97.

121. Ibid., 98.

122. Ibid., 97.

123. "[W]hen I pass on to the question, 'Can I love first?' what assurance can I legitimately hope for, as a lover? Evidently not the assurance to be able to continue or to persevere in my being despite the suspension of vanity, but the sole assurance appropriate to the radicalized erotic reduction—not the assurance of being [*l'assurance d'être*], nor of being itself [*ni de l'être*], but *the assurance of loving* . . . understood as the pure and simple assurance of the precise fact that [I love]." Marion, *The Erotic Phenomenon*, 73.

124. Ibid., 76.

125. Ibid., 78.

126. Marion, *The Erotic Phenomenon*, 100–101; Gschwandtner, *Marion and Theology*, 91.

127. Marion, *The Erotic Phenomenon*, 99.

128. Ibid., 98.

129. Ibid.

130. Ibid., 101.

131. Ibid., 104.

132. Marion, "The Intentionality of Love," 87.

133. Ibid., 84.

134. Ibid., 88.

135. Ibid.

136. Ibid., 89.

137. Ibid., 99.
138. Ibid.
139. Ibid.
140. Marion, "What Love Knows," in *Prolegomena to Charity* (New York: Fordham University Press, 2002), 165.
141. Marion, *Le phénomène érotique*, 131; Marion, *The Erotic Phenomenon*, 80.
142. Marion, *The Erotic Phenomenon*, 107.
143. Ibid., 108.
144. Ibid.
145. Ibid., 108–109.
146. Ibid., 109.
147. Ibid., 111, 112.
148. Ibid., 126.
149. Ibid.
150. Ibid.
151. Ibid., 151.
152. Ibid., 142.
153. Ibid., 152.
154. Ibid., 175.
155. Marion argues that free love is love liberated from the automatic or un-chosen nature of the flesh. Ibid., 179–83. Indeed, he claims that the lover can only actually reach the other person as such in speaking rather than touching. Chasity may be the erotic virtue par excellence. Ibid., 183. See also, Gschwandtner, *Marion and Theology*, 92; Robyn Horner, *Jean-Luc Marion: A Theo-Logical Introduction* (Surrey: Ashgate, 2005), 139–40.
156. Marion, *The Erotic Phenomenon*, 184.
157. Ibid., 185.
158. Ibid., 195.
159. Ibid., 197.
160. Ibid., 205–206.
161. Horner, *Jean-Luc Marion*, 141.
162. Marion, *The Erotic Phenomenon*, 209.
163. Ibid., 212.
164. "[W]hen I say that reduced givenness does not demand any giver for its given, I am *not* insinuating that it lays claim to a transcendent giver; when I say that the phenomenology of givenness by definition passes beyond metaphysics, I do *not* say between the lines that this phenomenology restores metaphysics." Marion, *Being Given*, 5.
165. Horner, *Jean-Luc Marion*, 142.
166. Marion, *The Erotic Phenomenon*, 211.

167. Ibid.

168. Ibid., 212. Marion also describes God as the first lover whom we encounter in the final erotic reduction. There we find ourselves always already loved by the eternal witness that preceded us. While this assertion is less relevant to our present study, it is worth a brief comment. The reference to God as first lover again raises the question of ontotheology. How should we understand it? On the one hand, we can read Marion as proposing a straightforward theological solution to a phenomenological problem. But that reading does not take into account his earlier works distinguishing between theology and philosophy. On the other hand, we might read this reference to God in light of his previous work on language and God. According to this line of argument, references to God are pragmatic and undecidable. They are not metaphysical claims. Horner, *Jean-Luc Marion*, 144. But there is a third way of understanding Marion's God-as-first-lover in terms of hermeneutics. Recall that for Heidegger the answer to the question of Being in some way must precede its asking. The question reveals a hermeneutic circle: it is only because I already know what Being is—even if only vaguely and intuitively—that I can ask what Being is in the first place. I have a sense of the whole of Being that allows me to look at the parts of Being and clarify it through the method of hermeneutical phenomenology. Likewise, Marion can be seen as arguing not that God is "out there" loving us as the witness to the oath of faithfulness, but rather as a Heideggerian acknowledgment that to even enter into the erotic reduction means that we have already in some sense been loved and therefore know what to look for. Like the answer to the question of Being, the answer to the question of love precedes its very asking. The eschatological witness to the oath of faith is the sense of love that we must already have before we are even able to investigate love in the first place. The erotic reduction allows us to clarify what we already know about love just as the question of Being allows us to clarify what we already know of Being. The *adieu*, the witness, God, do not signify a loving God that exists "out there" but is the love itself to which we have always already been exposed. It is the condition that allows for the possibility of the reduction in the first place. Recall *God Without Being* and 1 John 4:8: "God is love." In this sense, to enter into the erotic reduction does indeed mean we have already been loved, even if the call of the lover remains "in silence."

169. Marion, *The Erotic Phenomenon*, 210.

170. Gschwandtner, *Marion and Theology*, 86.

171. Gschwandtner, *Degrees of Givenness*, 105–106.

172. Claude Romano, "Love in Its Concept," in *Counter-Experiences: Reading Jean-Luc Marion*, ed. Kevin Hart (South Bend: Notre Dame University Press, 2007), 323.

173. Robyn Horner, "The Weight of Love," in *Counter-Experiences: Reading Jean-Luc Marion*, ed. Kevin Hart (South Bend: Notre Dame University Press, 2007), 240–44. I agree with Horner's reading.

174. Stephen Lewis, "The Lover's Capacity," *Questions disputable* 1, no. 1 (2010): 235.

175. See, e.g., John Greisch, "L'herméneutique dans la 'phénoménologie comme telle.' Trois questions à propos de Réduction et Donation," *Revue de métaphysique et de morale* 96, no. 1 (1991): 43–63; Jean Grondin, "La tension de la donation ultime et de la pensée herméneutique de l'application chez Jean-Luc Marion," *Dialogue* 38, no. 3 (1999): 547–59; Richard Kearney, *Debates in Continental Philosophy: Conversations with Contemporary Thinkers* (New York: Fordham University Press, 2004), 15–32; Tasmin Jones, *A Genealogy of Marion's Phenomenology of Religion: Apparent Darkness* (Bloomington: Indiana University Press, 2011), 109; Gschwandtner, *Degrees of Givenness*, 14–24; Mackinlay, *Interpreting Excess*, 36.

Chapter 3

1. The imagination's relationship to time and space is more complicated than its relationship to the categories of understanding. "Kant wavers, saying in one place that the synthesis of the imagination depends on the conditions of experience in time and space, but elsewhere clinging to the idea that even conditions of experience in time and space, and hence the categories, are themselves founded on an overall synthesis of mind and nature that is performed by the imagination." James Engell, *The Creative Imagination: Enlightenment to Romanticism* (Cambridge: Harvard University Press, 1981), 133.

2. Ibid., 128–33.

3. Scholars disagree about the nature of the relationship between the unity of apperception and the transcendental imagination. It is not clear in Kant which is prior to the other. Kant writes, "The transcendental unity of apperception thus relates to the pure synthesis of imagination, as an *a priori* condition of the possibility of all combination of the manifold in one knowledge." Immanuel Kant, *Critique of Practical Reason*, trans. Lewis White Beck (New York: Bobbs-Merrill, 1958), 142. But shortly later, he writes: 'Thus the principle of the necessary unity of pure (productive) synthesis of imagination, prior to apperception, is the ground of the possibility of all knowledge, especially of experience." Ibid., 142–43. Heidegger, for example, argued that Kant grounds the transcendental ego in the productive imagination. Martin Heidegger, *Kant and the Problem of Metaphysics*, trans. Richard Taft (Bloomington: Indiana University Press, 1990). Patrick Bourgeois disagrees, critiquing Heidegger's read

as a misappropriation and emphasizing Kant's account of the mediating role of the productive imagination which connects the categories with intuition but does not itself construct the unity of apperception. Patrick Bourgeois, *Imagination and Postmodernity* (Plymouth, UK: Lexington Books, 2013), 70–77.

4. Martin Heidegger, *Kant and the Problem of Metaphysics*, trans. J. Churchill (Bloomington: Indiana University Press, 1962), 180.

5. Engell, *The Creative Imagination*, 132–39; Richard Kearney, *The Wake of the Imagination* (Minneapolis: University of Minnesota Press, 1988), 171, 176–77.

6. "Paul Ricoeur," by Kim Atkins, *Internet Encyclopedia of Philosophy*. http://iep.utm.edu/, Feb. 27, 2018.

7. Ibid.

8. Ibid.

9. Venema, *Identifying Selfhood*, 92–94.

10. Ibid., 93–94. Ricoeur critiques the tendency in philosophy to view imagination only in terms of "seeing" and "imaging." Kearney, *Poetics of Imagining*, 145–47. For Ricoeur, the imagination is verbal and linguistic. It is poetic. Championing "semantic innovation" as the primary function of the imagination, Ricoeur argues that through the "inherently symbolizing-metaphorizing-narrativizing-activity" of imagining we open ourselves up to the possibility of something else, something more (the Other, new meaning, utopia, etc.). Richard Kearney, "Paul Ricoeur and the Hermeneutic Imagination," *Philosophy and Social Criticism* 14 no. 2 (1988): 115–45. Metaphor is the paradigm example. Metaphor holds both identity and difference in tension by putting together words that both are and are not equivalent. This "clash of meanings" opens up the space of possibility for new meaning. It is the "invention" of innovation. But, importantly, innovation does not occur in a vacuum. The second meaning embedded in innovation is "inventory." Metaphor operates by drawing upon the preexisting inventory of language to invent a new meaning and produce a semantic innovation. This imaginative process gives rise to possibilities that were not otherwise available prior to the metaphor's construction.

11. Charles Larmore, *The Romantic Legacy* (New York: Columbia University Press, 1996), 3.

12. Ibid., 11.

13. Ibid., 8.

14. Ibid., 4–5.

15. Ibid., 22; emphasis in original.

16. Ibid., 31.

17. Bourgeois, *Imagination and Postmodernity*, 67.

18. Kearney, *Poetics of Imagining*, 16.

19. Ibid., 22.

20. Ibid., 25. See also, Brian Elliott, *Phenomenology and Imagination in Husserl and Heidegger* (New York: Routledge, 2005), 69–80.

21. Kearney, *The Wake of the Imagination*, 156.

22. The limits of the imagination and the problem of solipsism appear in their strongest form in Husserl's account of the Other. Scholars disagree as to whether Husserl's theory of intersubjectivity overcomes solipsism. See, e.g., Dan Zahavi, *Husserl's Phenomenology* (Stanford: Stanford University Press, 2003), 109–40; Kearney, *Poetics of Imagining*, 26–27. Richard Kearney argues that for Husserl "no matter how liberally it may vary the facts of the world, imagination can never transcend *itself* as transcendental consciousness." Kearney, *Poetics of Imagining*, 26. Paradoxically, Kearney observes, Husserl's best attempt at overcoming solipsism actually relies on the imagination (although the argument ultimately fails). Ibid., 26–27. Kearney adopts the traditional read of Husserl's theory of the Other as experienced through analogy:

Husserl's argument is based on the following program of imaginative variation: I am here (*hic*), the other is there (*illic*); but there (*illic*) is where I could be if I were to move. From over there (*illic*) I would see the same things but under a different perspective. Hence, through imagination I can co-ordinate the other perspectives to *my* place and to *my* perspective. But because the life of the other is not given to me in an "original production" (*Leistungen*), but merely in a fictive "reproduction" in the mode of the "*as if* I were there," the life of the other can never become for me the equivalent of the one life of which I have originary experience, that is, my own. Husserl cannot escape the self-enclosing mesh which his own theory of imagination has cast. Ibid., 26–27.

23. I will use a temporal metaphor to describe this process, but it is only a metaphor. I am not arguing that the phenomenon of individuation unfolds chronologically.

Chapter 4

1. There are some who problematize this reading of Marion. See, e.g., Stephen Lewis, "The Phenomenological Concept of Givenness and the 'Myth of the Given,'" in *Reason of the Gift* (Charlottesville: University of Virginia Press, 2011).

2. *In Excess, Prolegomena to Charity*, and *Reprise du donné*.

3. Jean Luc Marion, *Negative Certainties*, 194.

4. Ibid., 199.

5. Mackinlay, *Interpreting Excess*, 108–109.

6. Jean-Luc Marion, *Negative Certainties*, 198–99.

7. Mackinlay, *Interpreting Excess*, 42.

8. Claude Romano, *Event and World* (New York: Fordham University Press, 2009), 87.

9. Ibid., 51.

10. Mackinlay, *Interpreting Excess*, 48–49.

11. Romano, *Event and World*, 30.

12. Note here that I am *not* claiming the self absorbs the Other in any metaphysical sense. I am claiming that the amorous imagination "absorbs" the amorous event into the self's narrative in a meaning-making enterprise. The event always comes from "outside." As we will see, the Beloved's appearance is marked by distance and separation, not absorption.

13. To be clear, I am not arguing that the amorous event always occurs like a lightning strike out of nowhere. Clearly, strangers, friends, or colleagues can slowly grow to love one another. But that is not the point. The point is that on a basic level, in the very grammar of love, we seem to acknowledge its evental nature. Love upends us and reconfigures our horizons whether it emerges over time or hits us all at once. It is the structural dimension of the amorous event that concerns me, not whether it happens all at once or develops over a period of time.

14. Indeed, this is one reason why the traditional typology of love includes *philia*.

15. This description is not meant to be romantic in the common sense of the term. My goal is to describe love as it appears. That it appears as a *fait accompli* can in part explain our grammar of love, such as when we say one was "lovestruck" or "was destined" for another, or "fell in love," and so on. While this language may attest to a cultural mythology of romantic destiny it also characterizes the amorous phenomenon as a certain kind of appearing. One must look "behind" or "below" the language of love to uncover its structures, which are expressed in and at times covered over by the language we use to describe it.

16. More on this in the next chapter.

17. For a full treatment of Marion's theory of desire, see Jason Alvis, *Marion and Derrida on the Gift and Desire: Debating the Generosity of Things* (New York: Springer International, 2016).

18. "Bold Lover, never, never canst thou kiss, / Though winning near the goal—yet, do not grieve; / She cannot fade, though thou hast not thy bliss, / For ever wilt thou love, and she be fair!"

19. Edmund Husserl, *Ideas Pertaining to a Pure Phenomenology and to a Phenomenological Philosophy*, Second Book, trans. R. Rojcewicz and A. Schuwer (Dordrecht: Kluwer, 1989), 153.

20. Richard Kearney, "The Wager of Carnal Hermeneutics," in *Carnal Hermeneutics*, ed. Richard Kearney and Brian Treanor (New York: Fordham University Press, 2015), 27.

21. Ibid.

22. Paul Ricœur, *Freedom and Nature: The Voluntary and the Involuntary*, trans. Erazim Kohák (Evanston: Northwestern University Press, 1966), 94.

23. Jean-Paul Sartre, *Being and Nothingness*, trans. Hazel Barnes (New York: Philosophical Library, 1958), 354.

24. Ibid., 389.

25. Levinas, *Totality and Infinity*, 257.

26. Ibid., 257–58; see also, Kearney, "The Wager of Carnal Hermeneutics," 33.

27. Kearney, "The Wager of Carnal Hermeneutics," 37–38.

28. Ibid., 38.

29. Maurice Merleau-Ponty, *The Visible and the Invisible*, trans. Alphonso Lingis (Evanston: Northwestern University Press, 1979), 155.

30. Ibid., 149, 209, 215–16, 228, 246; Christopher Ben Simpson, *Merleau-Ponty and Theology* (New York: Bloomsbury, 2014), 42–45.

31. Maurice Merleau-Ponty, *Nature: Course Notes from the Collège de France*, trans. Robert Vallier (Evanston: Northwestern University Press, 2003), 218, 272–73; Simpson, *Merleau-Ponty and Theology*, 42–45.

32. Merleau-Ponty, *The Visible and the Invisible*, 149–51.

33. Ibid., 150–51; Simpson, *Merleau-Ponty and Theology*, 44.

34. Merleau-Ponty, *Nature*, 218; Simpson, *Merleau-Ponty and Theology*, 44.

35. Merleau-Ponty, *The Visible and the Invisible*, 261; Simpson, *Merleau-Ponty and Theology*, 45.

36. Merleau-Ponty, *The Visible and the Invisible*, 151, 212; Simpson, *Merleau-Ponty and Theology*, 44.

37. Merleau-Ponty, *The Visible and the Invisible*, 152.

38. Kearney, "The Wager of Carnal Hermeneutics," 39.

39. Maurice Merleau-Ponty, *Phenomenology of Perception*, trans. Colin Smith (London: Routledge, 1962), 160.

40. Kearney, "The Wager of Carnal Hermeneutics," 40.

41. Ibid., 41.

42. Ibid., 46. Of course, there are stark differences between Marion's and Merleau-Ponty's accounts of the self, flesh, and world. My point here is not to conflate their views but to highlight the role of receptivity in Marion while adding the role of carnal hermeneutics in Merleau-Ponty. Merleau-Ponty's account of the flesh as expressive, opening, and double provides a more robust account of the flesh than Marion's as the site of meaning making, and Marion's view benefits from the richness of Merleau-Ponty's account.

43. Ibid., 47.

44. Ibid.
45. Paul Ricoeur, *Freedom and Nature*, 99; Kearney, "The Wager of Carnal Hermeneutics," 48–49.
46. Kearney, "The Wager of Carnal Hermeneutics," 54.
47. B. Keith Putt, "A Love that B(l)inds," in *Transforming Philosophy and Religion*, ed. Norman Wirzba and Bruce Ellis Benson (Bloomington: Indiana University Press, 2008), 127.
48. Ibid.
49. Ibid.
50. Ibid., 128.
51. Ibid., 133.

Chapter 5

1. *Heidegger, Kant and the Problem of Metaphysics*, 248–49.
2. How, if at all, does the amorous imagination differ from other types of imagination? The answer is twofold. In one sense, it doesn't. The amorous imagination is a particular *way* of imagining. It is a manifestation of the imagination, or better, a certain way the imagination manifests in light of the amorous event. Insofar as it exhibits the classical productive and reproductive qualities of the imagination, it is not in itself a separate transcendental activity. It is a subset or type of imagining. In another sense, however, the amorous imagination is unique insofar as it contributes to a new way of "seeing" the world and "responding" to it amorously, a new *as if* that emerges in the wake of the amorous event. Because of its role in love the amorous imagination merits its own phenomenological description.
3. Alain Badiou, *In Praise of Love*, trans. Peter Bush (Paris: The New Press, 2009), 29.
4. For a concise and thoughtful explanation of the phenomenological difference between perception, memory, and imagination, see Robert Sokolowski, *Introduction to Phenomenology* (Cambridge: Cambridge University Press, 2000), 66–76.
5. Kneller, *Kant and the Power of the Imagination*, 22 (citing Novalis, II: 545, #105).
6. Ibid.
7. Ibid., 23.
8. Safranski, *Romanticism: A German Affair*, 71.
9. Kneller, *Kant and the Power of the Imagination*, 23 (citing Novalis, 3: 601, #291).
10. Ibid.
11. Larmore, *The Romantic Legacy*, 14, 28–31.

12. Stendhal's notion of "crystallization" also illustrates this point. Although, for Stendhal, crystallization is a pseudo-psychological projection, considered phenomenologically, crystallization provides an apt metaphor for the way in which the lover envisions the Beloved through the amorous imagination. Following the amorous event, the lover is enamored with the Beloved. The event captures her imagination, she recounts her experience of the Beloved, relives moments spent with him, and "sees" him differently than she sees anyone else precisely because of the amorous encounter in which the lovers took part. Unlike any Other, the Beloved is imbued with a multiplicity of meanings, values, and adornments that arise from and are perpetuated by the amorous imagination. But, contrary to Stendhal's account, the crystals that form around the Beloved as a result of the amorous imaginings are not mere fabrications or fancy. They are "romanticizations" in Novalis's sense of the term. They are the lover's creative-responsive expression to the saturated phenomenon of the Beloved. The lover answers to the call. Indeed, amorous imaginings are themselves the lover's response to what gives itself as excess. Amorous imaginings are not freewheeling fantasies that surrender the lover to indeterminacy. They draw from the Beloved as he gives himself phenomenologically. They are answerable to the call of the Beloved, a call that can never itself be fully answered.

13. Brian Treanor, "Mind the Gap: The Challenge of Matter," in *Carnal Hermeneutics*, ed. Richard Kearney and Brian Treanor (New York: Fordham University Press, 2015), 59–60.

14. And of course, like any imagining, amorous imaginings always carry with them an impressional manifestation of the flesh as well.

15. John D. Caputo and Michael J. Scanlon, "Introduction: Apology for the Impossible: Religion and Postmodernism," in *God, the Gift, and Postmodernism* (Bloomington: Indiana University Press, 1999), 2.

16. Ibid., 3.

17. "Not this, not that."

18. James Arbuckle, *Hibernicus's Letters* (2 Vols., 1729), No. 4, 28–36.

19. Todd May, "Love and Death," in *Thinking about Love: Essays in Contemporary Continental Philosophy*, ed. Diane Enns and Antonio Calcagno (University Park: The Pennsylvania State University Press, 2015), 29.

Chapter 6

1. Larmore, *The Romantic Legacy*, 2.

2. Carl Schmitt, *Politische Romantik* (Berlin: Duncker u. Humblot, 1919), 162.

3. Larmore, *The Romantic Legacy*, 3–5.

4. Whether Husserl truly made such a distinction is up for debate, but some critics do read him this way.

5. Ruth K. Westheimer and Jerome E. Singerman, *Myths of Love: Echoes of Ancient Mythology in the Modern Romantic Imagination* (Fresno: Quill Driver Books, 2014), 36 (quoting Ovid, *Metamorphosis*, 4).

6. Ibid.

7. Gschwandtner, *Marion and Theology*, 32.

8. Horner, *Jean-Luc Marion: A Theological Introduction*, 61–62.

9. We have already seen one version of violent merging in the myth of Hermaphroditus and Salmacis, although in that myth the delusional "lover" forces herself onto the Other. The lovers do not share a desire to merge.

10. Samuel Taylor Coleridge, *Shakespearean Criticism*, ed. Thomas Middleton Raysor (London: Dent, 1960), 2:106.

11. Singer, *Courtly and Romantic*, 289.

12. Coleridge, *Shakespearean Criticism*, 2:106.

13. Rougemont, *Love in the Western World*, 46; emphasis in original.

14. I use the terms *amorous* and *lover* loosely here. As we have seen, phenomenologically speaking, the lover ceases to be a lover when he mistakes the injunction for the call of the Beloved.

Bibliography

Aristotle. *Nicomachean Ethics*. Translated by F. H. Peters. New York: Barnes and Noble, 2004.
Armstrong, John. *Conditions of Love: The Philosophy of Intimacy*. New York: W. W. Norton, 2003.
Badiou, Alain. *In Praise of Love*. Translated by Peter Bush. New York: The New Press, 2012.
Barthes, Roland. *A Lover's Discourse*. Translated by Richard Howard. New York: Hill and Wang, 2010.
Beals, Corey. *Levinas and the Wisdom of Love: The Question of Invisibility*. Waco: Baylor University Press, 2007.
Benson, Bruce E., and Norman Wirzba, eds. *Transforming Philosophy and Religion: Love's Wisdom*. Bloomington: Indiana University Press, 2008.
Berlin, Isaiah. *The Roots of Romanticism*. Princeton: Princeton University Press, 1999.
Blanning, Tim. *The Romantic Revolution: A History*. New York: Modern Library, 2011.
Bornemark, Jonna, and Marcia Sá Cavalcante Schuback, eds. *Phenomenology of Eros*. Huddinge: Södertörn University, 2012.
Bourgeois, Patrick L. *Imagination and Postmodernity (Studies in the Thought of Paul Ricoeur)*. Plymouth, UK: Lexington Books, 2013.
Bruhn, Jørgen. *Lovely Violence: Crétien de Troyes' Critical Romances*. New Castle upon Tyne: Cambridge Scholars Publishing, 2010.
Capellanus, Andreas. *The Art of Courtly Love*. Translated by John Jay Parry. New York: W. W. Norton, 1969.
Caputo, John D. *On Religion* New York: Routledge, 2001.
———. *The Prayers and Tears of Jacques Derrida: Religion without Religion*. Bloomington: Indiana University Press, 2006.
———. *The Weakness of God*. Bloomington: Indiana University Press, 2006.
———, and Michael J. Scanlon, ed. *God, the Gift, and Postmodernism*. Bloomington: Indiana University Press, 1999.

Casey, Edward S. *Imagining: A Phenomenological Study*. 2nd ed. Bloomington: Indiana University Press, 2000.
Catalano, Joseph S. *A Commentary on Jean Paul Sartre's Being and Nothingness*. Chicago: University of Chicago Press, 1974.
Critchley, Simon. *The Problem with Levinas*. Edited by Alexia Dianda. Oxford: Oxford University Press, 2015.
Crowell, Steven. *Normativity and Phenomenology in Husserl and Heidegger*. Cambridge: Cambridge University Press, 2013.
———. *Husserl, Heidegger, and the Space of Meaning: Paths toward Transcendental Phenomenology*. Evanston: Northwestern University Press, 2001.
Daly, Gay. *Pre-Raphaelites in Love*. New York: Ticknor and Fields, 1989; repr. Schwartz, 2004.
Davey, Nicholas. *Unquiet Understanding: Gadamer's Philosophical Hermeneutics*. Albany: State University of New York Press, 2006.
Davis, Colin. *Levinas: An Introduction*. Notre Dame: University of Notre Dame Press, 1996.
Deleuze, Gilles. *Difference and Repetition*. Translated by Paul R. Patton. New York: Columbia University Press, 1994.
———. *Nietzsche and Philosophy*. Translated by Hugh Tomlinson. New York: Columbia University Press, 1992.
Deleuze, Gilles, and Felix Guatttari. *Anti-Oedipus*. Translated by Robert Hurley, Mark Seem, and Helen R. Lane. New York: Penguin, 2009.
———. *A Thousand Plateaus*. Translated by Brian Massumi. Minneapolis: University of Minnesota Press, 2016.
Dupré, Louis. *The Quest of the Absolute: Birth and Decline of European Romanticism*. Notre Dame: University of Notre Dame, 2013.
Elliott, Brian. *Phenomenology and Imagination in Husserl and Heidegger*. New York: Routledge, 2005.
Engell, James. *The Creative Imagination: Enlightenment to Romanticism*. Cambridge: Harvard University Press, 1981.
Enns, Diane, and Antonio Calcagno, eds. *Thinking About Love: Essays in Contemporary Continental Philosophy*. University Park: Pennsylvania State University Press, 2015.
Falke, Cassandra. *The Phenomenology of Love and Reading*. New York: Bloomsbury, 2017.
Ferber, Michael. *Romanticism: A Very Short Introduction*. Oxford: Oxford University Press, 2010.
Ferry, Luc. *On Love: A Philosophy for the Twenty-First Century*. Translated by Andrew Brown. Cambridge: Polity Press, 2013.
Fromm, Eric. *The Art of Loving*. New York: Perennial, 2000.
Foucault, Michel. *The History of Sexuality: An Introduction*. Vol. 1. New York: Random House, 1976.

———. *I, Pierre Rivière, Having Slaughtered My Mother, My Sister, and My Brother . . . : A Case of Parricide in the 19th Century*, New York: Pantheon, 1975.

Gardner, Sebastian. *Sartre's Being and Nothingness: A Reader's Guide*. New York: Bloomsbury, 2009.

Gasset, Jose Ortega Y. *On Love: Aspects of a Single Theme*. Translated by Toby Talbot. Mansfield Centre: Martino Fine Books, 2012.

Goethe, Johann Wolfgang von. *Goethe's Faust: The Original German and a New Translation and Introduction*. Translated by Walter Arnold Kaufmann. New York: Anchor, 1989.

———, and Stanley Appelbaum. *The Sorrows of Young Werther: Die Leiden Des Jungen Werther*. Mineola, NY: Dover Publications, 2004.

Gorman, Francis. *The Cambridge Companion to Victorian Culture*. Cambridge: Cambridge University Press, 2010.

Gschwandtner, Christina M. *Degrees of Givenness: On Saturation in Jean-Luc Marion*. Bloomington: Indiana University Press, 2014.

———. *Marion and Theology*. London: Bloomsbury, 2016.

———. *Reading Jean-Luc Marion: Exceeding Metaphysics*. Bloomington: Indiana University Press, 2007.

Hall, W. David, 2007, *Paul Ricoeur and the Poetic Imperative: The Creative Tension between Love and Justice*, Albany: State University of New York Press.

Harpur, James. *Love Burning in the Soul: The Story of Christian Mystics from Saint Paul to Thomas Merton*. Boston: New Seeds, 2005.

Hart, Kevin, ed. *Counter-Experiences: Reading Jean-Luc Marion*. Notre Dame: University of Notre Dame, 2007.

Heidegger, Martin. *Basic Writings from Being and Time to The Task of Thinking*. Edited by David Farrell Krell. London: Harper Perennial, 2008.

———. *Being and Time*. Translated by John Macquarrie and Edward Robinson. New York: Harper and Row, 2008.

Horner, Robyn. *Jean-Luc Marion: A Theo-logical Introduction*. Burlington, VT: Ashgate, 2005.

———. *Rethinking God as Gift: Marion, Derrida, and the Limits of Phenomenology*, New York: Fordham University Press, 2001.

Husserl, Edmund. *Ideas: General Introduction to Pure Phenomenology*. New York: Routledge, 2012.

———. *Logical Investigations, Vol. 1*. Translated by John N. Findlay. New York: Routledge, 2008.

———. *Logical Investigations, Vol. 2*. Translated by John N. Findlay. New York: Routledge, 2001.

———. *The Crisis of European Sciences and Transcendental Phenomenology: An Introduction to Phenomenological Philosophy*. Translated by David Carr. Evanston: Northwestern University Press, 1970.

———. *The Phenomenology of Internal Time Consciousness*. Translated by James Churchill. Bloomington: Indiana University Press, 1964.
Ihde, Don, *Hermeneutic Phenomenology: The Philosophy of Paul Ricoeur*, Evanston: Northwestern University Press, 1971.
Janicaud, Dominique. *Phenomenology and the "Theological Turn": The French Debate*. Translated by Bernard C. Prusak. New York: Fordham University Press, 2000.
Kant, Immanuel. *Critique of Pure Reason*. Translated by Paul Guyer and Allen W. Wood. Cambridge: Cambridge University Press, 1999.
Kearney, Richard. *Anatheism*. New York: Columbia University Press, 2010.
———. "Paul Ricoeur and the Hermeneutic Imagination." *Philosophy and Social Criticism* 14, no. 2 (1988): 115–45.
———. *Poetics of Imagining: Modern to Post-modern*. New York: Fordham University Press, 1998.
———. *The Wake of Imagination: Toward a Postmodern Culture*. Minneapolis: University of Minnesota Press, 1989.
———. "What is Carnal Hermeneutics?" *New Literary History* 46 (2015): 99–124.
Kearney, Richard, and Brian Treanor, eds. *Carnal Hermeneutics*. New York: Fordham University Press, 2015.
Kierkegaard, Søren. *Works of Love*. Translated by Howard Vincent Hong and Edna Hatlestad Hong. New York: HarperPerennial, 2009.
Kneller, Jane. *Kant and the Power of Imagination*. Cambridge: Cambridge University Press, 2007.
Kreeft, Peter. *Three Philosophies of Life*. San Francisco: Ignatius Press, 1989.
Large, William. *Levinas' Totality and Infinity*. New York: Bloomsbury, 2015.
Lehtinen, Virpi. *Luce Irigaray's Phenomenology of Feminine Being*. Albany: State University of New York Press, 2014.
Lennon, Kathleen. *Imagination and the Imaginary*. New York: Routledge, 2015.
Levinas, Emmanuel. *Alterity and Transcendence*. Translated by Michal B. Smith. New York: Columbia University Press, 2000.
———. *Ethics and Infinity: Conversations with Phillippe Nemo*. Pittsburgh: Duquesne University Press, 1995.
———. *Otherwise than Being, or Beyond Essence*. Translated by Alphonso Lingis. Pittsburgh: Duquesne University Press, 1998.
———. *Time and the Other*. Translated by Richard A. Cohen. Pittsburgh: Duquesne University Press, 1987.
———. *Totality and Infinity: An Essay on Exteriority*. Translated by Alphonso Lingis. Pittsburgh: Duquesne University Press, 1969.
Lewis, Stephen. "The Lover's Capacity," *Questions disputable* 1, no. 1 (2010): 235.
Lilar, Suzanne. *Aspects of Love in Western Society*. Translated by Jonathan Griffin. London: Thames and Hudson, 1965.
Mackinley, Shane. *Interpreting Excess*. New York: Fordham University Press, 2010.

Makkreel, Rudolf A., *Imagination and Interpretation in Kant: The Hermeneutical Import of the Critique of Pure Reason*. Chicago: Chicago University Press, 1990.
Marion, Jean-Luc. *Being Given: Toward a Phenomenology of Givenness*. Translated by Jeffrey L. Kosky, Stanford: Stanford University Press, 2002.
———. *Dieu sans l'être; Hors-texte*. Paris: Librarie Arthème Fayard, 1982.
———. *De surcroit: études sur les phénomènes saturés*. Paris: Fresses Universitaires de France, 2001.
———. *Étant donné. Essai d'une phénoménologie de la donation*. Paris: Presses Universitaires de France 1997.
———. *In Excess: Studies of Saturated Phenomena*. Translated by Robyn Horner and Vincent Berraud, New York: Fordham University Press, 2002.
———. *Givenness and Hermeneutics (Pere Marquette Lectures in Theology)*. Milwaukee: Marquette University Press, 2013.
———. *God without Being*. Translated by Thomas A. Carlson. 2nd ed. Chicago: University of Chicago Press, 2012.
———. *La Croisée du visible*. Paris: Presses Universitaires de France, 1996.
———. *Le phénomène érotique: Six méditations*. Paris: Grasset, 2003.
———. *Le visible et le révélé*. Paris: Les Éditions du Cerf, 2005.
———. *L'idole et la distance: Cinq études*. Paris: B Grasset, 1977.
———. *Prolegomena to Charity*. Translated by Stephen E. Lewis. New York: Fordham University Press, 2002.
———. *Prolégomènes á la charité*. Paris: E.L.A. La Différence, 1986.
———. *Reduction and Givenness: Investigations in Husserl, Heidegger, and Phenomenology*. Evanston: Northwestern University Press, 1998.
———. *Réduction et donation: recherches sur Husserl, Heidegger et la phénoménologie*. Paris: Presses Universitaires de France, 1989.
———. *The Crossing of the Visible*. Stanford: Stanford University Press, 2004.
———. *The Erotic Phenomenon*. Translated by Stephen E. Lewis. Chicago: University of Chicago Press, 2007.
———. *The Idol and Distance: Five Studies*. New York: Fordham University Press, 2001.
———. *The Visible and the Revealed*. Translated by Christina M. Gschwandtner. New York: Fordham University Press, 2008.
May, Rollo. *Love and Will*. New York: W. W. Norton, 1969.
Mcgann, Jerome J. "The Beauty of the Medusa: A Study in Romantic Literary Iconology." *Studies in Romanticism* (1972): 3.
Mensch, James R. *Levinas's Existential Analytic: A Commentary on Totality and Infinity*. Evanston: Northwestern University Press, 2015.
Moran, Dermot. *Edmund Husserl: Founder of Phenomenology*. Cambridge, UK: Polity Press, 2005.
———, ed. *The Phenomenology Reader*. London and New York: Routledge, 2002.

Moyn, Samuel. *Origins of the Other: Emmanuel Levinas between Revelation and Ethics*. Ithaca: Cornell University Press, 2005.
Norton, David L., and Mary F. Kille. *Philosophies of Love*. San Francisco: Chandler, 1971.
Novalis. *Henry Von Ofterdingen: A Novel*. Translated by Palmer Hilty. New York: F. Ungar, 1972.
———. *Hymns to the Night and Other Writings*. Translated by Charles E. Passage. Indianapolis: Bobbs-Merill, 1960.
Nygren, Anders. *Agape and Eros*. Translated by Philip S. Watson. Chicago: Chicago University Press, 1982.
Platoni, Kara. "The Sex Scholar." *Stanford Magazine*. Web. November 22, 2015.
Polt, Richard. *Heidegger: An Introduction*. Ithaca: Cornell University Press, 1999.
Popova, Maria. "Stendhal on the Seven Stages of Romance and Why We Fall Out of Love: Timeless Wisdom from 1822." *Brain Pickings*. November 29, 2012; November 21, 2015; https://www.brainpickings.org/2012/11/29/stendhal-on-love-crystallization/.
Praz, Mario. *The Romantic Agony*. 2nd ed. London: Oxford University Press, 1951.
Richards, I. A. *Coleridge on Imagination*. Bloomington: Indiana University Press, 1965.
Reeve, C. D. C., ed. *Plato on Love: Lysis, Symposium, Phaedrus, Alcibiades, with Selections from Republic, Laws*. Indianapolis: Hackett, 2006.
Ricoeur, Paul. *Fallible Man*. Revised and translated by Charles A. Kelbley, New York: Fordham University Press, 1986 (1960).
———. *Freedom and Nature: The Voluntary and the Involuntary*. Translated by Erazim Kohak, Evanston: Northwestern University Press, 1966 (1950).
———. *Hermeneutics and the Human Sciences: Essays on Language, Action and Interpretation*. Edited and translated by John B. Thompson, Cambridge: Cambridge University Press, 1981.
———. *Husserl: An Analysis of His Phenomenology*. Translated by Edward G. Ballard and Lester E. Embree. Evanston: Northwestern University Press, 1967.
———. *Oneself as Another*. Translated by Kathleen Blamey, Chicago: University of Chicago Press, 1992 (1990).
———. *The Conflict of Interpretations: Essays in Hermeneutics*. Edited by Don Ihde. Translated by Willis Domingo et al. Evanston: Northwestern University Press, 1974 (1969).
———. *The Rule of Metaphor: Multi-Disciplinary Studies in the Creation of Meaning in Language*. Translated by Robert Czerny with Kathleen McLaughlin and John Costello S. J. Toronto: University of Toronto Press, 1978 (1975).
———. *The Symbolism of Evil*. Translated by Emerson Buchanan, New York: Harper and Row, 1967 (1960).
———. *Time and Narrative*. Translated by Kathleen Blamey and David Pellauer. 3 Vols. Chicago: University of Chicago Press, 1984, 1985, 1988 (1983, 1984, 1985).

Romano, Claude. *Event and Time*. New York: Fordham University Press, 2015.
———. *Event and World*. New York: Fordham University Press, 2009.
———. *Il y a: essais de phénoménologie*. Paris: Presses Universitaires de France, 2003.
———. *L'Aventure temporelle: Trois essais pour introduire à l'herméneutique événementiale*. Paris: Presses Universitaires de France, 2010.
———. *L'Événement et le Monde*. Paris: Presses Universitaires de France, 1999.
———. *L'Événement et le Temps*. Paris: Presses Universitaires de France, 1999.
———. *There is: The Event and the Finitude of Appearing*. New York: Fordham University Press, 2016.
Rougemont, Denis de. *Love in the Western World*. Translated by Montgomery Belgion. Princeton: Princeton University Press, 1956.
Sallis, John. *Force of Imagination: The Sense of the Elemental*. Bloomington: Indiana University Press, 2000.
Safranski, Rüdiger. *Romanticism: A German Affair*. Translated by Robert E. Goodwin. Evanston: Northwestern, 2014.
Sartre, Jean Paul. *Being and Nothingness*. New York: Routledge, 2012.
———. *The Imaginary*. Translated by Jonathan Webber. New York: Routledge, 2010.
———. *The Imagination*. Translated by Kenneth Williford and David Rudrauf. Abingdon: Routledge, 2012.
Schlegel, Friedrich. *Lucinde and the Fragments*. Translated by Peter Firchow. Minneapolis: University of Minnesota, 1971.
Schwartz, Regina, ed. *Transcendence: Philosophy, Literature, and Theology Approach the Beyond*. New York, 2004.
Sharples, Robert W. *Stoics, Epicureans, and Sceptics: An Introduction to Hellenistic Philosophy*. London: Routledge, 2005.
Simms, Karl. *Hans-Georg Gadamer*. New York: Routledge, 2016.
Simpson, Christopher Ben. *Merleau-Ponty and Theology*. London: Bloomsbury, 2014.
Singer, Irving. *The Nature of Love: Plato to Luther*. 2d. ed., Vol. 1. Chicago: University of Chicago, 1987.
———. *The Nature of Love: Courtly and Romantic*. Vol. 2. Cambridge: MIT, 2009.
———. *The Nature of Love: The Modern World*. Vol. 3. Chicago: MIT, 2012.
Smith, Daniel W., ed. *Essays on Deleuze*. Edinburgh: Edinburgh University Press, 2012.
Smith, David Woodruff. *Husserl*. New York: Routledge, 2013.
Sokolowski, Robert. *Introduction to Phenomenology*. Cambridge: Cambridge University Press, 2000.
Sousa, Ronald de. *Love: A Very Short Introduction*. Cambridge: Cambridge University Press, 2015.
Stendhal. *Love*. London: Penguin Books, 2004.

Stockitt, Robin. *Imagination and the Playfulness of God: The Theological Implications of Samuel Taylor Coleridge's Definition of the Human Imagination*. Eugene: Pickwick, 2011.

Vaughan, William. *Romanticism and Art*. London: Thames and Hudson, 1994.

Venema, Henry Isaac. *Identifying Selfhood: Imagination, Narrative, and Hermeneutics in the Thought of Paul Ricoeur*. Albany: State University of New York Press, 2000.

Vilhauer, Monica. *Gadamer's Ethics of Play: Hermeneutics and the Other*. Lanham, MD: Lexington Books, 2010.

Wagoner, Bob. *The Meanings of Love: An Introduction to Philosophy of Love*. Westport, CT: Praeger, 1997.

Warnock, Mary. *Imagination*. Berkeley: University of California Press, 1978.

Westheimer, Ruth K., and Jerome E. Singerman. *Myths of Love: Echoes of Ancient Mythology in the Modern Romantic Imagination*. Fresno: Quill Driver Books, 2014.

Wu, Duncan. *Romanticism: An Anthology*. 4th ed. Chichester: John Wiley and Sons, 2012.

Zahavi, Dan. *Husserl's Phenomenology*. Stanford: Stanford University Press, 2003.

Index

absence, 127
  of the Beloved, 116, 120, 123, 129, 131
  and death, 152
  of God, 157
  and imaginings, 79, 124, 128–29
  and the invisible world of thought, 102, 105
  and the Other, 96
  and the saturated phenomenon, 41
adieu, 64–65, 68, 136, 139, 159
adonné, 3, 6, 40, 67, 76–77, 95, 107, 160
  and the flesh, 99, 103
  and hermeneutics, 67
  as receptive, 40–41, 80, 86–87, 94, 104, 107, 122
  and resistance, 41
  and the saturated phenomenon, 42, 81, 145
advenant, 88
affectivity, 106
agape, 1, 6, 9–11, 155
alterity, 20, 34–38, 50, 58–59, 96, 103, 126–27, 143–44, 149, 156
amorous event, 5, 69, 85, 87, 89, 91–93, 101–13, 118–20, 128, 133, 139, 160–61

the call, 91, 93–94
cause and effect, 91–92
and culture, 112
and delusion, 146–47
distance and separation, 96–97
the encounter, 90–91
and the endless hermeneutic, 93, 95, 97, 99, 105, 109, 111
the flesh, 99, 106, 109–10
hermeneutical, 92–93, 99, 104–5, 108–9, 111–12, 119
and the imagination, 110
individuation, 92, 109
irreversible, 92
and knowledge, 145
and misapprehension, 146–47
the response, 96, 109
saturated phenomenon, 105, 123
saturates, 109
similar to friendship, 90–91
and solipsism, 144
time, 115–16, 118
amorous expressions, 111, 116–17, 162
amorous imagination
  embodiment, 99, 101
  enamors, 98
  individuation, 137

INDEX

amorous imaginings, 31, 97–98, 111, 120, 124, 152
  appearance of, 124
  and death, 137
  as envisioning, 125–26
  and fidelity, 136
  and the flesh, 126
  hidden away, 134–35
  and impossibility, 131–32
  impressional, 128–29
  and narcissism, 148
  presence and absence of, 127–30
  and solipsism, 142–44
apperception, 72, 110, 117
auto-affection, 52–54, 63

Being Given (Marion), 30, 39, 44–45, 49, 51
Beloved
  appearance of, 90–91, 93, 108, 118, 133–34
  call of the, 94
  and distance, 126
  and the endless hermeneutic, 96, 108
  as an event, 3, 66, 68, 89–90
  givenness of, 61, 66, 68, 84–86, 89–90, 94–96, 98–99, 118, 126, 128–29, 133, 143, 160–61
  individuation of, 88, 92, 99–101, 104–5, 107, 119, 137, 139, 161
  as saturated phenomenon, 61, 84–85, 159
birth, 42
body
  and the amorous event, 110
  and carnal hermeneutics, 99, 101, 103, 106
  as opposed to flesh, 63
  and signification, 63, 74, 77–78, 83, 99, 105, 127
  as site of imagination, 77–78, 83, 105
  and value, 106
  versus flesh, 100
Boétie, 48, 82, 90, 156

Caputo, John, 36–37, 130, 163
caress, 45, 101, 110, 145
child, 64, 73, 125, 130, 137, 156–57
confluence (of phenomena), 78, 83, 106, 112, 116
consciousness, mode(s) of, 25, 31, 121–23
counterintentionality, 59, 66, 94
crystallization, 12, 15, 19–20, 77
Cupid, 95, 145–46, 153

Dasein, 26, 28, 74, 104, 117
death, 96, 134, 139, 146
  of the Beloved, 119–20, 129, 138, 152
  of Elaine, 143
  impending, 120
  love is haunted by, 137
  love of, 96–97
  as merging in myth of Hermaphroditus and Salmacis, 147
  as merging in romance of Tristan and Isolde, 150
  and metaphysical merging in Romanticism, 19–20
  Novalis on, 11, 13–14
  as wish in *The Sorrows of Young Werther*, 151
deconstruction, 36–37, 131, 163
delusion, 13
  the danger of, 20, 144–47, 151–52
  imagining as, 123

imagining is not, 14, 19, 77, 122–24, 126
Derrida, Jacques, 37, 65, 130–31
distance
   and the amorous event, 96–98
   between lover and Beloved, 107–8, 119, 130
   collapse of is violence, 149
   as a condition for the possibility of love, 107, 149–50, 160
   as dangerous, 127
   in deconstruction, 37
   diacritical reading across, 38, 111, 126–27, 151, 162
   and the face, 55, 62
   and the flesh, 63, 78, 101, 103, 106–8
   in Percy Bysshe Shelley's "Love's Philosophy," 18
   in phenomenology, 38

effects, event's, 47
embodiment, 101, 103
   the imagination's, 78–79, 100, 105, 109
   and values, 106
empiricism, 2, 21–24
envision
   the Beloved, 126, 128
   the Other, 35, 56, 73
   the world, 75, 126, 137
envision(ing), Romantic, 16, 18
eros
   in *The Erotic Phenomenon* (Marion), 52, 63
   as part of love's traditional typology, 1, 6, 9–11, 155
   versus ethics in Levinas and Marion, 34, 37, 56, 59, 62
erotic call, 56, 91, 93–94, 105, 146, 160

erotic phenomenon, 51–52, 56–57
Erotic Phenomenon, The (Marion), 3, 6, 29–30, 34, 38, 51–52, 56–57, 64, 78, 85, 90, 155, 158–59
erotic phenomenon
   and flesh, 53, 62–63, 66, 78
   and individuation, 57, 62–63, 66–67, 107, 109, 135
   and the oath, 64–65, 136
   and suspicion, 53
erotic reduction, 57, 65
eternity, 56, 61, 64, 66, 132, 136, 138
ethical injunction, 28, 33–35, 56, 59–60, 91, 93, 147, 157, 160
ethics, 34–35, 37, 62
event, 42–43, 73
   the amorous, 89–93, 95–96, 104, 106, 109, 112, 123, 160
   death as, 120, 137
   and friendship, 46, 48, 90–91, 156
   hermeneutical structure of, 68, 86–89, 92
   and history, 47
   personal nature of, 88–89
   as saturated phenomenon, 47, 82–83, 85–86
   unforeseeable, 47

faith, 63, 111
fidelity, 64–66, 95, 135–36, 138
flesh
   the crossing of, 61–63, 66, 78, 99, 156
   and distance, 107, 126
   eroticized, 63–64
   the hermeneutical nature of the, 99–101, 138
   in Husserl, 100

flesh *(continued)*
  and its relationship to the imagination, 77–78, 83, 101, 105–6, 108, 110, 122–23, 161
  in Merleau-Ponty, 101–5
  as saturated phenomenon, 45, 50–55
  as site of the amorous event, 104, 123
friendship, 46, 48, 56, 89–92, 156

gaps, 42–43, 63, 66, 102–3, 107–8, 126
gaze
  and the idol, 49–50, 94, 98, 147
  and its impact on what appears, 43, 87
gazes, 87, 98
  adonné's, 43, 87
  the crossing of, 38, 48–49, 56–57, 59–60, 66, 83, 91, 93, 139, 156
  and the idol, 148
  lover's, 94–95, 148
gift, 30, 40, 67–68, 98, 155, 157
givenness
  of the amorous event, 92
  of the Beloved, 56, 68, 83, 91, 95, 108, 128, 135, 145, 156
  degrees of, 39–40, 44–45
  of the event, 86
  excessive, 108, 126
  God is not, 65
  and idolatry, 148
  and the impossible, 131
  and initiative, 40
  and misapprehension, 147
  of the Other, 50, 58, 73, 144
  pure, 23, 30, 43, 87
  reduction to, 29–30, 39, 43
  and resistance, 41

  saturating, 56, 68, 83, 108, 128, 156
God, 41, 64–65, 145, 157, 162–63
Gschwandtner, Christina M., 67

Heidegger, Martin
  hermeneutical phenomenology as a method, 23, 26–27
  on Kant's account of the productive imagination, 117
Heidegger, Martin, Marion's critique of, 30, 39–40, 45
Hermaphroditus, 146
hermeneutic(s), endless, 97–113, 115, 117, 125, 127, 131–33, 136, 138, 144–45, 148–49, 151–52, 156, 160
  and the amorous event, 92
  amorous imagination as site of, 72
  and the Beloved's individuation, 55, 83, 85
  and individuation (generally), 5, 32, 56, 82
  as proper response to saturated phenomenon, 3, 32, 42, 49, 68, 84
  as proper response to the saturated phenomenon, 86
hermeneutical structure
  of the event, 88–89, 93, 104
  of the flesh, 55, 99, 104–5
  of the imagination, 71, 74–75, 82
hermeneutics
  carnal, 54, 79, 100–101, 103, 106, 108, 110, 162
  in Claude Romano's theory of the self, 88
  as critique of empiricism, 22
  of suspicion, 1, 21

in tension with phenomenology, 4, 23
hetero-affection (of the flesh), 52–54, 62, 99
Horner, Robyn, 68
Husserl, Edmund, 22, 25, 27, 39, 71, 79–80, 100, 108, 130–31, 142, 158–59
 on double sensation of the flesh, 100, 102
 eidetic phenomenology as a method, 24–25
 and the empty signifier, 130
 on imagination as a mode of consciousness, 79–81
 on the imagination as a mode of consciousness, 121, 123, 128
 and solipsism, 142–43
 view of phenomenology preceding empiricism, 22

icon, 49, 55–56, 94, 147
idol, 49–50, 94–95, 98, 101, 127, 147–49
idolatry, 7, 76, 95–96, 127, 147, 151–52
illusion, 13–14, 77, 105, 122–24
imagination, 75, 77
 accountable to the given, 122
 and the amorous event, 110
 the amorous event captures the, 91
 carnal, 106
 castle-building, 132–33
 creative-responsive, 75–77, 122–23, 125
 and the death wish, 150–51
 as delusion, 146
 and disillusion, 152

embodied, 55, 77–78, 83, 99, 105–6, 108, 121, 123, 160
enamored, 98
imagination *(continued)*
 hermeneutical structure of, 74–75
 in Husserl, 79–81
 and individuation (generally), 31, 71, 73, 76–77, 80–83
 in Kant, 72
 key features, 71
 lover's, 15, 67, 96, 110, 123, 139
 in Merleau-Ponty, 77–78
 and misapprehension, 146
 as a mode of consciousness, 25, 31, 79–81, 121–23
 in Novalis, 12–14, 125
 in Percy Bysshe Shelley, 16–19
 productive, 3, 72–73, 117
 in Ricoeur, 74
 Romantic, 3, 11–12, 17, 19–21, 125, 141
 as site of the endless hermeneutic, 95, 97–98, 105, 108, 112–13, 119, 156
 as solipsistic, 142–43
 in Stendhal, 15–16
 sympathetic, 13, 18
 in time and culture, 115–17
 transcendental, 72
 and violence, 148–49
imaginings, 79–81, 97–98, 106, 123, 131
 and the flesh, 78, 106
 as hermeneutical response to the Beloved, 123
 and idolatry, 50
 as a kind of hymning, 98
 as narcissistic, 98
 as negation, 119

imaginings *(continued)*
  as phenomenological intuitions, 79–80, 98, 122
  as solipsistic, 81, 97–98
  and time, 116
  See also amorous imaginings
impossibility, 93, 130–31
individuation, 62, 93
  and the adieu, 64
  and the amorous event, 92–94
  of the Beloved, 83, 108–13, 115, 121, 124, 128, 138, 156
  called into question by death, 137
  and the crossing of flesh, 63
  and the crossing of gazes, 48–49, 59–60
  definition of, 4–5
  in eros (Marion) and ethics (Levinas), 33–34, 36, 38
  and the erotic call, 59
  in *The Erotic Phenomenon*, 30, 57, 61, 65–66, 68
  and the face, 56
  and the flesh, 99, 101, 105, 107
  of the friend and the child, 157
  and the hermeneutical nature of events, 89
  and imagination (generally), 71–73, 82
  and the lover's advance, 58, 67–68
  and the oath of fidelity, 136
  and the Romantic imagination, 11–12, 125
  through embodied imagination, 78–79
  through imaginative narrativizing, 75
  through the endless hermeneutic, 3, 108, 115
  through the imagination as a unique mode of consciousness, 80–81
initiative
  of love, 60
  lover's, 65, 67, 84, 90
  of the Other as saturated phenomenon, 81
  of the Other in the eroticization of the flesh, 53
  of the phenomenon (or the given), 40–42, 86, 122
injunction
  as one-directional, 59
  as universal command lacking particularity, 35–36
  versus call, 94, 109, 146
insufficiency, 18, 58, 132, 161
intention (phenomenological)
  the Beloved saturates, 125
  constraining pure givenness in Marion, 30
  and the crossing of gazes, 38, 59
  and the event of friendship, 48
  and the flesh, 52, 63
  and the idol, 49–50
  and impossibility in Derrida and Marion, 130–31
  the Other exceeds all, 35
  and proper response to the saturated phenomenon, 145
  role played in constituting phenomena, 39, 43–44
  some phenomena saturate, 30, 40, 45
  as structure of consciousness in Husserl, 25
intuition (phenomenological)
  of the event, 46
  and the flesh, 52

and impossibility in Derrida and
  Marion, 130–31
as linguistic in Ricoeur, 23
of poor and common phenomena,
  30, 39
the productive imagination does
  not show itself as, 117
restricted by intention to
  constitute an object, 43–44, 105
of saturated phenomena, 40
as structure of consciousness in
  Husserl, 25
as vague "loving to love" in
  lover's advance, 58, 61, 66

Kant, Immanuel, 3, 46, 71–72, 79,
  117–18
Kearney, Richard, 100, 102–3, 157,
  162–63
knowledge, 25, 72, 80, 94, 96, 117,
  145–46

Lancelot, 143
Levinas, Emmanuel
  and the caress, 101
  and the face, 55–56, 93
  and the limits of phenomenology
    as a method, 27
  and the Other, 33, 59
Levinas, Emmanuel *(continued)*
  and the problem of intimacy, 135
  and violence, 95–96
Levinas, Emmanuel, Marion's
  critique of, 34–37, 93

Mackinlay, Shane, 53, 86–89, 107–8
Marion, Jean-Luc
  and the adieu, 64
  answer to the question of
    individuation, 65–68
  and the crossing of flesh, 62–63
  and the crossing of gazes, 38,
    59–60
  critiqued for failing to
    account for hermeneutics in
    phenomenology, 68, 87–88
  endless hermeneutic proper
    response to saturated
    phenomenon, 144
  endless hermeneutic proper
    response to the saturated
    phenomenon, 108, 111
  and erotic individuation, 57–59
  on ethics versus eros, 34–36
  on the event as saturated
    phenomenon, 46, 48
  on the face as saturated
    phenomenon, 55–56
  on the flesh as saturated
    phenomenon, 51–54
  on God, 64–65
  on hermeneutical reception of
    the given, 41–43
  on the idol as saturated
    phenomenon, 49, 147
  on the individuated Other, 33
  and the limits of deconstruction's
    account of the Other, 37
  on love's univocity, 157
  on the need to rethink love, 1–2
  on the reduction to givenness,
    29–30, 39
  on the saturated phenomenon,
    44–45
  on the self (*l'adonné*), 40–41
  versus Derrida, 131
meaning
  human, 26, 163
  inventory of, 119, 160
  preexisting, 26–27, 143
  ultimate, 48, 130

merging (metaphysical), 11, 17, 19–20, 63, 96–97, 103, 112, 132, 146, 148–51
Merleau-Ponty, Maurice, 77–78, 101–6, 108, 121, 144
metaphysics
    Heidegger's conception of, 26
    as idolatry, 95, 147
Montaigne, 48, 82, 90, 135, 156

narcissism, 21, 73, 76, 98, 127, 147–48, 151
Narcissus, 95, 147–48
narrative self, 75, 118, 120
Negative Certainties (Marion), 42–43, 87
Novalis, 3, 11–16, 18–20, 77, 124–25, 127, 148

oath, 61, 64–66, 68, 136, 138–39, 156
"On Love" (Shelley), 16–17, 20

passivity, 41, 52, 61–62
perception
    the imagination is accountable to, 143
    as mode of consciousness, 79–81, 83, 115, 121–23, 127
    and the Romantic imagination, 19–20
phenomenology
    and deconstruction, 36–38
    of givenness, 39
    hermeneutical, 23–24, 28–29
    and hermeneutics in Marion, 87
    Marion's conceptual tools as they relate to the amorous imagination, 67–68
    as a method (generally), 2, 4–5, 22–24

as a method
    Heidegger, 26
    Husserl, 24–25
    Levinas, 27–28
    Marion, 29–30
    Ricoeur, 28
    and Romanticism, 30–31
    versus empiricism, 21–23
philia, 1, 6, 9–11, 155
philosophy of love, 2, 10, 57, 161, 163
Plato, 3, 17, 19, 72, 149
Psyche, 145–46, 153

response
    the amorous event calls for a, 92
    and call are not reciprocal, 109
    the call is shown in the, 41
    as an endless hermeneutic, 42, 93–94, 108, 113
    improper to the givenness of the Other, 95
    lover's, 94–95
    proper to the saturated phenomenon, 41
    proper to the saturated phenomenon, 145
    as resistance to the given, 41
responsibility, 28, 36–37, 55–56, 81
Ricoeur, Paul, 28, 74, 77, 101, 106–7, 121
Romano, Claude, 67–68, 86–89, 92, 107–8
Romanticism, 19, 24, 30–31, 141

Schmitt, Carl, 76, 141
self
    as *advenant* in Romano, 88
    as attestation, 28
    becomes a lover, 65
    called into question in Levinas, 27

constructed through narrative, 29, 74–75
dissolution of, 11
and the flesh, 54, 99–100, 102–3, 106, 108
individuation of the, 5
as *l'adonné* in Marion, 40–42, 67, 145
reconstituted in terms of the Beloved's appearance, 113–21, 139, 161
role in showing what gives itself, 87
Shelley, Percy Bysshe, 3, 11–12, 16–20, 77
similitude, 37–38, 144
solipsism, 76, 81, 97, 122, 127, 142–44, 151
Stendhal, 3, 15–17, 19–20, 77, 123
stranger, 4, 73, 94, 157
sympathy, 11–14, 18, 133, 143–49

time, 16, 115
the amorous event's relationship to, 115–16
Being as projection over, 110, 117
being-in-, 117
and eternity, 61, 64, 136, 163
and the event as saturated phenomenon, 47
experienced in light of the amorous event, 118–19, 161
experienced in relationship to death, 119
and God signified in the oath, 65
an impressional amorous imagining, 129
oriented around the Beloved's appearance, 133
phenomenological, 29, 74
touch, 52, 62–63, 78, 83, 99–100, 103, 106, 111, 119, 163
transcendence, 11, 19, 28, 36, 55, 63, 93, 102
Treanor, Brian, 36
Tristan and Isolde, 91, 97–98

univocity, love's, 9, 57, 155, 157–58

violence, 7, 20, 37, 96–97, 148, 151

wager, 111, 137, 139
witness, 19, 64

www.ingramcontent.com/pod-product-compliance
Lightning Source LLC
Chambersburg PA
CBHW020737230426
43665CB00009B/461